# To Barcelona and Beyond

# To Barcelona and Beyond

*The Men Who Lived Rangers' European Dream*

PAUL SMITH

BIRLINN

This edition first published in Great Britain in 2011 by
Birlinn Ltd
West Newington House
10 Newington Road
Edinburgh
EH9 1QS

*www.birlinn.co.uk*



ISBN: 978 1 84158 995 4
e-book ISBN: 978 0 85790 085 2

British Library Cataloguing-in-Publication Data
A catalogue record for this book is available on request from the British Library

Typeset by Iolaire Typesetting, Newtonmore
Printed and bound by CPI Group (UK) Ltd, Croydon, CR0 4YY

To Coral, Finlay, Mia and Zara

# Contents

# ACKNOWLEDGEMENTS

Thanks firstly must go to the eleven men at the heart of this book and the select band of additional players who had a part to play, from the smallest cameo to a leading role, in helping Rangers to the Barcelona final in 1972. Without them there would be no story to tell, no triumph to celebrate. All eleven members of Willie Waddell's team from that night graciously spared me their time and shared with me their memories to make this project possible. Thanks also go to Neville Moir, Peter Burns and the rest of the dedicated team at Birlinn for their support in bringing the updated version of *To Barcelona and Beyond* to fruition as well as to photographer Eric McCowat, whose wonderful images tell their own story. My eternal appreciation also goes to my dad for my love of football and mum for a love of writing that stems back to her help with my first book as a five-year-old (that one never did get published). Last but far from least, heartfelt thanks to my son Finlay and daughters Mia and baby Zara for keeping a smile on my face and a bounce in my step, even when deadlines loom, and my wife Coral for her patience, love and support.

# Introduction

On a balmy Barcelona evening in 1972, eleven men joined forces to create a piece of sporting history none could have predicted. Yes, Rangers were favourites to become the European Cup Winners' Cup champions, but nobody inside the famous Nou Camp stadium would have dreamt it would prove to be the club's one and only continental success in the otherwise trophy-laden years that have passed since then.

A second European trophy has become the Holy Grail for generations of players and fans who have followed in the footsteps of the stars who took on and beat Moscow Dynamo and 25,000 foot-soldiers who formed a formidable supporting cast on the cascading terraces of Barca's towering home.

Almost four decades have passed and still a repeat of the winning formula has not been found to match the late Willie Waddell's group of likely lads. Every one of the eleven players was home-grown, plucked from a variety of football outposts by a succession of Rangers managers in the years leading up to 1972.

When Walter Smith's side ran out at Eastlands in 2008 in the final of the UEFA Cup, they became the first Gers team to reach the climax of a continental competition in 36 years. Unlike in '72, the side that night in Manchester had just half a dozen Scots in the starting eleven. For 72 gallant minutes Smith's troops held firm and the dream lived on. Then, with two killer blows from the Russians of Zenit St Petersburg, all hope was gone. Now, with the 40th anniversary of the Barcelona triumph looming, the quest for European success continues. The heroic 2008 run remains the most notable effort at equalling the achievements of the Barca Bears.

Before that, the 1993 Champions League campaign had hearts fluttering and pulses racing. On that occasion the Light Blues negotiated preliminary ties against Lyngby of Denmark and Leeds United before tackling a group featuring Marseille, Bruges and CSKA Moscow. Walter Smith's men were unbeaten in ten ties but missed out on a place in the final of that year's tournament by a single point, with Marseille booking the prestigious berth. With few exceptions, the other post-Barcelona campaigns have brought nothing but pain and anguish for the Rangers faithful. European Cup quarter-final defeats at the hands of Cologne, in 1979, and Steaua Bucharest, nine years later, are the only near misses in the seasons since the celebrations in Spain.

Ally McCoist is entrusted with finding the solution to the ongoing European conundrum, hoping to succeed where Dick Advocaat, Walter Smith, Graeme Souness and the others before and after Waddell have failed. In truth there was no magic recipe, no secret to success. The wily manager's eye for detail, as the infamous sun-bathing ban at the Spanish pre-match hideaway bore testament to, was a key part, as was his ability to piece together an eclectic group and form a solid unit which proved capable of matching the best Europe had to offer. For proof, just ask Franz Beckenbauer or Gerd Muller – just two of the world superstars who fell at the feet of Waddell's men.

Football has changed since then and it is safe to say the Barcelona mix will never, ever, be repeated or rediscovered in a game that is now dominated by overseas imports and one-season wonders. Take the 2005 Champions League encounter with Slovakian side Artmedia Bratislava as a case in point. The bottom seeds held Rangers to a 0–0 draw at Ibrox but could have been forgiven for thinking they were in Amsterdam or Auxerre after looking at the home side's team sheet. Barry Ferguson ploughed a lone furrow as the solitary

Scot, with Steven Thompson and Chris Burke appearing as substitutes. In place of the Scottish talent in the starting eleven were two Dutchmen, two Frenchmen, a Greek defender and his Trinidadian partner, an Argentinian striker, a Danish winger and two North Africans. The face of the game had changed and Rangers have moved with the times, although they still wait to reap the rewards for the cosmopolitan approach.

In '72 there were big-money signings such as Colin Stein, Alex MacDonald, Tommy McLean and David Smith. There were youth recruits who came good in the form of John Greig, Derek Johnstone, Willie Johnston, Willie Mathieson, Alfie Conn and Sandy Jardine. They mixed with the shrewd addition of Peter McCloy, who was swapped by Motherwell for two Ibrox players who had been surplus to requirements.

They came together from all corners of the country, from Aberdeen to Ayrshire. Each followed a different path to the Nou Camp and each took a different route once the euphoria had subsided. For some it marked the beginning of the end of their Ibrox career, for others, such as Johnstone, just the start of a love affair with the Ibrox club. For two, Jardine and Greig, the ties with Rangers still remain through their positions on the staff and board.

Many others are still regulars at Ibrox as part of the pre-match hospitality team, others return simply as supporters. Some have retired, but the bulk can be found working in everything from the pub trade to the world of golf. While McCloy, McLean and Greig played out their careers at Ibrox, Stein and Johnston made for the exit door just months after winning the European Cup Winners' Cup. They sampled life in England, along with two other team-mates, while America and South Africa were amongst the other pit stops for members of Waddell's most famous team. They have drifted apart, but all savour the memory of one night above any other in their football lives.

Each has a story to tell of how they came to be in the blue

of Rangers on that momentous evening and where they have ventured since. Almost 40 years have been and gone, but the memories of that game still live vividly in the memories of those who took centre stage.

It should be remembered that seven of the eleven who celebrated in Barcelona had played on a day when the dark side of football came to the fore. Jardine, Mathieson, Smith, Greig, Stein, Johnston and MacDonald were all in the team on 2 January 1971, when 66 Rangers supporters died as barriers on stairway 13 at Ibrox collapsed at the end of an Old Firm encounter. Each of those players had their career and life influenced by the horrific events of that awful day. John Greig, captain on the day, dedicated an entire chapter of his own book, *My Story*, to his recollections of the disaster and speaks for every player who witnessed events unfold when he says: 'More than 30 years on, I still can't fully get my head round the fact that 66 people died as a consequence of attending a football match. It just seems utterly absurd that such a tragedy could occur. The tragedy was not just the deaths of so many, but the effect their loss had on so many others. The suffering continues to this day for many of the families who lost a loved one.' It made football inconsequential but the success the following year in Barcelona was at least a fitting memorial to those who did not survive to witness it.

The path to Barcelona began in inauspicious surroundings on 15 September 1971, in the confines of the home ground of provincial French side Rennes. They may not be recognised as giants of the game in France but they had made an impact in their domestic game in the early 1970s and held Rangers to a 1–1 draw in the home leg of the first-round tie, with Johnston on target, before being eased out 1–0 at Ibrox when MacDonald scored.

Next on the agenda came Sporting Lisbon, a talented crop of Portuguese internationalists who were defeated 3–2 in Glasgow after a Colin Stein double and Willie Henderson goal, but inflicted a 4–3 defeat on Rangers on their home patch when Stein again bagged two and Henderson added another. After finishing locked 6–6 on aggregate, the Scots lost a penalty shoot-out before discovering well after the tears had dried that in fact they would progress to the third round thanks to the recently introduced away goal rule.

In the quarter-final it was Torino of Italy's powerful Serie A who went toe to toe with Rangers and lost out, drawing 1–1 on the continent, Johnston on the score-sheet again, and losing by a single goal in the return leg at Ibrox when MacDonald was the match-winner. That teed up a semi-final against the imposing Bayern Munich, as feared as, if not more feared than the current Bundesliga stars now wearing the famous red shirts. Over two tense ties, Rangers claimed a 1–1 draw on foreign soil courtesy of an own goal before finishing the job with a 2–0 victory in Govan, thanks to an early strike from Jardine and Derek Parlane's goal. Jardine described the first-leg draw as the 'biggest hammering' of his entire career, but his side rode out the storm. In the return game they overran the highly fancied Bundesliga team, who even started fighting amongst themselves as their bruised egos realised they were heading out of the competition. Six of the Munich players helped their national side to a 3–1 win over Sir Alf Ramsey's England ten days after seeing their club dream shattered in Britain. Two years later the core of the Bayern team became World Cup winners.

After victory against Munich, only 90 minutes and the eleven Russian stars of Moscow Dynamo, the first club from the Soviet Union ever to reach a major final, stood between the Light Blues and the prized silverware. The legendary goalkeeper Lev Yashin was in charge of the Russians but even his influence was not enough to halt a Rangers team who grew in confidence with every passing round, still on a massive high from their performance against Bayern by the time the final piece of the jigsaw fell into place in Spain.

Five players appeared in all the ties in the European campaign: goalkeeper McCloy, defenders Jardine and Mathieson, midfielder MacDonald and striker Stein. Six players scored goals on the way, Colin Stein leading the charge with five strikes and Willie Johnston just one short of that after their contributions in the grand finale.

The preparations for that ninth tie in Barcelona began later than Waddell had hoped. Breaking through the Iron Curtain proved difficult, even on football business, and his plans for a spying mission were continually blocked by Russians not keen to have their team laid bare. Eventually, with little more than a week to go, he was granted entry to the country to see Dynamo in action on one solitary occasion. According to those who made the trip with him, the initial welcome extended as far as giving the Rangers manager special dispensation to jump to the head of the queue to buy tickets for the match. When Waddell's suggestion that he should have been awarded a seat in the stand as a matter of courtesy was raised, the curt response was: 'You will take whatever tickets they can give you at the stadium.'

Waddell saw the Moscow side draw 1–1 against Kairat and returned to Scotland knowing his team faced a tough time in Barcelona, remarking at the time: 'No team can ever reach a European final without being a good team, without being a team you must respect.' And Waddell, who passed away in 1992, always paid the opposition respect. This was taken to the limit in the days leading up to the final, when nothing was left to chance.

Between the high of clinching their place in the final on 19 April with victory against Bayern and the Nou Camp date, there was a five-week lull for Rangers to endure. Four league games, two wins and two defeats, filled 12 days but a 23-day break from competitive action followed. Although friendly fixtures were arranged to keep the squad on their toes, the delay was a nuisance. The European bliss that was about to unfold was not replicated at home in the previous months.

Rangers finished third in the league, behind champions Celtic and challengers Aberdeen, had not got past the group stage in the League Cup and were edged out by Hibs in a Scottish Cup semi-final replay. Barcelona was the last chance saloon.

Tucked away in the Gran Hotel Rey Don Jaime on the outskirts of the Catalonian resort of Castelldefels while their Russian counterparts vied with Spanish tourists in the heart of the town, the Rangers squad were quite literally wrapped in cotton as they obeyed strict instructions not to bare their Scottish skin to the Spanish sun for fear of burning or suffering sunstroke. Nothing was overlooked by the manager, who took three goalkeepers to Barcelona to compensate for his fear that more than one could be struck down by stomach trouble on the latest foreign excursion. He went mob-handed, a manager who had every angle covered. While Waddell and his coach, Jock Wallace, maintained their traditional calm, signs of tension in the Russian camp were beginning to show. Scottish journalists were met by the type of obstructions Waddell himself had faced while players complained of the noise and disruption surrounding their hotel.

For Conn, the last player to be confirmed in the Rangers eleven, the countdown was a tense time: 'We had gone through the final training session and the team was basically picked. I've read since then that Derek Johnstone feared he was the one who would miss out, but I think I was the one who got lucky. I had picked up an injury in a friendly against St Mirren the week before the final but was fit enough in Barcelona. The team, or what everyone thought was the team, had actually been announced back home on television and, after speaking to family, I got wind of that in Spain. Andy Penman had been picked as far as I knew. It wasn't until the pre-match meal that the side was confirmed by the manager – and I was in it. I left the table to visit the toilet pretty soon after! As far as the match is concerned, it is a complete blur for me. I don't think anyone can take that type of occasion in, you're on such a high.'

Waddell and Wallace had the trusty McCloy in goal, Jardine on the right side of defence and Mathieson on the left to flank sweeper Smith and centre-half Johnstone. Greig anchored the midfield with MacDonald, Conn and McLean while Johnston was given freedom to roam in support of Stein, who led the attack.

Greig, suffering from a broken bone in his foot, was passed fit to lead the side out and dispelled any fears about his participation in an instant, snapping into the first tackle of the match to send out a message that the Scots meant business and putting in the type of energetic box to box performance that made him a mainstay. He said: 'Within seconds of the kick-off I was given the answer I wanted concerning my foot. I clattered into their captain, Sabo, and emerged unscathed. He was an exceptionally good player and I ended up having a running battle with him. There were no hard feelings and we actually met up again years later in Kiev.'

Rangers were forced to be patient, McLean almost forcing the issue early on with the first shot of the match but having his effort well saved: 'I tried my luck a couple of times, the first one charged down and the second well saved by their keeper. We had to be patient but at the same time it was important to get ahead early on. The build-up to the final was difficult. There was a long gap between our last league game and the final and one of our two friendlies in between was against Inverness Clachnacuddin from the Highland League, not an ideal warm-up to a major European final. We were a very fit team but the lay-off had an impact – by the end of the final we were out on our feet. I honestly think if the Russians had got an equaliser they would have gone on to win it, but we held out.'

With the Russians packing their defence, space was at a premium. The attacking players were being frustrated and many of the early Rangers forays came from deep as Jardine, Mathieson, Johnstone and Smith were given licence to roam. Jardine says: 'We were probably the first Scottish side to use overlapping full-backs. Although I was a defender, I wasn't interested in kick and rush so it suited me. In the final there was scope to get forward and put them under pressure.'

Mathieson adds: 'Sandy and I were encouraged to go forward. Before Rangers started using that system, full-backs weren't even encouraged to cross the half-way line. Against Dynamo, we had our share of defending to do as well. They weren't a bad side and had a lot of pace – the guy I was up against was a professional sprinter, or at least it seemed that way. I was one of the fastest at Rangers but he gave me a run for my money.'

Johnstone too found the time and space to break and probe the Russian defence, marauding into attack with a succession of surging runs into enemy territory: 'Although we were defenders, Davie Smith and I were given the freedom to get forward. Sandy Jardine and Willie Mathieson would tuck in to cover if we went forward. We both liked to attack and we got the opportunity to do that in the final – but we knew if it broke down we had to get back and defend.'

MacDonald worked tirelessly in the engine room and was almost rewarded for his efforts, denied a penalty after falling under a Russian challenge after a lung-bursting run into the box. He says: 'We were all as fit as fiddles, as well prepared physically as any team could ever be. Training was great – we trained hard, rested well, trained hard, rested well. In the final, John Greig and Alfie Conn were both struggling with injuries but they had the stamina to pull through and do their jobs. Jock Wallace and his approach in training was important. Whereas before maybe three would go here and four would go there, he welded us together as one solid unit in games, training and outside of football. It was one for all and all for one.'

It was Smith who found the space to turn provider for the opening goal in 24 minutes. He recalls: 'I was playing at the back but I always tried to be creative. I preferred to dribble out of my own box than give the ball away or hammer it up the park. I didn't change that approach just because we were playing in a cup final and it was one of the most enjoyable games I played in. I saw a lot of the ball and was able to play my part in the first two goals.'

For Stein, who had been powerfully patrolled by the Russian rearguard, Smith's precise ball from deep into the heart of the opposition box down the right channel presented him with his first chance of the game and the outcome was clinical. He says: 'The ball came through over my shoulder, it bounced at the right height and I got a good strike on it. When it hit the back of the net I thought we were close to something really special. When the second went in I thought we were really close. To win 3–2 in the end was a travesty in my eyes because we actually hammered them.'

Johnston, who had come closest to opening the scoring before Stein's strike with a dipping shot from the left wing, was getting a flavour for the match with some neat flicks and tricky runs. He made it 2–0 to Rangers in the 40th minute when he darted to the front post to power a header past the keeper from Smith's left-wing cross, after the sweeper had cut in and beaten two defenders on the right wing. Just four minutes into the second half the mercurial winger latched onto an enormous McCloy drop kick, sneaked in behind the Moscow defence, and calmly slotted the ball low past their No.1. He admits: 'I remember more about the build-up than the game itself. I think I've seen the goals once. I remember the run to get off the pitch at the end well enough though – it was the only time Colin Stein had beaten me in a race. I remember him standing in the tunnel afterwards and asking me what had kept me. I was one of the players who had lost in the 1967 European Cup Winners' Cup final and I remember coming home from that game in Nuremberg – there was nobody there to meet us. I promised myself it wouldn't happen again and made sure of it in Barcelona.'

Three goals up and cruising, or at least that was the theory. In practice it turned out to be a different story as the resilient Russians came back in waves, battering their opponents and forcing them onto the back foot.

The Moscow side pulled a goal back after 59 minutes, the Rangers defence caught out trying to play possession football on the edge of their own 18-yard box and substitute Eschtrekov made them pay. It was 3–2 in the 87th minute: this time, Makivikov slipped through the back-line to give his side hope in the closing stages of a match that had seemed dead and buried.

Behind the Rangers back-line, McCloy had a busy night. A diving save low to his right in the first half proved to be as crucial as his through ball for the goal that gave Rangers what looked to be a comfortable three-goal lead. He says: 'As a goalkeeper you don't expect to play in big games against the best teams in Europe and have a quiet night. You have to learn to deal with the pressure. Because we had beaten Bayern Munich we were favourites, but the final wasn't easy. Even when we were two goals up I would say it was a fairly even game. We went three ahead and started to lose concentration, trying to pass the ball out of defence and giving it away for the first goal. After losing the second goal, the final whistle was a long time coming. John Greig wasn't fit and we could have done with fresh legs, but we made it over the finish line in the end.'

Mathieson recalls: 'We were so far ahead, so quickly, I think an element of doubt crept in. Subconsciously, we didn't know whether to settle for three goals or go for more. I passed to Sandy Jardine and he seemed to jump out of the way of it for their first goal. Then John Greig started throwing handbags at their No.8 and it was 3–2. The supporters started coming onto the field, so there were stoppages for that. It seemed like the longest three minutes in the world from their second goal to full-time. We didn't want interruptions, it allowed the Russians to get themselves together.'

And so the celebrations began, prematurely. With jubilant Rangers fans pouring onto the pitch, Spanish police wielded their batons as if faced by a full-scale riot and chaos ensued. The results have been well documented, with the one and only European triumph in the club's proud history marked by a presentation to captain Greig in a committee room in the bowels of the Nou Camp, far from the thousands who had made the cross-Channel trip to will their heroes to victory. The aftermath could not detract from the achievement, as eleven names were etched into Ibrox folklore for all time.

As unthinkable as it sounds now, the dramatic events in Barcelona were not broadcast live in Scotland. The SFA did not want competition for the national side's home international match against Wales on the same night. For the record, Scotland won 1–0 at Hampden in front of just 21,000 people.

The cup final highlights were only recorded in black and white by the Spanish film crew, although the Scottish broadcasters had been told they would receive colour images. Commentator Archie Macpherson noted the bemused looks upon the faces of the Spanish fans in the ground as the Rangers fans celebrated, describing it as: 'Pandemonium and a bedlam of noise rolled up together and let loose.' He spoke of the scenes in the stands around him as the Scottish followers went 'berserk'. The written press catapulted the victorious team to the front pages and heralded them as heroes. The *Rangers News* went one step further and proclaimed them as kings of Europe.

Rangers won many admirers that season as they blazed a trail across the continent. Dutch legend Rinus Michels, then manager of host club Barcelona, gave his Scottish guests a glowing endorsement after casting an eye over the final build-up in Spain, heralding them as clear favourites. Even a delegation from Russia, coincidentally in the area for a youth tournament, admitted on the eve of the showdown that Dynamo would be no match for the grit and skill of their opponents. Torino manager Gustavo Giagnoni was another convert, setting aside the pain of his club's exit to fly to Barcelona for the final. He arrived later at the Rangers team hotel to congratulate the winners and heaped praise on Smith's performance in the 3–2, the sweeper vying for the unofficial man of the match award with goal-scoring hero Willie Johnston according to the Scottish media.

The Barcelona eleven revelled in the compliments that followed their triumph, led by Waddell. He was known as a man of steel, but even he could not fail to be caught up in the emotion of the occasion. He gathered the players, their wives and the Scottish press in the team hotel to open the first of six cases of champagne and express his appreciation in a speech laden with sincerity and typical passion. At midnight he ushered the guests back to their Barcelona retreats, leaving him alone with the players who had made his dream come true and the squad continued the celebrations through to the next morning. Waddell labelled his winning team as Rangers 'immortals', claiming at the time: 'It was a display which stamped the team as a match for any club in Europe. The names of the eleven players will go down in history along with the Ibrox greats of the past . . . as is only right.'

The squad were well rewarded, collecting a win bonus of £2,000 for their efforts. It was the richest pay-out the club had ever offered, four times what was on offer for success in any of the domestic competitions, and an indication of just how important the prize was to the board who controlled the purse strings.

The team and their precious cargo flew out from Barcelona the day after the final, fans on neighbouring planes flocking onto the runway to catch a glimpse of the cup. They touched down at Prestwick airport for chairman John Lawrence to be greeted by Glasgow's Lord Provost John Mains and another army of adoring supporters. The famous old tale of an over-zealous customs officer halting Greig as he strolled through the 'nothing to declare' channel with the towering trophy was one of the quirks of the day, the captain's explanation that he hadn't bought the cup and didn't need to declare it eventually being accepted.

The jubilation at the airport was mirrored inside Ibrox as the team took their belated lap of honour. Before the grand entrance from the players, the 20,000 crowd had been warned that action would be taken against anyone who ventured onto the pitch. In the end the fears were unfounded, with the parade passing without incident. Only a couple of arrests were made afterwards on the streets around Ibrox as the crowd dispersed.

After the scenes in the Nou Camp, Rangers waited until the following week to discover the punishment UEFA would hand down. An emergency meeting of the European game's governing body was called and the disciplinary committee also considered the issue. Rangers pointed to similar pitch invasions when Ajax had won the European Cup in 1971, when Celtic had done the same in Lisbon four years earlier and when they themselves had been beaten by Bayern Munich in the 1967 European Cup Winners' Cup final in Nuremberg. None of those incidents had led to bans, but that was exactly the conclusion UEFA reached – barring the Scottish side from defending their crown and from continental competition for two years in total. The Spanish press called for Rangers to be banned from playing on their soil again, even though the home referee had claimed the fans were 'exuberant' rather than violent. Waddell fought the suspension and eventually it was reduced to a single year.

As the years roll on and the odds of a repeat performance lengthen, the magnitude of the occasion has been put in sharp focus. Reunions marked the 20th and 25th anniversaries while the winning team have, since 2000, had a walk-on part at Ibrox to be saluted by the current generation of fans and taken to Canada as guests of honour of the North American Rangers Supporters' Association. While the club stands accused of playing down the achievement, perhaps even being embarrassed by it after investing heavily and failing to engineer a repeat, the same argument cannot be levelled at the fans, who have masterminded various reunions and testimonials over the years.

Regardless of what happens in the future, all eleven were rewarded at the time with memories to cherish and pass through the generations. For those who shared in the joy of 1972, the following chapters represent a nostalgic trip down memory lane with some of Scottish football's greatest characters, and for the generations too young to have witnessed the triumph in Barcelona, an education on the men who etched the proud name of Glasgow Rangers onto the European Cup Winners' Cup for all time.

## CHAPTER ONE

# PETER McCLOY

Behind every great goalkeeper is a great goalkeeping coach – one of the mantras of modern football but an alien idea not so long ago. Rewinding through the decades, it is easy to pinpoint the sea change in attitude and the self-taught keeper Peter McCloy is the perfect case study.

He made the No.1 jersey his own at Ibrox for 16 years, turned out for Scotland and went on to pass on the tricks of the trade to the next generation when goalkeeping coaching was still a novel idea. When he made his name as a player, the idea of specialist training for the last line of defence was practically unheard of. Yet McCloy became established as one of the most dependable keepers Rangers have ever laid their hands on in an honour-laden career, testament to the theory that no amount of coaching can compensate for ability and instinct.

The Girvan-born shot-stopper was made for his role, standing 6ft 4in tall. Much has been made of McCloy's physical presence, the stuff of myth and legend. Delve into the archives from his first few seasons and you will find early newspaper reports claiming the young keeper stood at 6ft 7in. Maybe it just looked that way for forwards bearing down on him.

He proved to be an immovable obstacle for a succession of men who tried and failed to dislodge him from his place at the head of the team sheet under Willie Waddell, Jock Wallace and John Greig. It wasn't until his 40th birthday loomed that McCloy called time on his possession of the gloves. He helped the club to two league titles, four League

Cup wins, two Scottish Cup victories and success in Europe in his time at Ibrox.

The towering keeper's recruitment in 1970 made Rangers a better team and McCloy also believes the switch from Motherwell made him a better goalkeeper. He says: 'When I joined Rangers it was the first time I had any specialist coaching. I worked closely with Jock Wallace, although I wasn't spared any of the physical work the rest of the squad endured either. Even then, the goalkeeping coaching was nothing like as intense or well developed as it is now – I sometimes wonder what difference today's coaching would have made to my game. I'll never know.'

When he retired from playing in 1986, the pupil turned teacher with a move into coaching in his own right just as the Graeme Souness era was launched at Ibrox. 'I stayed on to work with Chris Woods but I also ended up taking on responsibility for the reserves. I enjoyed that involvement with the young lads – there was a good bunch coming through at that time – but the manager and I didn't see eye to eye in the end. These things happen in football and I knew it was time to move on.'

McCloy was a man in demand and worked with a host of the country's leading clubs after leaving Rangers in 1988 and with some of Scotland's most revered goalkeepers. Jim Leighton was one student and Andy Goram at Hibs was another, with Rangers going on to reap the rewards of his development. As a coach he was even drafted in by Caley Thistle manager Steve Paterson to work with the Inverness keepers the season before that Scottish Cup victory against Celtic at Parkhead in 2000.

'When I started in goalkeeping coaching I felt it was going to be a big thing and I've been proved right. It has come on in leaps and bounds: every club at a decent level has a specialist to work with their keepers. I worked with a few clubs, going through to Edinburgh to work with Hearts a couple of days each week and with Andy Goram at Hibs as well as Jim

Leighton at Dundee and some work with the likes of Motherwell and Ayr United. The travelling became a bit of a burden and now I'm working closer to home as the head starter at Turnberry – it's a great place to call your office. I had a four-year spell running a golf complex at Brunston, nearby, and it has always been another of my big sporting passions. I try to get on the course as often as I can.'

Still based in his home town of Girvan, McCloy's sons Peter, a PE teacher, and Steven, a fire-fighter, are joined by daughter Justine, a graduate of Aberdeen University. McCloy juggles family life with his work in golf. Relaxed after a sunshine golfing break in Portugal, he makes clear his love of the fairways as he mulls over a career dominated by highs and punctuated with very few lows. He represented his country at golf as an amateur but, as the son of a former St Mirren goalkeeper, football was his first sporting love. He was a youth international keeper and had no hesitation in dedicating his life to the profession.

'My parents had wanted me to get an apprenticeship but I had broken my collarbone playing amateur football and then joined Motherwell when I recovered from that, so there was no time. It was always going to be football for me anyway.'

He signed for Motherwell from Crosshill Thistle in 1964 as a 17-year-old. The Fir Park club were in the top flight of Scottish football with Bobby Ancell at the helm. The manager moved on a year into McCloy's stay, replaced by Bobby Howitt, but it did not halt the young goalkeeper's progress. In six years with the Steelmen he played around 150 games. Even in his formative years at Fir Park he made an impact, capped by the Scottish League four times, well before his switch to Ibrox.

Motherwell made steady progress, finishing 14th in the 18-team First Division in 1964/65 before climbing one place and then a further three in the following campaigns. Relegation in 1967/68 brought 'Well back down to earth, but they regrouped as McCloy and his team-mates cruised to the

Second Division championship the following season. The 1969 league title was a clear contest with Motherwell, 11 points clear of runners-up Ayr and 16 ahead of East Fife in third place, having conceded just 23 goals in 36 games.

They consolidated with 11th place in the First Division on their return, but their finish would not be the Ayrshire man's concern as he was plucked from Lanarkshire early in 1970 to embark on the most fruitful spell of his career.

'I spent six years at Motherwell, part-time for the first season. I signed for Rangers on Friday the 13th in March 1970 – it wasn't an unlucky day for me. I had known Willie Waddell as a player and a journalist before he took on the job at Ibrox. He must have seen something he liked in me. I had been playing in the Motherwell reserve side after losing my place in the first team when he signed me, making me the first he took to the club. I remember going in at night with Motherwell, when the full-time boys would train with the part-time players, and being called over by the manager to tell me I would be going to Rangers and the wing-half Bobby Watson and Brian Heron would be going in the opposite direction. I went through the next day to Ibrox and everything was signed and sealed before I left. I didn't hesitate – I couldn't afford to.'

The manager was just three months into the job at Ibrox and saw his new No.1 as the man he wanted at the foundations of his team. The talents of German keeper Gerry Neef had failed to persuade the new top man that the answer to his goalkeeping conundrum was already at the club and he looked to Fir Park for the solution.

Rangers, as they had been for the four previous seasons, were destined to finish runners-up to Celtic and conceded 40 goals in 34 league games in the season that McCloy was added to the pool. He made his debut on 14 March 1970, in a 2–1 defeat at Dunfermline. Only five team-mates from the starting eleven that day would feature in Barcelona two years down the line as the manager began to ring the changes. John Greig, Colin Stein, Dave Smith, Willie Johnston and Willie Mathieson were the others.

Willie Waddell wanted to run a tight ship and the following term the number of goals leaked was cut by six, but the goals-for column also saw a reduction, his side bagging nine fewer goals in 1970/71 than they had the year before and falling to fourth in the table. It was McCloy's first full season after a brief introduction before the summer break and he missed only three league games as, in his early twenties, he staked his claim for the long-term right to the goalkeeper's jersey.

League disappointment was tempered by success in the League Cup. It is easy to be blasé about Rangers and cup wins – after all, there have already been more than 100 trophies brought back to Ibrox and the counter is still rolling. Every win has to be put in context and the League Cup success in the 1970/71 season was vital. The last prize the club had picked up was the Scottish Cup in the 1965/66 season and the League Cup had been absent from the trophy room since the campaign before that. In the interim, Celtic had the monopoly on the league and had won one or both of the knock-out competitions every year. The supporters needed hope, the manager wanted to send out a message and the players were in need of a confidence boost.

On their way to the final, Rangers conceded just a single goal in six group games against Dunfermline, Motherwell and Morton before defeating Hibs 6–2 on aggregate over two legs in the quarter-final and minnows Cowdenbeath 2–0 in the semi-final to foster genuine optimism in the dressing room and on the terraces. Derek Johnstone's goal on 24 October 1970, at last gave them and the blue half of the 106,000 crowd at Hampden some silverware to cherish. McCloy says: 'The League Cup win was important because it was the first trophy the club had won in four and a half years and it broke Celtic's grip a little.'

He got his first taste of life as a winner with the Light Blues in that final and it was a flavour he would become accustomed to, even though he feared his days as first-choice keeper could have ended before they had properly begun. 'There were only five games of the season left when I joined. I played well in those but missed out on the pre-season tour of Germany with a virus. That little spell on the sidelines didn't do me any harm because I got to know the club and everyone around it that bit better. My replacement in Germany was a young keeper called Bobby Watson. He got good reviews and kept his place for the first game of the season but fortunately I got back in after he had played in the Glasgow Cup final, which Celtic won 3–1. I got in and stayed in.'

Over the years the Rangers keeper locked horns with Celtic's attack over and over again. He got used to the experience in time but still remembers his early days in the Old Firm arena. 'The League Cup in 1970 was a derby final and you need to get a few of those games under your belt before you really get a feel for them. Old Firm games are just a bedlam of noise and were even louder then because of the number of people squeezed into the grounds.'

With domestic success under his belt, it was time to broaden his horizons. McCloy was still only 25 when he played such an influential role in the club's night of European glory. A keeper, rightly or wrongly, will always be judged on shut-outs and in that respect McCloy's contribution to the run to Barcelona was vital. He kept a clean sheet against Rennes in the first round but it was against Torino and Bayern Munich, both at Ibrox, that the most vital defensive operations were conducted. Against the Italians, McCloy and his rearguard stifled the attacking threat and held out for a single-goal victory after sharing two goals in the away leg. Against the Germans, again following a 1–1 draw on foreign shores, the goalkeeper would face one of the most tense nights of his life as he and his team-mates endured a torrid time against superstar striker Gerd Muller and his colleagues. Wave after wave of German attacks were thwarted and two goals on the counter had the Rangers fans grabbing for their sombreros and booking their flights for Barcelona.

The keeper had another decade and a half in front of him, but did not take that for granted: 'I don't think I ever imagined I would spend so long with the club – it may be an old cliché, but you never look beyond the season you are in. Coming from a smaller club, it's not all about ability when you move to a bigger one. It's about adjusting mentally as well.'

That mental strength was tested to the limit in the 1972 European Cup Winners' Cup final. After turning from net minder to creator, his long clearance catching out the Moscow Dynamo defence for Willie Johnston to run on and score the third goal, he reverted to defensive duties as the Russians clawed back two goals and threatened to make it 3–3. McCloy believes a lack of competitive action could be at the root of the late jitters: 'When we came to the end of the season there was a two or three-week gap until the final in Barcelona. We played friendlies but I don't think we were at our sharpest. Our league form hadn't been great but in Europe we were stronger – we had the right system and the players to make it work.'

He more than anyone had to hold his nerve in the pressure-pot atmosphere of a European final as Rangers protected a one-goal lead with the clock running down. McCloy insists he did not feel the strain: he had of course seen it all before in the run to the final. 'I think once we had beaten Torino in the quarter-final we started to believe we could win the competition. They were at the top of Serie A and we had got past them. Once you're into the last four, you're in the mix and any team from that stage has to fancy their chances. We were a team that could stand up to a lot of pressure. It was a siege in Munich but we got through it.'

McCloy is well placed to make comparisons between the

Rangers of old and the current crop. He, like a host of his fellow Barcelona veterans, is part of the pre-match hospitality team at Ibrox and admits the game has moved on since he helped the club conquer Europe. 'People talk about the changes in the game, that it is much quicker than it used to be. There's no doubt it is true but a lot of that is down to the surfaces now. Before, a player had to take a touch but now they can play one-touch football because the pitches allow for that. I don't necessarily think the essence of the game has changed or that technically it is far superior.'

That leads to the other big question: when will we see their like again?

McCloy says: 'It doesn't help that so many clubs in European competition have far greater financial resources. Teams are also expected to play far more games now, with the group stages in both European competitions. That can work in your favour in that if you have a bad night you get a second bite at it, but it also means you need a decent-sized squad to cope with all the games.'

McCloy is a voice with experience, having sampled life on the international stage as well as scaling the heights at club level. He won four caps for Scotland over the space of two months in 1973. National manager Willie Ormond handed him his debut against Wales in the home international series on 12 May. The team included the likes of Kenny Dalglish and Pat Stanton, and McCloy kept a clean sheet as a double from George Graham sealed a 2–0 win in Wrexham.

The Rangers keeper retained his place for subsequent games against Nothern Ireland, Switzerland and Brazil but was edged out by Celtic counterpart Ally Hunter and then David Harvey when the qualification campaign for the 1974 World Cup began that winter. It was Harvey who had the starting spot for the World Cup finals in Germany in 1974, and it is ironic that an Englishman kept Girvan's most famous football son out of the Scotland team for the tournament. Harvey, an FA Cup winner with home-town team

Leeds in 1972 under Don Revie, qualified for the Scotland team through his father. He won 16 caps for the national team from 1972 to 1976 and proved to be the main obstacle for McCloy in a period crucial to his international aspirations.

McCloy may not have made it to the national team's hall of fame but he did hold a place in the national football museum at Hampden. His shirt from the Barcelona final was placed alongside the world's oldest match ticket, Archie Macpherson's sheepskin coat and Kenny Dalglish's 100th cap after he stepped in to answer a plea from the museum for memorabilia from the occasion to be loaned to them. Today, Rangers fans can still buy T-shirts with McCloy's image and name emblazoned across the chest. The legend lives on.

At club level, with two cups from two years, McCloy could have been forgiven for thinking life would be easy at Rangers. More weight was added to that argument when he completed a trophy hat-trick with victory in the 1973 Scottish Cup final. Again Celtic were the opponents, and this time he was in for a busy afternoon as his side shaded it with the odd goal in five.

It was all or nothing on 5 May 1973, as McCloy lined up in his latest Old Firm final. The league had already gone to Parkhead and the League Cup to Easter Road with Hibs. To reach the showdown, Rangers had beaten Dundee United 1–0, Hibs 2–1 in a replay, Airdrie 2–0 in the last eight and Ayr United 2–0 in the semi-final. That set the scene for another Glasgow duel to mark the centenary final of the Scottish Cup. Kenny Dalglish scored the opener after 24 minutes but Rangers hit back ten minutes later through Derek Parlane. Alfie Conn made it 2–1 to the Light Blues within seconds of the second-half starting, but just nine minutes later it was all square, McCloy going up against George Connelly's penalty but being left with no chance. It was a Tom Forsyth tap-in that wrapped it up for Rangers in a tumultuous 90 minutes.

The cup wins were one thing, league supremacy was

another. The vice-like grip Celtic had on the Scottish crown was broken in 1975 but Stewart Kennedy was the ever-present goalkeeper that term. It was one of the rare occasions when McCloy was not between the sticks for Rangers over the course of the 1970s, eventually outlasting Gerry Neef, Bobby Watson, Stewart Kennedy and Jim Stewart.

Watson, not to be confused with the wing-half by the same name who was swapped for McCloy, could not shift him, Neef moved back home to Germany in 1973 after failing to dislodge McCloy, while Kennedy, a £10,000 signing from Stenhousemuir in the same year, was next to try his luck. He had greater success than most, playing a season in 1975/76 and mustering almost 100 games for Rangers, but moved on to Forfar in 1978 before turning his hand to coaching. Stewart signed from Middlesbrough in 1980 but managed to just pass the half century of appearances in four years before going out on loan to Dumbarton and then seeing service with St Mirren and Partick Thistle.

McCloy recalls: 'There were a lot of goalkeepers who came in during my time at the club but I kept my head down and worked away. I've always believed a loss of form is temporary but ability lasts a career. I suppose people had a notion that it was time for me to move on at different points, when I wasn't in the team, but I never saw it like that. I was prepared to work to get back in and I had a helping hand from you guys in the media – you could never answer negative comments or criticism as such, but you could do your talking on the pitch and I tended to respond that way.'

Rangers showed loyalty to their reliable keeper and it was mutual, with McCloy happy to continue to sign contract after contract at Ibrox even when most of his team-mates had been tempted to try their luck elsewhere. He admits: 'Of course there were other clubs interested at various points and maybe I should have seen if the grass was greener elsewhere, but I've got no regrets. I had 18 good years at a great club. The only reason players moved to England was because clubs down there could offer two or three times what Rangers could pay – in any profession that is an opportunity that's difficult to turn down but I felt happy at Ibrox.'

Gordon Marshall, a future Scotland internationalist, was one of the understudies to McCloy in the early 1980s. Marshall was still turning out for Motherwell into his forties and cited his old mentor as the wiliest fellow member of the goalkeepers' union he ever encountered, learning from his one-time Rangers colleague's willingness to knuckle down in the face of competition for the jersey.

The man known as the Girvan Lighthouse hit back from the disappointment of being ousted for the 1974/75 league winning season and the following term played in 24 of the 36 Premier Division fixtures as Rangers clinched the first of two trebles under Jock Wallace.

The league marathon is always the most gruelling leg of the race to the finish line in a treble season. In 1976 Rangers pinned their hopes on solidity and it worked. Celtic were beaten to the title by six points despite scoring 12 more goals than the champions – the key was a stingy defensive record that saw Rangers concede just 24 goals in 36 league outings compared to the 42 that the Hoops had leaked. They kept clean sheets in half of their league games, McCloy registering 15 of those 18 shut-outs.

It took Alex Ferguson's Aberdeen until 1983 to match the Premier League goals-against record set by Rangers in 1976 and the following year for the Dons to beat it by three goals. It wasn't until 1986/87 that a Rangers defence beat it by a single goal.

In the 1975/76 season an Alex MacDonald goal in the League Cup final against Celtic had put the first part of the treble in the bag, the Parkhead side struggling as so many sides did that term to find the net. On the way to that final the group section, including Airdrie, Clyde and Motherwell, had been negotiated before Queen of the South and

Montrose were swept aside in the knock-out rounds. The opposition on the way to the Scottish Cup final against Hearts were East Fife, Aberdeen, Queen of the South and Motherwell. Within a minute of the final Rangers had sight of the treble, Derek Johnstone scoring the opener after 42 seconds. Alex MacDonald added another, Johnstone grabbed the third and the Edinburgh side could only muster a consolation goal.

It was the first treble the club had won since 1964 and the first Scotland had seen since Celtic claimed the full set of honours in 1967, but the next was just around the corner. In 1977/78 the league flag was again taken back to Ibrox, the League Cup was claimed with a 2–1 win against their Old Firm rivals and the Scottish Cup decked in red, white and blue after the same scoreline in the final against Aberdeen.

McCloy says: 'I was only in my second year when we did the whole Barcelona thing. It was a good time to be at the club – the 1970s as a decade was a good time to be a Rangers player. I caught the last four years of nine in a row and there's no doubt the two trebles we won after that were sweet. Just to win your league is an achievement but to win the cups as well was fantastic. Still, as the years go on you realise just how big a thing it was to win in Europe.'

The 1978 treble marked the end of the Jock Wallace era and the start of John Greig's quick-fire transition from player to manager. 'When Jock left, the team was getting a bit long in the tooth. John took over but it didn't work out as well. We had a lot of good players, all internationals, and replacing that type of quality was difficult. It wasn't possible to swap like for like.'

McCloy emerged to become Waddell's longest lasting legacy on the playing side of the club, outlasting any of his other signings by a considerable margin. Tommy McLean, another notable signing by Mr Rangers, played his last game in 1982, a full four years before McCloy's swansong. The keeper was also the last man standing from the two treble-winning teams and from the European Cup Winners' Cup champions, with the break-up beginning in the wake of the 1978 success.

John Greig was the first to go, hanging up his boots to concentrate on his new role as manager, while in the years that followed Derek Parlane was sold to Leeds and Alex MacDonald and Sandy Jardine moved on to Hearts. By the time McCloy played his last game a new breed was coming through. He was behind a defence featuring Stuart Munro and Dave McPherson, the midfield included Ian Durrant and Derek Ferguson while Ally McCoist was the new kid on the block in attack.

The 1978 league championship was the last McCloy would play a part in, with Aberdeen and Dundee United emerging as a powerful opposition force to the Old Firm in the remainder of his playing days.

That frustration on the league front was tempered by continued success in the country's other competitions. In 1978/79 Greig's team, with McCloy as the last line of defence, did the cup double. The League Cup was claimed after a 3–2 semi-final win over Celtic and 2–1 final victory against Aberdeen while the Scottish Cup was taken back to Govan after an epic three-legged final against Hibs. In the first match McCloy and his side shut out their Edinburgh opponents but failed to score and the 0–0 result was repeated in the replay. It took a second replay before the gates opened and the men in blue put a 3–2 win on the board. They had made heavy weather of the campaign, with the semi-final against Partick also going to a replay.

Jim Stewart was the man in possession of the No.1 shirt by the time the 1981 Scottish Cup title and following season's League Cup were added to the Rangers honours list but McCloy, true to form, was back in charge and able to supplement his own precious metal collection when they returned to Hampden in later years.

McCloy was no stranger to Old Firm drama and the

1983/84 League Cup final is a case in point. It took extra-time to separate the two Glasgow giants, with an Ally McCoist hat-trick enough to earn a 3–2 win and put another medal in the locker for the veteran goalkeeper.

His final prize came in the 1984/85 season as Rangers lined up against Dundee United in the pre-Christmas final of the League Cup at Hampden. McCloy and his defence held firm as Derek Ferguson's goal clinched victory.

He eventually bowed out in a 1–1 Premier League draw against Aberdeen at Pittodrie on 26 April 1986. By that time Walter Smith was holding the fort as Rangers waited for new manager Graeme Souness to fly in from Italy and revitalise the club, with McCloy playing a part in the early stages of that through his position on the coaching staff and still on occasion pulling on the gloves again in friendlies.

McCloy spent more than a quarter of a century at the top level in Scotland, going in where it hurt time and time again and getting involved in some bone-crunching challenges in his pursuit of success. Surprisingly he bears few battle scars, although he is given a sharp reminder of the amazing range he offered with his clearances: 'I played until just short of my 40th birthday and wasn't really troubled with injury. The only problem I have now is with a bit of pain in my kicking foot, wear and tear. The long clearance for the third goal in the Barcelona final was just a wee loft in comparison to some – I used my lob wedge for that one.'

## CHAPTER TWO

# SANDY JARDINE

Brazilian players have provided Scottish fans with hours of entertainment in their pursuit of the beautiful game, but surely only one Scot can claim to have captured the imagination of the South American football superpowers.

Sandy Jardine made his name as a defender but he was no ordinary stopper – just ask former Brazil coach Mario Zagalo. After watching his side being held to a 0–0 draw by Scotland in the 1974 World Cup, Zagalo heaped praise on the cultured Rangers player.

Famously the national side returned home unbeaten from the finals, missing out on a first ever appearance in the second stage on goal difference. Jardine had time to make an impact and was included in FIFA's all-star team along with Celtic's Danny McGrain as the competition's best full-back pairing.

The 1974 tournament was an undisputed international highlight for the Edinburgh-born player but at club level it is impossible to pick out a defining moment in a distinguished career.

Twice crowned Scotland's player of the year, Jardine collected an array of honours with Rangers in an amazing 18-year stint as a player at Ibrox. More than 40 years since he first walked into the stadium as a teenager, he still bounds through the front door with the same enthusiasm. The difference is training gear has been swapped for a suit, and playing exchanged for the role of marketing and sales manager in a multi-million pound enterprise.

As a schoolboy his father helped to secure a place for him

on the Rangers payroll but would never have predicted it would be the beginning of a four-decade association with the Light Blues. Jardine recalls: 'I signed straight from Tynecastle School, in the shadow of the Hearts stadium, when I was 15. I was at an age where I wanted to leave school and asked my dad to look for a job for me . . . he told me not to worry, he had something in mind and he'd talk to me about it later. It turned out to be a place on the Rangers ground staff and I moved through to Glasgow.'

The east coast boy began his career at Ibrox in 1964, the year the Ibrox side secured their second consecutive championship and both domestic cups. It would be 11 years until the league trophy returned, 12 until all three were brought together under one roof in Govan, and Jardine was still there to savour both occasions.

After following the familiar trainee's first step on the football ladder as part of the ground staff, the teenager did not take long to earn playing privileges. At the age of 18, he made his debut in the first team in a 5–1 win over Hearts at Tynecastle in February 1967. Jardine, who had made his mark as a skilful attacking player as a schoolboy, wore the No.4 jersey in a team that had been reshuffled following the shock 1–0 Scottish Cup defeat at Berwick just one week before.

That upset in the Borders caused shock-waves at Rangers, but presented a chance to take advantage of the inevitable changes that followed: 'I made my debut quite quickly after joining the club. I'd been doing well in the third team and then the reserves, but the Berwick game, because of the impact of the result, was a factor. It provided me with my opportunity.'

And he grabbed that opportunity with both hands, making it impossible for manager Scot Symon to ignore him. In his debut season as a first-team player, Jardine sampled life at football's top table as Rangers marched into the 1967 final of the European Cup Winners' Cup in Nuremberg. Irish outfit Glentoran and Borussia Dortmund, of Germany, had been accounted for by the time the versatile youngster came into the side for the third-round clash with Real Zaragoza, winning 2–0 in Spain and being defeated 2–0 at home before going through on the toss of a coin. Jardine retained his place for the semi-final games against Slavia Sofia, of Bulgaria, as two single-goal victories saw his side ease through.

The mighty Bayern Munich were the opponents in the final but the rookie in the Rangers ranks was not fazed by the imposing presence of legends Sepp Maier, Franz Beckenbauer and the well-oiled machine they led. In the Nuremberg final, close to a home tie for Bayern, he impressed the hosts and Beckenbauer spoke highly of Jardine's contribution after going head to head with him.

It was so close to a dream start to his career, but Bayern clinched the trophy with a single goal from Franz Roth in extra-time. It was all part of the learning curve for Jardine, and the experience stood him in good stead. 'I was only 18 at the time, the youngest player ever to feature in a European final at that time. I was just happy to be involved, and I didn't realise the magnitude of the game until afterwards. As the years pass, you begin to realise just how rare an occasion like that is for any player. Back then, everything was new to me and I took it all in my stride. I wasn't overawed, just glad to be playing and testing myself against some fantastic names.'

His ability to cope with the pressure of life as a Rangers player proved a valuable quality as the Ibrox side tried to compete with the Celtic nine-in-a-row side. He rode through that period to enjoy the good times, and the years spent in the red-hot environment of the Old Firm rivalry have given Jardine a unique insight.

The Scottish contribution to the modern day derby may be limited, with continental players just as likely to earn a starting berth as the home-grown stars, but that has not diminished the importance of the event. According to the

Rangers staff man, the competition with Celtic has evolved in his 46-year attachment to the famous fixture but the core elements of the world's fiercest city rivalry remain the same.

'In my early days we were up against Celtic's best ever team, but the other side of the coin is that I experienced it from the opposite perspective, when Rangers dominated in the 1970s. The rivalry has never changed and I don't think it ever will. Football's different now, like every industry, because there's more freedom of movement and more foreign players at clubs like Rangers, but the current team feels the rivalry with Celtic just as much as we did with a team made up of 90 per cent Scottish boys. The pressures for the players now are the same as they were back then. We were judged ultimately on how we did in the handful of games against Celtic each season and that remains the case.'

The battle to break Celtic's dominance in the late 1960s and early 70s saw Jardine being used as a pawn in the tactical games that were played. He went on to carve out a career as one of Scotland's best defenders but always had attacking instincts. In fact, during a spell as a centre forward in the late 1960s he boasted 11 goals from 12 consecutive games. It was an enviable scoring ratio, but his talents extended beyond poaching and were seen as perfect for the role of overlapping full-back, a new innovation in the Scottish game.

He explains: 'I went to Ibrox as a forward but I played in midfield, where I made my debut, as a sweeper and at full-back. I settled down to become a defender but I was a skilful player, not interested in kick and rush.'

The first taste of success came in the 1970 League Cup final as Rangers, in front of a six-figure crowd at Hampden, dumped Celtic 1–0 thanks to a goal from another of the rising young stars, Derek Johnstone. It ended the barren spell for the club and weeks later Jardine achieved another personal landmark to add to his first winners' medal as he took his international bow.

Bobby Brown was the manager who awarded the first cap,

throwing the 21-year-old in as a substitute for David Hay in a 1–0 win over Denmark at the national stadium in Glasgow. The new boy would go on to become a Scotland captain.

The appearance against the Danes was the first of 38 caps won by Jardine, all as a Rangers player. As well as skippering the side on nine occasions, he added international goalscorer to his list of credits with a strike against Wales to help the country to a 2–0 victory in the home international championship in 1974. The best moments of that particular year were still to come, with the World Cup finals confirming Scotland's place among the elite of the game.

'Scotland were very fortunate to have an awful lot of quality players. We had the likes of Denis Law, Kenny Dalglish and Billy Bremner at their peak at that time. The 1974 World Cup in Germany was the first time the finals had become commercialised, they were the first big finals in that sense, and it was a great experience. We were in a really hard group, with Brazil, Yugoslavia and Zaire, but came through the group undefeated.'

Joe Jordan and Peter Lorimer helped Scotland get off to a perfect start, on target in the 2–0 win over Zaire to set the ball rolling in Germany. A spirited performance against Brazil saw Scotland match their esteemed opponents, holding them to a 0–0 draw. In the third and final game a spirited 1–1 draw with Yugoslavia proved to be not enough to earn a passage to the next stage, although it remains the nation's best ever showing in a major competition.

Jardine adds: 'To go out on goal difference was painful because if we had got past the group stage I think the team we had would have got stronger and stronger.' He wore the No.2 shirt in each game and brought the superb club form the Rangers fans already knew all about to the world stage.

Of course, those talents had already reached a Europe-wide audience two years previously when he had helped his club to the European Cup Winners' Cup title. It was Jardine who scored the crucial goal in the second leg of the semi-final against Bayern to open up the path to the Nou Camp. He remains modest about his contribution but not about the team's: 'Barcelona was a fantastic occasion, and the fact I had played in the 1967 final stood me in good stead for '72. Being honest, the Cup Winners' Cup was often the easiest of the European competitions to win but nobody could say that about that year's tournament. We played quality teams at every stage and that made it even sweeter.'

No team could boast a finer pedigree than the German outfit he helped dump from the competition, Rangers drawing 1–1 in Germany and winning the return leg in Glasgow 2–0 thanks to that Jardine strike and Derek Parlane's goal. 'Bayern Munich had the nucleus of the West German team who went on to win the World Cup two years later and that team is the best I ever played against. We matched them, and deserved to go through. Getting the goal in the semi-final was the icing on the cake after a fantastic team performance.'

Today, Jardine is part of a commercial operation at Ibrox that attempts to provide the financial clout to allow the club to compete on the European stage. Even with substantial investment, success at that level has been hard to come by. Now simply qualifying for a place in the group stages of the Champions League is classed as a triumph, not least because of the revenue stream that relatively modest achievement can bring.

To compare and contrast, failing to reach the latter stages of a European competition in Jardine's playing days with Rangers was seen as a huge disappointment: 'There were no set expectations going into the competition in 1972 but we always hoped to do well. From the mid-1960s to 1972 I played in two European Cup Winners' Cup finals as well as a quarter and semi-final in Europe – Rangers did very well at that level at that time. We would defend frantically away from home, knowing we were strong and capable of beating anyone at Ibrox.'

Only some top-class opposition prevented Jardine from

adding to his tally of European final appearances. The season after the 1967 showpiece against Bayern Munich, Leeds United accounted for their Scottish opponents in the quarter-final of the Fairs Cup. In 1968/69, in the same competition, it was Newcastle United who got the better of Rangers in another cross-border tie, this time at the semi-final stage. Cologne edged out the Light Blues in the quarter-final of the 1978/79 European Cup with a 2–1 aggregate win. Jardine recalls: 'We were very well prepared, right down to the pictures of our individual opponents, and all of those things you take forward with you and use in later life, particularly in coaching and management.'

In the aftermath of Barcelona, Rangers could rightly approach domestic football with renewed confidence. They had matched the best the continent had to offer, and now it was time to get the better of the team who had laid claim to the title of best in Scotland for nine long years. Celtic's domination was ended in 1975 and that sparked a period in which the other half of the Old Firm was in the ascendancy.

Events in Spain three years earlier had an impact. Jardine explains: 'The team that won in Barcelona was at the core of the squad that went on to do so well throughout that decade. It was a very successful period in the club's history, we were winning regularly and were the team everyone else had to beat.'

For their No.2, there was no time to sit back and revel in that 1975 league title win. According to Jardine, nobody at Ibrox was happy to savour a one-off occasion – they wanted to keep bringing trophies back to the club. That approach paid dividends, particularly in the treble-winning seasons of 1976 and 1978, in which he continued to play an influential part.

'It wasn't a case of relief when we won the league for the first time – we knew we were the better team at that stage and wanted to make the most of the opportunities we had in front of us. I'd say we did that, particularly in the two treble seasons.'

In truth a single chapter barely scratches the surface when it comes to detailing the defender's achievements at Ibrox. His list of medals reads more like a Christie's catalogue than one man's collection of honours. After winning his first medal in 1970, he went on to collect a further 13. The European Cup Winners' Cup was next in 1972, the Scottish Cup the next year and the league title in 1975, followed by another in 1976 to add to the Scottish Cup and League Cup that same season. The treble of 1978 took his tally into double figures before the Scottish Cup and League Cup haul was supplemented in 1978/79. Another cup double in 1980/81 completed the collection, with the final medal collected in the 1981/82 2–1 win over Dundee United at Hampden in the League Cup.

In that incredible Ibrox career he made 674 competitive appearances, to add to the 38 Scotland caps he amassed as a Rangers player, and scored 77 goals. Among the most memorable strikes was a mazy solo effort against Celtic in the 1979 Drybrough Cup final, starting from the edge of his own penalty area and ending at the opposition box with an unstoppable drive. Mr Zagalo would have been proud.

In fact, the chance to shine alongside the likes of Brazil would not come again. After the highs of the 1974 World Cup, Jardine sampled the finals for a second time four years later in Argentina. It was a very different experience, with Scotland crashing out after a 3–1 defeat at the hands of Peru, a 1–1 draw with Iran and 3–2 win over Holland which proved too little too late and ended Ally MacLeod's bold pre-tournament claims and predictions of Scottish glory.

Jardine's involvement was hampered by injury, and he played only in the match against Iran. The ill-fated MacLeod adventure would still prove useful in later life as Jardine's experiences with Scotland, playing under a succession of international managers in a decade with the national team, coloured his coaching career.

After Bobby Brown handed the full-back his first taste, caps followed under Tommy Docherty, Willie Ormond, Ally MacLeod and Jock Stein. It was Ormond who appointed him captain, and he took the armband for the first time in a 3–0 win over East Germany at Hampden in October 1974.

Jardine played his last game for Scotland as captain in a 3–1 defeat against Belgium in 1979. He finally called time on his Rangers career in the summer of 1982, having been an ever-present in his final season. By that time he had risen to third in the all-time appearance list, behind only John Greig and Dougie Gray. In the post-Bosman era, that pecking order is almost certain to remain untouched.

Well past his 30th birthday, he reasoned his best days were behind him – but he was about to be treated to a pleasant surprise with a renaissance to be proud of. 'As I saw it then, I was coming to the end of my playing career. I was 32 and the team I'd been part of was breaking up. After everything I'd gone through in 18 years, I knew my time at Ibrox was coming to an end and I was keen to get involved in management. The opportunity to go to Hearts as a coach cropped up, and Rangers were good enough to let me go on a free transfer.'

He left Ibrox to assist his former Rangers team-mate Alex MacDonald, who had just accepted the post of manager at Hearts. It was the first rung on the coaching ladder for Jardine, but the move also gave him a second wind as a player.

He made his debut for his home-town club on 9 August in a 1–0 defeat to Hibs at Easter Road and amazingly went on to play at the top level for a further 62 months, showing some of his finest form as he switched from full-back to sweeper. As touched upon previously, the defender had been named as the Scottish Football Writers' player of the year in 1975, a fitting tribute to his contribution in the season

Rangers were crowned champions as he missed not even a single game in that league campaign.

Eleven years later, he became only the fifth man in the history of the award to win it for a second time, in good company alongside John Greig, Brian Laudrup, Henrik Larsson and Barry Ferguson. When the 1986 honour was bestowed upon him, Jardine was approaching his 38th birthday – proof positive that age is no barrier if a player has the talent, intelligence and natural fitness to make it totally irrelevant.

'In both cases, it was great to get the awards but I wouldn't have been in that position without the help of my team-mates. It's impossible to say one meant more than the other, but when you start getting into your thirties you don't expect to be singled out as the best in Scotland. The second was more unexpected rather than more appreciated.'

He averaged more than 30 games a season for the Tyne-castle side. That type of reliability was nothing new: at Rangers, he strung together a staggering run between 27 April 1972 and 30 August 1975, in which he played in every single one of the club's 171 games.

His player of the year award in 1975 was part of an Old Firm monopoly on the prize, and the fact he repeated his achievement with the less fashionable Hearts after a season in which the team ended empty handed puts that feat in context. The statistic that he is one of only 12 players from outside of the Glasgow giants to have taken the individual title in 40 years of the post-season ceremony puts it in even sharper focus.

In addition to quality, he can boast records in terms of quantity and became the first player in Scottish football to smash through the 1,000 appearances barrier; fittingly, Rangers provided the opposition for the landmark game at Tynecastle in November, 1985. Almost two years later, on 3 October 1987, the same side provided the opposition as Jardine made his final run at the end of an incredible innings, playing his last match in a 0–0 draw in front of an Edinburgh crowd close to 29,000.

In 21 seasons as a first-team player he had stayed loyal to the two Scottish clubs. Everton and Tottenham were among a long list of suitors, but Jardine had pinned his colours to the mast. 'I played a lot longer than I expected to. When I left Ibrox I knew I'd carry on a bit longer, but in the end it was another seven years and I went on until I was 39. I'd always been fit and athletic, looking after myself, and it paid off for me.'

Of course Jardine's career was not confined to playing, his coaching role going hand in glove with his on-field commitments for the majority of that chapter in his football life. Having played under Scot Symon, David White, Willie Waddell, Jock Wallace and John Greig at Rangers, his inspirations were many and varied. He drew upon those influences, and his vast playing experience, when he linked up with MacDonald at Hearts.

When the duo took over, the club was at a low ebb and stuck in the First Division. Funds were not plentiful but Hearts had recruited a coaching team who had been there and done it as players and went on to demonstrate an ability to translate that wisdom into coaching nous in their first assignment. Both continued to play, but their influence extended beyond that.

Jardine, the perfect example when it comes to football longevity, is credited by MacDonald as the man responsible for the core fitness of a Hearts team who built their game plan around their ability to go the distance. It was he who set about bringing in fitness specialists, including sprint guru Bert McNeil. 'I'd always been interested in the physical side of the game and that was something Alex and I took with us to Hearts. We had them in good shape and well organised.'

Within a season, the capital city side had been restored to the Premier League as runners-up in the 1982/83 First Division and that place in the top flight was consolidated the following term. The club won a place in Europe in three of Jardine's seven seasons as part of the management team, while he helped the side to the runners-up spot in the Premier League twice and the comfort of fifth place a further two times.

Despite finishing sixth and seventh in two of those seasons, they never looked in danger of slipping back to the league MacDonald and Jardine took them from. The achievement of second place in 1986 will always be regarded as the most crucial part in the lifespan of that managerial pairing, as his side kick elaborates on in Chapter 10.

Hearts were just seven minutes from being crowned champions of Scotland for only the fourth time in their history, the last title coming in the dim and distant past of 1960. In those seven minutes, the Jambos lost two goals in the closing stages of their game at Dundee while second placed Celtic were hammering St Mirren 5–0 at Love Street. The end result saw roles reversed, with the Hoops leapfrogging Hearts on goal difference.

It was a crushing blow at the end of a season which promised to make Jardine a legend in the Gorgie district in which he took his first steps to football stardom as a fresh-faced player in his school team. Hearts had the sympathy of a nation, save for the Celtic and Hibs fans who revelled in their failure to cap a season of outstanding form with one last push.

While Jardine's playing contribution was recognised by the football writers in their annual awards, he would gladly have sacrificed that honour to enable the team to get their hands on the Premier League trophy or even the Scottish Cup. The Jambos lost out on the cup a week after their league disappointment when Alex Ferguson's Aberdeen emerged 3–0 winners in the final at Hampden.

It was Ferguson's crowning glory as Pittodrie boss, before leaving for Manchester United in the summer of 1986. That created a vacancy in the Dons dug-out and, not surprisingly, the MacDonald and Jardine partnership stirred interest from the Aberdeen boardroom, with Jardine emerging as a candidate for the top job in his own right. Hearts took no risks, and the pair were tied to new long-term contracts which also saw the assistant officially promoted to the post of co-manager as the Tynecastle hierarchy and MacDonald recognised his behind-the-scenes contribution.

Chairman Wallace Mercer was proud of the innovation, but failed to show the courage to match his earlier convictions in the years that followed. In the first season under dual control, 1986/87, Hearts finished fifth and in the second again finished runners-up to Celtic. The coaching team hoped it would be third time lucky but were not afforded the opportunity to discover if that would be the case, because Mercer dismissed Jardine in November 1988, claiming a single pair of hands was needed at the tiller.

The good Tynecastle memories far outweigh the bad: 'I still look back on Hearts as being very successful. We may not have won anything, but we were in the First Division when I joined and ended up back in the top half of the Premier League, qualifying for Europe three times and finishing runners-up in the league three times. Going so close in 1986 was painful, but every club in the country would love to be able to sustain a challenge to the Old Firm over the course of a season now.'

Ironically, it was a 3–0 defeat at the hands of Rangers that proved the final blow to the pairing. Gary Mackay, captain at the time, praised the departing co-manager for his dignity, admitting the farewell had left many of the squad overwhelmed with emotion. Despite the storm created by Mercer's decision, internally and externally, Jardine retained his customary calm and remained philosophical. He took stock, broadened his horizons and moved away from football's frontline to tackle the commercial world with one of Scotland's leading brewers, leading eventually to his current role with Rangers.

'Some clubs came looking, but I was 40 by then and wanted to test the water outside of football. It's always been an up and down game and the idea of getting involved in another business was appealing. Having been a player, a manager and worked on the other side of the fence with McEwans and their sponsorship of Rangers, has given me some good tools to work with now.'

Jardine has thrown himself wholeheartedly into his Ibrox role, being one of the first into the stadium in the morning and darting about the country for appointment after appointment in his attempts to drum up new business for the rapidly expanding and diversifying commercial arm.

Being back at his old stamping ground has not rekindled any desire to dig out his boots again. 'I still keep fit and enjoy a game of golf but I never kicked a ball after I stopped playing professionally. I suppose I got that out of my system in the 23 years I played week in and week out. I'm kept busy at work and with my grandkids, so I've got plenty to keep me occupied.'

He played his final Premier League game three months before his 40th birthday – the Davie Weir of his time. Of course, Weir is the exception rather than the rule in an era in which the average retirement age is creeping forward with every passing season. The reason is not physical, according to Jardine, more financial.

He said: 'The back-up and support clubs provide now is fantastic, the playing surfaces, both at the grounds and training pitches, have come on leaps and bounds. I think too many players stop too soon. There's a clamour to retire after they hit 30. Maybe they lose a bit of their hunger because they have made their money by that stage in their career.

'We had to play as long as we could because that was how we earned a living – you're more hungry when you are poor! We were always looking out for our next job, whereas players now have to worry about how they're going to fill their day when they stop – they don't have to work. I don't begrudge them anything, it's a different era and the world has moved on. I enjoyed every minute I had and wouldn't change it for anything. I had 18 years at a wonderful club, and I doubt any player now or in the future will enjoy that.'

CHAPTER THREE

# WILLIE MATHIESON

Thirteen days after guiding Rangers to victory in Barcelona, manager Willie Waddell announced his decision to hand control of the team to Jock Wallace. In the intervening days, Waddell, an accomplished journalist as well as coach, took time out to reflect on the team he rightly predicted would always have a place in the history of his proud club.

Writing in the club's official handbook, he paid tribute to the men who had clinched the previously elusive European title Rangers craved. He singled out the pace, precision and skill of the eleven who stormed into a three-goal lead against Moscow Dynamo less than two weeks earlier and he was quick to pick out two individuals. The first was Alex MacDonald, the second Willie Mathieson.

Waddell said: 'The hard work, tireless efforts and character of these two players meant a lot to the team. Their contribution to the Rangers success may not always have been noticed by the public . . . but we at Ibrox fully recognise and appreciate what these two loyal players have done for the club.'

The appreciation was mutual. Mathieson spent 15 years at Rangers and served under four different managers: Scot Symon, Davie White, Willie Waddell and Jock Wallace. It was during Waddell's tenure that he rose to prominence and enjoyed the richest spell in his football career.

Now retired from his post-football career in the electrical industry and living the quiet life in the Highland capital of Inverness, he says: 'It really started to take off for me when Willie Waddell took over. Davie White, his predecessor, was a good coach but didn't have the authority a Rangers manager needs. Maybe that was because he had been a player at the same time as us – I'd played against him a few times myself. Waddell, on the other hand, had that authority. He put a lot of faith in me. I was a hard and fast player, the type he needed when he took over. He came in on the back of a disappointing European defeat at the hands of Gornik, an unknown Polish side, in 1969. I played in a reserve game the day he took over and must have done something right. I went straight into the team and never looked back.'

Mathieson had already been with Rangers for nine years before Waddell took the reins, supporting the praise lavished upon him for his loyalty. By the time he savoured his finest hour in light blue, the Fife-born defender had spent 12 years with the club and was nearing his 30th birthday.

Loyalty was one quality, resilience was another. That character was built in the toughest environment of all, working in the pits surrounding his childhood home on Scotland's east coast. Having spent two years as a teenager working beneath the surface, it is understandable that Mathieson was prepared to bide his time at Ibrox. Coming from an area steeped in football heritage, it was no surprise he found his way to the top.

But for Mathieson, the mines were an insurance policy his family wisely insisted upon.

'I was born in Cardenden in Fife, on the same street as the Celtic goalkeeper John Thomson. He died in 1931 as the result of a collision in an Old Firm game but his name and reputation lived on. At school, Willie Johnston was a year or two below me. We weren't friends as such, because of the age difference, but we knew of each other before we joined up again at Rangers and long before the win in Barcelona. Football was always my game. We would play every spare minute, on any piece of waste ground we could find or on the street.

'People talk about the shortage of young players coming

through in Scotland now, about the need for coaching, but that's the big difference – there's no waste ground or open space for kids to play on, nowhere for them to develop a love of the game.'

Mathieson went on to establish himself as one of Scottish football's most consistent defenders under Waddell, but that particular die was cast long before he ever set foot inside Ibrox. As a boy on the streets of Fife he honed his skills, turning out for his school team, district select and local juvenile outfit West End Strollers.

Even early on, the budding player discovered that the politics of football are not always easy to fathom. It was an important lesson, and one revisited when it was time to end his Ibrox career. He recalls: 'I actually got put out of the school team because I played for the juveniles, and the school master didn't approve. He went on to become a first-class referee, so our swords crossed again in my Rangers days. I don't think he ever held it against me in later life.'

His early promise was spotted by St Andrews United, who introduced him to the man's world of junior football as an enthusiastic 15-year-old and later profited, albeit modestly, from his switch to the big time with Rangers. 'I finished school when I was 14 years and 11 months old and went down the mines to work a week later. I was an electrician in the pits. It was a tough shift, but a good experience. I would be able to work the day shift and come off that and go to play football – I fitted work and football around each other. Mind you, there were days we would come off the night shift and stay on to play football at seven in the morning.'

The tale of how Mathieson came to become a Rangers player illustrates the changes Scottish football has seen, not simply in monetary terms but in culture. While Catholics and Protestants now sit side by side in the Ibrox dressing room, he would never have pulled on the famous shirt had he been a follower of what the club, at the time, deemed the wrong religion for its stars.

'I had come off working a day at the mine and gone back home to an empty house. My mother, father, brother and sisters had gone out and I was dozing on the settee when a guy came knocking at the door. I'll always remember the first thing he asked me when I opened the door: "Which foot do you kick with?" I said, "I'm left footed." He looked at me straight and asked again: "But what foot do you kick with?" I said, "I'm a left back, I'm with St Andrews." Eventually he asked: "What side of the fence are you on, what's your religion?" I told him I was a Protestant and he just said: "That's right, good. Rangers want to sign you then." That's the way things were then.

'My father and I went through to Glasgow and I signed part-time for two years. My father wouldn't let me go full-time until I had finished my apprenticeship. He had my best interests at heart and it stood me in good stead outside of football. There were quite a few part-time players going in at night at that time. I was just one of them. My squad number, for my training gear and basket in the dressing room, was 54 – that's an indication of the people who were ahead of me when I signed as a 17-year-old.'

When Mathieson lined up in the Rangers team that swept aside Moscow Dynamo, he was alongside £100,000 signing Colin Stein. Dave Smith had cost the club £50,000 while Alex MacDonald commanded the same fee. In contrast, the No.3 was a steal: 'I got a £20 signing-on fee, £6 a week wages and St Andrews got a £250 transfer fee.'

He went from a pit worker to professional football player, mixing with a cast of legends in the space of just 24 hours. Despite swapping the harsh realities of life in the mines for the more plush surroundings of Ibrox, he never left his Fife roots behind. Remaining on the east coast, outside of Glasgow's intense Old Firm spotlight, helped Mathieson shelter from the interest he was beginning to create.

'A group of us used to travel through. We used to get the train at 7 a.m. in Kirkcaldy, grab a cup of tea in Glasgow then go into training. We had to report, stripped and ready to start for 10 a.m. and were usually finished by noon. I'd be back home in Fife and in the house by 2 p.m., so it wasn't a bad life and better than being down the mines, that's for sure.

'I suppose I started to be recognised once I was in the first team. But it was different for us. The press weren't interested in us as people – just as footballers. That suited me fine – there wasn't the same intrusion into our personal lives as Old Firm players face now. I went full-time in June 1962, the day my apprenticeship ended. There were some great lads at the club. Willie Johnston was already full-time, although he had been farmed out to play in the juniors, while eight or nine young boys started on the same day as I turned full-time. Colin Jackson was one of those and we've been good friends ever since.'

When Mathieson arrived as a fresh-faced teenager in the early 1960s, the team was under the control of Scot Symon. A shrewd operator, Symon was also regarded as a true gentleman. He had assembled a solid side, with the formidable full-back pairing of Eric Caldow and Bobby Shearer providing a rock-solid foundation, and had added the flair of Jim Baxter, another of the Fife colony imported to Govan. Goalkeeper Billy Ritchie was the last line of defence, Harold Davis was at the heart of the back-line and Ralph Brand and Jimmy Millar provided attacking impetus. Waiting in the wings were a clutch of young upstarts, John Greig and Willie Henderson among them.

'On the first day we did some laps round the track, some sprints and then went over to the Albion training ground and broke off into groups of three. I was put with Eric Caldow and Bobby Shearer, two idols of mine. I wasn't daunted, just excited. I went into the third team, which was coached by Tiger Shaw. He was like a father to me. As a left full-back in his playing days, I think he took to me straight away.'

Competition for places was fierce. The men in possession

helped Rangers to the league title and Scottish Cup in 1962/63, going one better the following season with a domestic treble.

In all, Mathieson had to wait patiently for three years for his moment to arrive. 'I moved up into the reserve team but still had Eric Caldow and Davie Provan in front of me. Then, Eric broke his leg and Davie did the same. The circumstances weren't great, but it meant I got my chance. That was in 1965, when I made my debut against Hamilton in a 3–0 cup win. I was playing behind Jim Baxter in that first game. Scot Symon pulled me to one side after training on the Friday and told me I was playing and that I should let Jim know. I did that and Jim told me quite simply: "No matter where you are, win the ball and give it to me. Win the ball and give it to me." That's exactly what I did.'

Baxter was sold later that year, moving to Sunderland in a £72,500 transfer. For Mathieson, the chance to play alongside him before the flit to England was another box ticked. 'Jim was a hero to me, the best football player I have ever seen in my life. Obviously he had a different lifestyle to the rest of us, he was a star, but he was still one of the boys.'

His first game came in front of 22,814 supporters at Ibrox on 6 February 1965, in the first round of the Scottish Cup. Hamilton had been performing well in the old Second Division but were swept aside 3–0 by Rangers. The team went on to beat Dundee United in the next round before falling 2–1 to Hibs in the third round.

The 1964/65 debut season was the same year as the club narrowly missed out on a place in the semi-final of the European Cup, going out 3–2 on aggregate in the quarter-final against Inter Milan. It was a mark of the quality at Symon's disposal and the task facing players aiming to break into the side. 1965 proved a big year personally for Rangers' debutant, marrying his wife Edith in the months that followed his first-team breakthrough.

After a five-year wait from signing as a part-time player to taking his first-team bow, the loyal Ranger waited a further seven years for his crowning glory. 'We won the reserve league year in and year out, but to qualify for a first-team championship medal you had to play a certain number of games – I fell short on a couple of occasions. I played in the semi-final in the League Cup-winning run in 1970 but not the final. That was the way it was and I had no complaints. You were only as good as your last game, you didn't moan if you were out of the team. I managed over 300 appearances, including friendlies, so I didn't do too badly. I played a few games in midfield but mainly in defence. When you're playing for Rangers, it doesn't matter what position you're asked to play – I was happy to be part of it.

'Barcelona was the highlight for me. In 1972 we had a special bunch of guys and it all came together for us in Europe that year. We weren't team-mates, we were friends. Like brothers almost. If one went for a walk, we all went for a walk. If one went for a beer, we all went for a beer. That togetherness translated into amazing spirit on the park. That side had everything you need in a football team: thinkers, doers, workers . . . we had the lot, the best mix you could find. We didn't have a good season in the league but were a great cup team and suited to Europe.'

The 1971/72 campaign was a purple patch for Mathieson, moving into his prime as a 28-year-old with more than a decade of full-time football behind him. That term he missed only four league games, played every League Cup tie and, including replays, seven Scottish Cup ties. Including his European performances, Mathieson started 51 matches, culminating in the Nou Camp showpiece. Only Peter McCloy, Sandy Jardine and Alex MacDonald played more games that season.

The full-back was an ever-present in the march to the European Cup Winners' Cup final of 1972. His contribution to the win over Torino in the quarter-final was particularly telling as he silenced the intimidating Italian crowd at the

Communale Stadium in Turin with a vicious cross that was spilled by the home keeper to present Willie Johnston with an early gift. The Serie A side did equalise, but the Rangers goal on European soil proved crucial and they went on to win 1–0 at Ibrox to book a berth in the semi-final.

Mathieson was earmarked to play a spoiler's role in the famous encounter against Bayern Munich in the last four of the competition, a game which provided a revealing insight to the methodical approach Rangers adopted in the successful campaign. Waddell watched the formidable semi-final opponents in action against Stuttgart before dispatching coach Jock Wallace to Munich to see them defeat Cologne 3–0 in a German Cup game. Wallace compiled a comprehensive man-by-man dossier, as had been the practice throughout the competition.

Bayern fielded six West German international regulars in the shape of Franz Beckenbauer, Gerd Muller, Sepp Maier, Paul Breitner, Georg Schwarzenbeck and Uli Hoeness. The conclusion was that the bigger they were, the harder they would fall. Wallace reasoned that if Munich were put under pressure, the cracks would begin to show in their star-studded side after signs of infighting in their win over Cologne.

Mathieson explains: 'We could adapt depending on which team we were playing against and were tremendously prepared. Willie Waddell would give us a photograph of the player we would be up against and on the back he noted all of that player's strengths and weaknesses. Against Bayern Munich, I was detailed to mark their No.7. I ended up playing right-half most of the match, but that didn't matter because the job was done.'

Rangers came up against some famous names and mighty reputations, but Mathieson insists the team of Scots never considered themselves to be underdogs as they went in against French, Portuguese, Italian, German and Russian opposition. 'We were confident in every round that we could get at least a draw away from home and win the tie at Ibrox. That's exactly how it worked out for us. French football was the top of the tree at that time, so we took a lot of confidence from beating Rennes in the first round. After that we faced Sporting Lisbon, Torino and Bayern – there were no easy ties. The final, against Moscow Dynamo, was probably the easiest of the lot but we almost messed that up.'

The Russians scored their second goal in the 87th minute, leaving a tense wait for the final whistle. Those 180 seconds, extended by the interruptions created by the exuberant Rangers fans, capped a 12-year wait for Mathieson to get his hands on one of the game's biggest prizes.

'It was a huge relief, sheer elation, but a disappointment at the same time. In the first instance because we didn't get to celebrate properly and secondly because we were banned from Europe, for two years reduced later to one year. The team started to break up. If we had stayed together and been allowed to defend the title, I'm sure we would have done well. We didn't fear any team in Europe.'

As the history books show, that did not happen and the cup-winning team did indeed disintegrate – but not before Mathieson played his part in another famous victory. After retaining his place under Wallace, who filled Waddell's shoes in the aftermath of Barcelona, he lined up in the Scottish Cup final against Celtic in 1973 in front of 122,714 supporters.

He was one of eight survivors from the European triumph and played a key role in the build-up as Derek Parlane grabbed a first-half equaliser to cancel out Kenny Dalglish's opener. Rangers went on to win 3–2. The Scottish Cup victory was a sweet end to a tremendous season personally for Mathieson. He and Sandy Jardine were the only ever-present players in the league. Mathieson went one better in the League Cup, then including six group matches and two-leg knock-out ties, when he played in all 11 fixtures. That run ended in a 1–0 semi-final defeat against Hibs. Mathieson then turned out in all six Scottish Cup ties in the run to Hampden glory to complete another 51-game marathon season.

The 1973/74 campaign would prove a disappointment for the club. By the time the championship was brought back to Ibrox in May 1975, the full-back's days at Rangers were drawing to a close. During the title-winning season he rejected two transfer proposals but was resigned to leaving. The closing season was a frustrating one for Mathieson, who saw John Greig and Alex Miller share possession of the No.3 shirt that had previously been his own.

In the year of league reconstruction, moves to Motherwell and Partick Thistle were mooted. Both were battling for top-flight survival as the 18-team league became ten. In the end, Motherwell survived the cut while Partick missed out on a Premier League spot and fell to the new First Division along with Arbroath, Mathieson's chosen club.

'I left in 1975 under a bit of a cloud. I remember being called into Willie Waddell's office to be told I was signing for Motherwell – I told him I wasn't. I had six months left to run on my contract and, after 15 years man and boy at Ibrox, felt I deserved a free transfer. The club felt differently. Soon after, they told me they'd agreed a fee with Partick, but my response was the same. At the end of the season I got my free and moved to Arbroath.'

It was the same route followed by fellow Barcelona veteran Dave Smith and not as outlandish as a transfer between the Old Firm and the Angus club would seem in the current football climate. Whereas a modern-day Rangers star could expect to earn 500 times the £50 weekly wage of an average Arbroath part-timer in 2010, the gap between the rich and poor in Scottish football was nowhere near as vast in the mid-70s. In fact, Arbroath did not even fall into the latter category, thanks to the careful management of Albert Henderson and the volunteer committee who made the modest coastal town side, with an average gate of 1,000 at that time, an attractive proposition to a long list of leading players who made the switch during that era.

'I had options to go south, but it was an important time in the boys' schooling and that was the most important thing to Edith and I. Arbroath was close to home, one of the wealthiest and best run clubs outside of the big names at that time, and there was the extra lure of the promise of a job with an electrical manufacturer arranged through the club. It allowed me to fall back on my electrician's apprenticeship.'

Like his father before him, Mathieson's commitment to the future of his children paid off. Mark, the couple's eldest son, is a director with Scottish and Southern Energy in Reading while their youngest son, Ross, is involved in IT with Scottish Hydro Electric in Perth.

When he joined Arbroath, the club was aiming to bounce back from the disappointment of losing the top-flight status it had held so dearly. In his first season, Mathieson turned out 25 times as the club finished fifth in the new First Division, short of the ambitious target of clinching promotion to the Premier League. In truth, the Gayfield club was finding its level in Scotland's lower leagues, a position befitting its relatively modest gates and catchment area, and Mathieson too was making the transition from full-time football to the part-time game.

He maintained his enthusiasm for the game but, while the mind and soul was willing, the rigours of more than a decade and a half in Scottish football began to catch up with him. Injury, ultimately, sped up his decision to call time on a playing career that had taken him full circle, back to his native Fife. Not before he could fulfil one last childhood wish.

'By that time my years were advancing and I was having trouble with my knee, the cap was loosening. I played a season with Arbroath and another at Raith Rovers. Raith were my local team, the team I watched as a boy – Willie

McNaught was my hero. I was happy to play on for them, but the knee was shot by then. Doctors told me I could stop playing and the kneecap might tighten again or carry on playing and end up a cripple.'

Having started the 1976/77 season in possession of the Raith No.3 jersey, he put all of his years of experience to good use in 13 consecutive Second Division games before hanging up his boots for the final time. More than 16 years after arriving at Ibrox as a rookie professional, Mathieson bade farewell to the game as Raith fell to a 1–0 defeat against Airdrie at Broomfield.

As the playing chapter closed, another opened as two Barcelona old boys united to take their first steps on the coaching ladder at Berwick Rangers. Previously the worst team in Scotland, Berwick provided Mathieson with that winning feeling for one last time as he helped them to the Second Division league title in 1979.

After doing his bit for Rangers in their unique European win, Mathieson can also lay claim to a hand in the Wee Rangers' first ever trophy success. 'When Dave Smith came back from playing in America, he asked me to help out with the coaching at Berwick, where he was manager. I enjoyed it and we had some success, but after three years the travelling to training in Edinburgh and Berwick was getting more difficult with my increasing work commitments. I was with Edmundson Electrical in Edinburgh for 20 years and became president of the Electrical Wholesalers Federation. Work took priority and I enjoyed life outside of football.'

Having resisted the lure of Glasgow as a Rangers player, he and his wife waited until retirement to finally bid farewell to Fife. Fortune played a major part in the decision to move to Inverness, but there's no sign of a change of heart: 'My son had been up in Inverness. Edith and I always enjoyed visiting the city, especially as our two grandchildren, Carrie and Calum, were there. When we retired, we decided to head north. It is a lovely place to be and we see more of our friends than ever before – it's like a mini guest house at times. We love it and are settled here. We go out to Lanzarote three or four times a year, so we're kept busy.'

Indeed his affinity to Rangers has been passed on to his two grandchildren, who never let him forget the answer to a familiar question. 'People often ask what it means to be a Rangers player. Being a Ranger not only affects you, but everyone related to you. The pride and passion you get when you pull on that blue jersey is awesome. It's not only yourself who is affected, but your wife and all of your family, including grandchildren, many years later. It's quite incredible. When my grandson was six years old he came home from school one day and told his mother that the next day everyone in his class was to take something to the school and stand in front of the class to explain what it was and why they were proud of it. His mum thought he would take a favourite toy, but he disappeared to his room and came back with a Rangers programme and said: "This is what I'm taking mum, it has granddad's photograph in it and I'm going to tell the class how proud I am of him." It was a touching moment – 43 years after I first climbed that famous marble staircase inside Ibrox it still had an effect on my grandchild.'

Mathieson can look back on his career with few regrets. He was his own man and made his own decisions, signing for Rangers when the time was right for him and leaving on the same terms. Unlike so many in football, he chose to step off the coaching treadmill to concentrate on his business commitments and sidestepped the pitfalls and vagaries of life in management. For a man who made a point of controlling the factors that influenced his career, the only lingering niggle is totally outside his domain: 'I don't think the 1972 team has ever got the credit it deserves. It's almost as though we're an embarrassment because the club hasn't been able to repeat it. If you contrast that with Celtic, you can't get past the front door at Parkhead without seeing a picture of the Lisbon

Lions team or a replica of the European Cup. While the Celtic team are included in everything, we seem to be kept out of sight. That saddens me. We all share a love of Rangers and it's a team and an achievement that deserve to be remembered.'

CHAPTER FOUR

# JOHN GREIG

Rangers captain, manager, director and fans' favourite. Scotland captain, two-time winner of the nation's player of the year award and a Member of the Order of the British Empire. Where do you begin when it comes to John Greig's career? It is not a new problem or one I can claim to have tackled alone. Indeed, the man himself knows at first hand the potential perils of trying to compact almost half a century of football memories and put them into words.

When I interviewed Greig, he was enjoying some brief respite at his desk at the Murray Park training ground in the midst of a hectic nationwide book-signing tour, promoting his autobiography *My Story* following its release in 2005.

Long overdue, some might argue, but the subject insists there was no hidden motive behind the timing, no agenda and no attempt to produce an exposé. 'It took 18 months all in all. As you get older you start to have senior moments, so I thought it would be good to do it before they start happening more often. A lot of people have said to me over the years that I should do a book and, eventually, I decided to give it a go. I don't believe in slaughtering this person or that, it isn't what the book is about. It's about some fantastic memories I have taken from football. It is also about marking the bad times and remembering them. The Ibrox disaster was a terrible time but it shouldn't be forgotten or ignored and that is important to me.'

The aftermath of the book's release also put Greig back in touch with the club's far-flung supporters, stopping off in Inverness and Stornoway on a tour that took him to all corners of the country. It also reinforced the affection that saw him named as the greatest Ranger of all time in a post-millennium fans' poll organised by the club.

'It was great to get out and about. A lot of people don't realise that Rangers supporters don't just come from Glasgow, there are a lot of fans throughout the country. I've always had a good relationship with the supporters and it is nice to be able to meet with them.'

Not that there is any danger of Greig losing touch with Rangers or the club's supporters, as he is still firmly entrenched at Ibrox and Murray Park. Appointed to the board of directors in 2003, he is an all-seeing presence around the club and held up as a walking embodiment of what every trainee and young professional on the books is aspiring to emulate.

'I'm based at Murray Park now and very, very fortunate to have a day to day involvement with the club. I am in during the day to watch the young boys train in the morning and then at night to watch the schoolboys who are attached to the club. It gives me a lot of pleasure to see kids who come in at 13 years old earning themselves professional contracts.

'I try and build up relationships with them and their parents and help them understand what the club is about. I think you obviously have to have ability, but you also need the determination and dedication to make it as a player. I had a lot of help as a kid, I would never have done it on my own, and it is nice to be able to do my bit for the generation coming through now. I'll certainly never forget the people who helped me along the way.'

The memories of his own beginnings in football still burn brightly. As unlikely as it may sound from a man who went on to captain one of Britain's biggest clubs, Greig still recalls the pain of the rejection he felt when Hearts, his heroes as a schoolboy growing up in Edinburgh, never gave him his big break at Tynecastle.

Instead, in 1959, it was Glasgow Rangers who stepped

forward and took a chance on a slightly-built inside forward who had not yet turned 17 but would go on to become an unmovable defensive rock at club and international level. Greig had his arm twisted by his father and elder brother to sign for the Light Blues and can still recall the moment he was converted from a Jambo to a True Blue.

The transformation happened at Easter Road as Rangers played Hibs just days after he had pledged his future to the Ibrox side by penning a part-time contract. 'Rangers beat a decent Hibs side 6–1. Perhaps not surprisingly, my reaction was that this was some team I had signed for. Ralph Brand scored four of the Rangers goals, with Andy Matthew and Jimmy Millar getting the others. From that day on I was a Rangers fan and not once in the past 46 years has my loyalty ever wavered.'

The progression from supporter to player happened remarkably swiftly. Greig began his Ibrox life by juggling his fledgling football career with his commitments to an engineering apprenticeship, but by 1960 had been summoned to Scot Symon's office to find a full-time deal, at £10 per week, on the table. He put pen to paper and the adventure began.

There was no Murray Park, no multi-million-pound training complex. Instead, Rangers worked out at the home of Benburb juniors and Greig was paired with the worldly-wise Ian McColl, a future Scotland manager, on his first day. He moved through the ranks from the third team to the reserves and made his first-team debut at the age of 18 in a League Cup tie against Airdrie at Ibrox. Rangers won 4–1 and the new boy scored the opener after just ten minutes.

The pre-match time-killer and nerve-settler was a game of head tennis instigated by Jim Baxter, with Greig admitting: 'We must have looked quite a sight standing in our jock straps, heading the ball back and forward. In those days the players weren't allowed to put on their shirts and shorts until just before kick-off because we always had to look immaculate.'

He made his league debut the same year and scored seven goals in 19 appearances as the club, defending champions, finished runners-up to Dundee. They compensated by completing the cup double, although Greig's involvement in both the Scottish Cup and League Cup was restricted to the early stages. The team at the time included the likes of Baxter, Willie Henderson and Ian McMillan.

Within a year of his arrival on the first-team scene, Greig had forced his way into the heart of the side after finding a new role as a defender. In the 1962/63 season he missed just seven league games as the men in blue marched to the league championship, nine points clear of closest challengers Kilmarnock, and Greig claimed his second winners' medal in that season's 3–0 win over Celtic in the Scottish Cup final replay.

Having taken his European bow the previous term, against Standard Liege of Belgium, he sampled Spanish football in a tie against Seville. Little did he know how important that European experience would prove in the years ahead.

In 1963/64 Greig completed his full set of domestic honours at the tender age of 21 as Rangers claimed the treble in devastating fashion, losing just six of 52 games in all competitions. The class of 64 is still referred to in some quarters as the best ever Rangers team, but Greig prefers to leave those conclusions to others. 'People can still rattle off the names of those who played in 1964, which tells its own story, but I feel the European team of 1972 is in the same bracket. The team that won in Barcelona didn't get the recognition it deserved.'

The men who played in the all-conquering team of 1964 could not have imagined what lay ahead. The following season Rangers fell to fifth in the league, with Killie crowned champions, and went out at the third round stage of the Scottish Cup in a tie against Hibs.

Victory in the League Cup final against Celtic was a small

consolation, although for Greig there was more room for personal optimism. Having been an ever-present in the 1964/65 campaign he was named Rangers captain at the end of the term, replacing Jim Baxter following his transfer to Sunderland. Greig recalls Scot Symon's ceremony for bestowing the honour, calling him to one side after training and telling him: 'I want you to be captain.' Simple words, but for Greig a life-changing sentence.

He went from a player to a leader and retained the role for more than 13 years, until his retirement in 1978. Unfortunately for Greig, his appointment coincided with another landmark in the Scottish game – the beginning of Celtic's nine-in-a-row sequence of championship wins. He jokes that if he had known what lay ahead he would have left the country, but in truth he came through the other side to experience highs that compensated for the lows of watching Jock Stein's men take the Scottish game by the scruff of the neck.

Rangers, led by their new skipper, were runners-up to Celtic in 1965/66 and finished in the same berth for the next four years. Greig did, however, collect his first trophy as captain as the Light Blues beat Celtic at Hampden in the Scottish Cup final with a solitary strike from Kai Johansen. He was also chosen as Scotland's player of the year by the country's football writers, the first of two occasions he would collect that particular honour. Crucially, the success earned Rangers a place in the European Cup Winners' Cup and marked the start of the club's most fruitful spell among the elite of the continental game.

Rangers have played in a European Cup Winners' Cup final three times. In 1961 Fiorentina proved too strong and won the showdown 2–1. In 1967 it was Bayern Munich who shaded it with a 1–0 win and in 1972 it was time for Rangers to claim the glory. Greig played in the last two finals but remembers all three games as if they were yesterday.

'I had watched the club's first European final, played and

lost in the second and finally won it in the third. It is always difficult to single out a career highlight but Barcelona is right up there. Making my debut and scoring in that game against Airdrie is one because it was the realisation of a dream. Being made captain of Rangers, after a succession of fantastic men, was another great honour while every cup final win and league championship success was tremendous. From the club's point of view, winning the European Cup Winners' Cup was a massive achievement and that is the case personally too.'

The 1966/67 run in Europe is vital to the story of the success five years later. It was the year Celtic became kings of Europe and Rangers were desperate to match their city rivals. Glentoran were the first side to fall, going out 5–1 on aggregate, and Borussia Dortmund followed as Rangers clinched a 2–1 win over two legs. Greig, in the days before penalty shoot-outs, won a coin toss to decide the quarter-final after his team had finished deadlocked at 2–2 with Spanish outfit Real Zaragoza. Slavia Sofia proved a more manageable hurdle in the last four, the Scottish hopefuls running out 1–0 winners in both the home and away legs.

That set up a clash of titanic proportions with Bayern Munich in Nuremberg with the trophy on the line. A Franz Roth goal deep in extra-time ensured the cup made the short trip back to Munich, with Greig admitting: 'The galling thing was that we had created as many scoring chances as Bayern and had generally outplayed them. I wept for the first time in my career as I walked off the pitch.'

Like some of his team-mates, Greig threw his silver runners-up medal away but his was retrieved and now sits side by side with the gold medal he collected in Barcelona. He was one of four players – along with Sandy Jardine, Willie Johnston and Dave Smith – to have played in both games and the pain of defeat in 1967 was undoubtedly a spur in future European adventures.

In 1972 it all came together. Greig steered the team safely through the first round against Rennes, 2–1 on aggregate, and then suffered the nail-biting wait to discover if the away goal rule would favour his side after a 6–6 draw with Sporting Lisbon over 180 minutes. It did, and Rangers faced up to the Italians of Torino in the quarter-final. The captain recalls being told by manager Willie Waddell to put Claudio Sala out of the game. His response was to ask whether he meant for one game or for good. It was not said in jest, although Greig was only red-carded three times in his lengthy career despite a reputation as one of the country's most uncompromising players.

Rangers emerged victorious against the Turin side, winning 2–1 over two legs, and held old sparring partners Bayern Munich to a 1–1 draw at Ibrox. Greig missed the second leg through injury and was touch and go for the final against the men from Moscow, being persuaded to declare himself fit on the eve of the single biggest game in the illustrious history of Rangers.

He admits: 'I should never have played in the final, it was an act of sheer folly.' But he did play, and did his bit in the 3–2 win despite the pain of a stress fracture to his right foot which had kept him sidelined in the weeks leading up to the showpiece game. 'It was especially important because of the success Celtic had enjoyed in Europe five years earlier. It was good to be able to give the Rangers fans a taste of that. Because I was the captain and because of my position now, I get a lot of recognition that the other ten players deserve. In fact, I needed particular help from all of them in that game because I wasn't fit.'

The final was tinged with regret for the captain, who was forced to collect the trophy deep within the Nou Camp due to the on-field problems after the match. 'The team, or the club, didn't get the credit it deserved because of the trouble after the match. It was a real blow to have to pick up the trophy in the stadium instead of out on the pitch in front of the tens of thousands of supporters who had paid a lot of money to be at the match.'

Despite the regrets, Greig does not hold the Rangers supporters responsible: 'There was no badness involved. The Spanish police and authorities had a taste of it before the match when a few fans ran on to wish us all the best when we were on looking at the pitch before we got changed. They over-reacted when the same thing happened, albeit in greater numbers, towards the end. They wanted to celebrate, not look for a fight – there were virtually no Russian supporters in the stadium.'

The million-dollar question is whether the Rangers supporters will ever again get the chance to celebrate a European trophy properly. Greig admits: 'I live in hope that it could happen again. The biggest problem is that Rangers are operating in the Bosman market while the likes of Real Madrid are going out and spending tens of millions on individual players. That makes it so difficult to compete but it would be great for Scottish football as a whole if it did happen again. What will always set us apart is that we were a team of 11 Scots. We had fantastic individuals but more importantly we gelled as a team. That may happen again one day and I can see progress being made in Scotland, particularly with the national team.'

By the time Rangers celebrated their finest hour in Europe, Greig was already well travelled as a Scotland regular. He made his debut in 1964 in a 1–0 win against England at Hampden in the home international championship, given his big break by former Ibrox training partner Ian McColl. Ian Gilzean scored the only goal of the game in the 78th minute.

Already an under-23 international and Scottish League select player, nothing could prepare Greig for the many twists and turns he would endure in the dark blue of his country. In total he was capped 44 times over 11 years and played under McColl, Celtic adversary Jock Stein, Bobby

Brown and Willie Ormond. His final cap came against Denmark in a 3–1 win in 1975, the 15th time he had captained his country. Greig was appointed Scotland skipper by Stein in 1965, just a year after taking his international bow, and led the side out for the first time against Italy in Naples in a 3–0 World Cup qualifying defeat.

It was not the end Greig had hoped for, having produced his most famous international performance in the first leg at Hampden when he scored the only goal of the game, a screamer from outside of the box to the top corner, to shock the Italians. That goal was one of three the Rangers captain scored for Scotland, the others coming against Finland and Wales. Despite his status, Greig's shrewd decision to remain based in his home city of Edinburgh relieved some of the pressure.

'When I went back to Edinburgh to promote my book, it was good to be able to walk down Princes Street again. That's something I hadn't done for a long time. We moved across to Glasgow 27 years ago when I was manager at Ibrox, but as a player I had stayed in Edinburgh. The beauty of that was, even as captain of Rangers and Scotland, I never really got bothered when I walked down the street. I think it might have been different walking down Buchanan Street or Sauchiehall Street in Glasgow.'

Greig never had the opportunity to represent Scotland in the World Cup or European Championship finals, suffering similar qualification problems to the current Scotland team. He believes the fortunes of the current crop of internationalists are about to improve.

'We haven't produced players of the calibre of Kenny Dalglish or Jim Baxter in recent years but there are signs of recovery. The Scotland team has been stuck in a rut – it's difficult when it is being drummed into them that they are the worst team the country's ever seen. Now it looks as though they are not afraid to go up against players with big reputations, the likes of Italy. Every player is only as good as their next game and I used to love going up against the big-name players to test myself and my own ability.'

After Scottish Cup success in 1966, Greig picked up another League Cup medal after the 1–0 win over Celtic in 1970. The Scottish Cup followed in 1973 and, finally, he got his hands on his third league winners' badge in 1974/75, the campaign that saw the Light Blues wrest power away from Celtic to end the latter's hopes of ten consecutive titles. He missed only 12 games that term, coming back from injury as a substitute in the victory against Hibs that clinched the league. The best was still to come for the captain, leading his side in the glorious treble season of 1975/76.

Rangers were back, and Greig was at the centre of it. He was there at the beginning, leading the side in the 2–1 opening day Old Firm encounter that saw Derek Johnstone and Quinton Young on target. He was there at the end, in the goalless draw with Dundee United at Ibrox, and was the only man to play in all 36 Premier League games as his side beat the Hoops by six points in the race to be crowned champions. In the League Cup the captain was ever present, at Hampden to collect the trophy after Alex MacDonald had scored the only goal of the game and completed a remarkable season when he played in every round of the Scottish Cup on the way to the 3–1 win over Hearts. Greig had waited 12 long years since his last treble and was determined to savour every minute of it.

He did not have to wait as long for the next to come around, even though the season after the 1976 treble proved an anti-climax as Rangers finished runners-up to Celtic and lost to their biggest rivals in the Scottish Cup. The League Cup title, courtesy of another Alex MacDonald Old Firm winner, was the only reason for cheer in 1976/77. Rangers roared back with a vengeance in the 1977/78 season and again swept the board domestically. It would prove to be their esteemed skipper's final term as a player, and what a way to go out.

Greig was 35 by the time the curtain fell, but advancing years were no barrier and he played in 29 of the 36 league fixtures despite injury disrupting his start. In fact, a change of attitude in his later days is credited with a renewed verve for the game. 'I always remember when I was 32 or 33 and I started having terrible problems with pulled hamstrings, even to the extent of having to shorten my stride when I was making longer runs. I knew that if it continued to be a problem I wouldn't be able to go on. I started treating every game as though it was my last and enjoyed every minute. In the end, I played on for another 100 games or so.'

In his 1977/78 swansong, Celtic had been accounted for, 2–1 after extra-time in the League Cup final earlier in the season, and Greig made his final competitive appearance of an illustrious Rangers career on 6 May 1978. It came in front of more than 61,500 people at Hampden as his side beat Aberdeen, runners-up in the league, 2–1 courtesy of goals from Alex MacDonald and Derek Johnstone to complete the third piece of the treble jigsaw.

It was the latest prize in a long list for Greig. When he collected his second Scottish player of the year award in 1976, he became the first man in the history of the game to do the double. Others have followed but he holds the achievement dear and still makes a point of attending the annual awards ceremony, to which all former winners have an open invite.

He heads his club's own hall of fame list as the player voted the best of all time, but it was an award away from the game that signalled to Greig just how far he had come. Awarded an MBE in the 1977 Jubilee honours list, he made the trip south with his wife Janette and son Murray to collect. 'From a non-playing point of view, to go from a wee boy kicking a tennis ball around the streets outside our tenement building in Edinburgh to taking my wife and son to meet the Queen at Buckingham Palace was the greatest honour.' He is now a grandfather, and it is another memory to pass on to the next generation of the Greig clan.

A month after Rangers had completed their second clean sweep under Jock Wallace, the manager shocked Scottish football. He cleared his desk at Ibrox and moved to the more lucrative English league with Leicester City. Despite his lack of experience in the dug-out, Greig was the only man Rangers were likely to turn to.

Having led the club with distinction on the park, he was entrusted with repeating that off it. He could have played on and juggled both roles, as team-mates Alex MacDonald and Sandy Jardine went on to do so successfully with Hearts, but felt the job was too big for that. He points out that being manager of Rangers in the 1970s didn't just revolve around picking the team, it enveloped everything from dealing with the cleaning staff to maximising revenue from the famous old stadium.

Having become the first Rangers player ever to be awarded a testimonial earlier that year, playing against the World Cup-bound Scotland team in front of 70,000 to mark the occasion, he had already been afforded the opportunity for a playing send-off. That left the path open to channel his energies towards management. He would discover just how draining that would be as the years spanned out in front of him.

Greig took over the reins in the summer of 1978 and was under no illusions about the task facing him. 'When Jock quit as manager he got out at the right time, in my opinion, because we were an ageing team. The upshot was that I was the one left with the onerous task of getting rid of the older players and bringing in the younger ones.'

His first league game in charge was a 1–0 defeat at home to St Mirren. He sent out a team featuring Barcelona veterans Peter McCloy, Sandy Jardine, Alex MacDonald, Tommy McLean and Derek Johnstone, but the presence of the old guard could not prevent Rangers from slipping to another defeat and four point-sapping draws in the five Premier League encounters that followed. Greig rallied the troops, getting his first league victory in a 4–1 home win against Motherwell at the end of September and by the close of business they were just three points short of champions Celtic.

The League Cup and Scottish Cup were retained in the Ibrox trophy room after final victories against Aberdeen and, by virtue of two replays, Hibs. It was an encouraging start to his reign, so close to a dream start. Maintaining that form proved to be difficult as the experienced side began to break up.

In 1979/80 his charges fell to fifth in the league as his old team-mate Alex Ferguson's influence began to tell at Aberdeen, the Pittodrie team picking up their first title since 1955. Celtic beat Rangers by a single goal in the Scottish Cup victory to compound the problems and the League Cup run had been ended by the Dons at the third-round stage.

Hopes of a dramatic improvement in 1980/81 were shattered, with Greig's side third behind Celtic and runners-up Aberdeen in the league, but his managerial CV was boosted by a fantastic Scottish Cup triumph in a Hampden replay against Dundee United. Neither team could break the deadlock in the first game but the replay was entirely different, a John MacDonald double and strikes from Davie Cooper and Bobby Russell leaving Dundee United shattered after a 4–1 defeat. It has been credited as the finest display produced under Greig's stewardship.

In 1981/82 it was Celtic who again came out on top in the marathon of the Premier League, with Aberdeen second over the line and Rangers third. The Dons won the Scottish Cup 4–1 after extra-time in the final, but the Gers were not empty-handed having beaten Dundee United 2–1 in the League Cup showpiece thanks to goals from Davie Cooper and Ian Redford – a player taken to the club by Greig from Dundee. It was fitting that one of his own recruits won the last trophy he would savour with the club to which he had devoted his entire career. In 1982/83 Rangers finished fourth, Dundee United taking the honours as the Old Firm struggled to compete with Scottish football's exuberant New Firm in the shape of the teams from Tannadice and Pittodrie.

Celtic had beaten Rangers in the League Cup final and Aberdeen were the conquerors in the Scottish Cup final. The pressure was beginning to tell, and three months into the following season, in October 1983, Greig told the board he was ready to walk away for the sake of his health and his family, who were beginning to learn for themselves the level of abuse a Rangers manager can endure when fortune does not shine on him. Greig recalls having to be driven home by members of the Ibrox staff, incapacitated by splitting headaches that were just one of the symptoms he suffered as a result of the strain.

For 23 years, man and boy, he had gone to work at Ibrox. He had chances to move on to fresh pastures, Everton and Newcastle both making approaches during his playing days, but chose to stay loyal. That loyalty earned him the right to sample what he considers the 'biggest job in British football', but five years was enough, and his career in coaching drew to a close. He did, however, leave a sizable legacy in the shape of his greatest ever signing . . . Ally McCoist.

When he walked out of the front door at Ibrox in 1983, no longer on the payroll, Greig did not envisage a return. That all changed in 1990, when owner David Murray, in the early days of his Graeme Souness-led revolution, offered him a public relations role with the club.

He worked alongside Souness and his successor Walter Smith in that capacity before seeing his involvement intensify with the arrival of Dutchman Dick Advocaat in 1998, just weeks after Greig had suffered a heart attack during a workout at the Ibrox gym. That health scare could have prompted a reduction in his workload: instead, he returned to the frontline as a member of Advocaat's inner circle.

'My role changed dramatically when Dick Advocaat came in as manager. As the first coach from overseas to take charge of the team, he had requested my help as he settled in. Even things like finding your way around away grounds can be difficult when you are new to a country, so I was able to introduce him to Scottish football. As time went on and our relationship developed, we would work together from 8 a.m. to 5 p.m. and talked a lot about tactics and the team. He put the fire back in my belly and I valued his faith in me.'

Greig was involved in most aspects, right down to the recruitment of some players. Claudio Reyna was one of his suggestions as a replacement for the injured Barry Ferguson and was promptly brought to Glasgow. Advocaat's tenure brought success, claiming the treble in his debut season of 1998/99, retaining the league the following year, and even awarding Greig an SPL medal for his efforts. Alex McLeish took over in 2001, by which point his old confidant, in anticipation of the appointment of a Scottish manager, had already begun working with the younger players at the club. Greig had instigated a youth programme at Rangers as manager which bore fruit in the shape of future Scotland internationalists Derek Ferguson, Ian Durrant, John Spencer and Dave McPherson.

Now he acts as ambassador and link between the current development programme and its young players. 'When Alex McLeish came in, I knew he wouldn't need the same type of assistance as Dick, so I asked for a different remit. For the first six months I helped him settle in at the club and then moved over to trying to help the younger players at the club. It has always been close to my heart.'

Working out of the luxurious and sprawling Murray Park complex on the outskirts of Glasgow, he is well placed to muse on the changes that have shaken the game since he signed on at Ibrox in the late 1950s. He admits: 'The biggest change in the game without a doubt has been the Bosman ruling. When I played, it was very difficult to leave a club – they could simply re-register you and deny any transfer request. Now the balance of power has shifted to the players and some aren't happy to let the ink dry on a contract before they are looking to the next move or next deal. Freedom of movement has had a big impact but I wouldn't necessarily say it has been for the good of the game.

'I don't envy players today – you can only play in the era you're born in. We were well paid. The basic salary was slightly more than a first-class tradesman may have earned, but the win bonuses on top of that could make it comfortable. The big difference was that players from my generation had to carry on working once they retired from the game. That isn't necessarily the case now.'

But does that mean the modern generation are less hungry? According to the man renowned for his never-say-die attitude, it shouldn't. 'I could understand somebody not having the desire to get up at 4 a.m. and go down the pits to work on their hands and knees in the cold and dark, but not when it comes to going out and playing football. I don't understand when people say players don't have the right attitude. You are never going to do anything better in your life than get paid to play the game you love.'

CHAPTER FIVE

# DEREK JOHNSTONE

Everton had Wayne Rooney, Liverpool had Michael Owen and, long before either of those had kicked a ball, Rangers had Derek Johnstone. He was the ultimate teen sensation and the central character in Scotland's best-known football fairytale. Like every 16-year-old boy he dreamt of scoring the winning goal in a cup final – but the difference is he woke up the next day and made it happen. I make no excuses for retelling the well-worn tale of his famous introduction to a national audience.

Too young even to drive, he was old enough to carry the hopes of the entire Rangers support on his shoulders as he scored the only goal of the game in the 1970 League Cup final. It was not his debut, but the game did mark his arrival on the big stage and he did it in style.

It also gave a huge hint that the new boy would go far in the game, although few could have predicted the glittering career that would follow for the rookie who went on to become Scotland's player of the year, captain at Ibrox and a Scotland internationalist.

Johnstone's career on the front line saw him sample life at Chelsea, fulfil another childhood dream by briefly turning out for his boyhood heroes Dundee United and ended with a foray into the world of management. In the late 1980s he crossed the divide and joined the media corps, carving out a role for himself as a radio analyst and newspaper columnist that he has held for close to two decades.

It all began for him on 19 September 1970, when he made his first appearance for the first team in a 5–0 First Division win over Cowdenbeath at Ibrox in torrential conditions. For the 30,000 fans who braved the elements, it gave them a glimpse of a star in the making as he knocked home a double to justify Willie Waddell's decision to throw the youngster into his side.

Waddell was in his first full season at Ibrox and in the midst of a rebuilding exercise after a disappointing barren spell under predecessors Davie White and Scot Symon. The last trophy to have been delivered to the famous old stadium was the Scottish Cup in 1966. While the club had waited more than four years, Johnstone would have to wait just a matter of weeks to get his hands on some silverware.

The previous season, in 1969/70, had seen the club finish runners-up to Celtic and scoring goals had been a struggle. With 67 in 34 league games, the club had scored more in every season since 1954/55. Waddell needed to find an answer and in Johnstone, who had arrived from school in his home town of Dundee, having first linked up with the club two years previously, he saw a ready-made, if raw, solution. He was used sparingly in that first campaign and again goals were at a premium, the club finishing fourth in the First Division with just 58 strikes to their credit, but he did enough to show that Rangers had a striker fit to rival record signing Colin Stein.

Johnstone was capped at youth level, but his rapid progress astonished everyone, not least his teenage club-mates whom he had joined just months earlier to start what he expected to be a lengthy apprenticeship in 1970.

'I wasn't long out of school and the other boys who had been at the club for a few years told me how it would be. I'd play a while in the third team, maybe get into the reserves after a couple of seasons and then try and get a game for the first team. Instead I was in the team within three months, that was how quickly it all happened for me. I was only 16 but I was 5ft 11in, could play anywhere on the park and was fairly confident. There were a lot of experienced players in the side, the likes of John Greig and Sandy Jardine, and they all looked after me. A lot of people think the cup final was my first game but it wasn't. I played a few weeks before against Cowdenbeath: the rain was pouring down but there were 30,000 inside Ibrox and I scored two goals. Never mind the cup final, that was the moment for me. That was when I realised my dream, my first game and my first goals.'

'Fairly confident' comes close. In fact, the 16-year-old showed in his first game he was capable of excelling in the first team. His self-assurance persuaded Waddell he was ready to sample the Old Firm experience and he handed Johnstone the No.9 shirt for the League Cup final on 24 October 1970. The previous month he had been a trainee, now he was leading the line in the biggest club game on the planet and had pinched Colin Stein's jersey into the bargain. Stein wore No.10 that day.

In front of a crowd of 106,000 he was thrown head to head with the might of champions Celtic at Hampden Park. Billy McNeill and Jim Craig were Scotland's most formidable defensive pairing at the time, but they were outfoxed by the teenager.

Willie Henderson fed the ball to Alex MacDonald in midfield, he released Willie Johnston down the right wing and his cross was bulleted home by Johnstone, despite being sandwiched between Craig and McNeill, to leave the Hoops keeper Evan Williams stranded. The drought was over and it sparked frenzied celebrations among the Rangers supporters who saluted their new great hope.

For the player, it capped an amazing 24 hours in which his world had been turned upside down by a ten-second conversation deep inside Ibrox stadium. Always a picture of composure on the field, Johnstone admits his nerves were jangling as the news he was about to take centre stage sank in during the build-up to that final.

'I wasn't expected to play in the final. Everyone thought Willie Waddell would go with the more experienced players.

He took me into the boot room on the Friday before the game and said: "Here's half a dozen tickets, get some friends and family along. You're playing." That was all the ceremony he needed. I was glad he had told me in advance because it meant I could go away and prepare myself for it. As a boy you lay in your bed at night dreaming of scoring the winning goal in a cup final. The next day I woke up and did it.

'I remember going out to look at the pitch after arriving at the stadium. Everyone was still out there but I was back in, stripped and ready to play. It was five past two, and there was still almost an hour before kick-off. I had to take my top back off and go away and calm myself down. I was just as excited during the game, running on pure adrenaline. It took a bit of beating.'

Having been introduced to the Ibrox faithful as a forward, it was during the summer of his first full season as a first-team player that his versatility first came to the fore. Rangers headed for Sweden for a training camp and during the course of the trip Johnstone was moved from centre forward to the centre of the defence.

He had played at the back as a schoolboy and Waddell liked what he saw in Gothenburg. The manager said at the time: 'Derek Johnstone is another John Charles in the making. He has still to prove to me which is his best position. I can play him at centre forward and he will score goals for me. I can pull him back into the defence and he will stop people scoring. Both roles come to him easily and he plays both so very well.'

In the 1971/72 season he started out wearing No.5, at the heart of the defence, but spent half of his time playing further forward in midfield or attack. He bagged seven goals in 16 league appearances, including his first hat-trick in a 6–0 win over Hearts, despite being deployed as a defender for spells. His side would go on to finish third in the First Division but fell at the preliminary stage in the League Cup and were beaten by Hibs in the semi-final of the Scottish Cup.

In Europe it was, of course, a different story entirely. Johnstone had dipped his toe in the water at that level as a substitute in the second leg of the 1970/71 Fairs Trophy first-round tie against Bayern Munich, a game Rangers drew 1–1 after losing 1–0 to a disputed goal in Germany.

The following season he had to bide his time but went on to make a crucial contribution to the successful run in the European Cup Winners' Cup. Johnstone was drafted in to the side for his first start in Europe against Torino in Italy in the first leg of the quarter-final. He helped his side to a 1–1 draw and again wore No.8 as Rangers won the home leg 1–0. In the last four against Bayern, Johnstone was a vital cog in the defensive operation that kept the Germans at bay in Munich after Paul Breitner's opener had been cancelled out by an own goal. They were shut out at Ibrox as the Scottish shock-troops won 1–0 and the golden boy, 18 by then, was on the cusp of another cup final.

When Colin Jackson limped out of the final training session on the eve of the Barcelona final, it cemented Johnstone's place in the side. He wore No.5 and partnered Dave Smith in defence but was still able to make some of his customary raids into enemy territory to supplement his team's attacking options. In the closing stages, with the three-goal lead cut to one, his defensive qualities were even more valuable.

He recalls: 'I had been in the side for 14 months by the time we played in Barcelona, so I had settled by then. Still, I didn't realise how big it was until I started to look back in later years at all the great Rangers teams that haven't been able to win in Europe. I was never going to play in the final but we lost Ronnie McKinnon in the earlier round against Sporting Lisbon and then Colin Jackson just before the Barcelona game. I hoped I would be one of the subs because we knew Colin was struggling with injury but when the team was named I was in – he hadn't made it.

'Although I considered myself a striker, even playing at

centre-half I was confident. I had Davie Smith behind me at sweeper and he was one of the best talkers in the game. He would lead you through every game and was the same with the opposition – he'd be asking the strikers why they had made that run or played that pass. He told me before we went out at the Nou Camp just to go for every ball and that if I lost out he would be at my back. For any centre-half that's great for confidence because the dangerous time is the split second when you decide whether to hold your position or go for the ball. I could throw myself at everything.

'I've always said that even though Colin Stein and Willie Johnston were marvellous, Davie was the man of the match. He was getting forward and causing all sorts of problems. The two of us were encouraged to go forward and we did. Davie went up the park a couple of times and so did I, with Sandy Jardine and Willie Mathieson tucking in to cover. We didn't play a strict 4–4–2, it was a good system and well suited to European ties. It was a great way to play.'

Like the rest of his team-mates, for Johnstone the joy of winning was tempered by the pain of having the shine taken off the occasion. 'The down side was when the punters started coming on the pitch, John Greig went away to pick up the cup with the manager and I'll always remember him coming back into the dressing room and throwing it into the bath where all the guys were.

'When you win, you want to show off the trophy. Instead we were on the back of a truck getting soaked by the rain at Ibrox the next day. It was the greatest day in the club's history, so it was disappointing not to get to celebrate it properly. In this game you can never say never, but who knows when it will happen again? Now the bigger clubs are getting richer and Rangers and Celtic are struggling to keep up.'

The Dundonian would have plenty of opportunity to celebrate in the seasons ahead as Rangers traded places with Celtic to become the dominant force in the Scottish game and he became one of the first names on Jock Wallace's team sheet. Wallace had taken over from Waddell for the 1972/73 season, when Johnstone became established as a virtual ever-present and missed only three league games as the club finished second. The bulk of his games were in defence.

He collected his third winners' medal in the Scottish Cup final that season, Rangers winning 3–2 against Celtic in front of 122,000 people, and played a key role in the winning strike as he rose to head Tommy McLean's free-kick towards goal only to see it kept out by the post and present Tom Forsyth with a tap-in to clinch the cup.

The 1973/74 campaign was another barren season for the Light Blues but the following year Johnstone, still flitting between defence and attack, collected the first of three league championship winners' medals. He contributed 15 goals in 27 First Division outings as his side won the title with games to spare, including the opening strike in the 3–0 win over Celtic in the second Old Firm meeting of the season, which hammered another nail in the Parkhead side's hopes of making it ten in a row.

It went from good to sublime when in 1975/76 the Ibrox men swept the board in Scotland. Again his goals were crucial to the championship effort, scoring the winner in the New Year derby against Celtic to start an unbeaten run to the end of the season that saw them overhaul their city rivals' lead. It was another Johnstone special that sealed the main prize, as he hit the net just 22 seconds into a game against Dundee United at Tannadice to win the league with two games left to play. Playing almost exclusively in attack, he was the leading scorer in the Premier Division with 15 goals in 32 starts.

The League Cup had brought another Old Firm victory thanks to a single Alex MacDonald strike and Johnstone got the third and final leg of the treble quest underway with the opener in the Scottish Cup against Hearts, grabbing a second late in the game to add to another MacDonald goal in a 3–1 win. He had scored seven goals in four cup ties.

Still life was not easy, and the pressure of being a Rangers player was never far away. 'We won the treble in 1976 and nothing at all the following year, that's how fickle the game can be. Three defeats in a row and the manager, and players, were under pressure – whether you had just won the treble or not. That's just the way of Scotland. If you look at Celtic, they went through six managers when Rangers were dominating in the 1990s.'

Rangers, Jock Wallace and Johnstone bounced back in style in the 1977/78 campaign with another stunning hat-trick in the domestic competitions. This time the maturing striker was even more potent, with 25 goals in just 33 league games, including hat-tricks of his own against Ayr and Motherwell. New partner Gordon Smith bagged 20 as Rangers crossed the finish line first.

The League Cup had been won earlier in the season with a 2–1 extra-time win over Celtic and fittingly it was Johnstone who had the last say in what had been a sensational season for him, scoring the second goal in a 2–1 Scottish Cup final win over Aberdeen for his 38th goal in all competitions.

It was a stunning goal-scoring record and he was rewarded when he was named Scotland's player of the year, beating Aberdeen goalkeeper Bobby Clark to the punch – not for the first time that season. Willie Miller and Scotland keeper Alan Rough trailed in third place, demonstrating the calibre of competition Johnstone had for the country's premier individual prize. He followed fellow Barcelona veterans Smith, Greig and Jardine in being crowned by the country's football writers.

After collecting that award in May, the summer of 1978 proved to be an eventful period in his career. When John Greig took over as manager at Rangers his first task was to persuade the unsettled striker to stay at Ibrox. He did that by handing Johnstone the captaincy, having groomed him for the role while he himself was skipper. Jardine was seen by many as the natural person to inherit the armband, but Greig was convinced it would be the making of Johnstone to take on the responsibility.

He had handed in a transfer request as he flew out with Scotland for the 1978 World Cup in Argentina, being courted by England's heavy weights who were reported to be ready to pay £500,000 for his services.

Instead he opted to go with his heart and stayed at the club that had given him his break. He withdrew his transfer request after a miserable time in Argentina, where he was not used once by Ally MacLeod in the ill-fated World Cup finals campaign.

The wasted World Cup trip was a bitter blow to Johnstone, who won 14 caps for Scotland between 1973 and 1979. He made his debut under Willie Ormond against Wales as Scotland sailed to a 2–0 win in Wrexham on 12 May 1973, courtesy of a double from George Graham. As he did at club level, Johnstone played both in defence and attack and grabbed two goals in international matches, ironically both in the warm-up to the 1978 World Cup in two 1–1 draws against Wales and Northern Ireland. His final appearance came a year later, in December of 1979, in a 3–1 defeat at the hands of Belgium, when Jock Stein played him in attack.

'My versatility probably didn't do me any favours in terms of the national team, although I don't suppose there are any other players who have played for Scotland as a defender and a striker. When you are playing for your country you don't care where you're asked to play. To get one cap was a dream come true. I don't think it matters as much now. Berti Vogts devalued it to a certain extent by giving 60 or 70 players debuts in a matter of years. Some would argue that he had to try different players but to me there's just not the same prestige when it comes to playing for Scotland any more.'

By the time his international career ended, Johnstone was the skipper at Ibrox but Greig's decision to hand him the honour was not the principal reason for him pledging his immediate future to the club. He has no regrets about choosing to stay with Rangers when he had considered leaving in 1978, reasoning: 'I won 14 trophies so I think I called it right. I look at much better players than myself who have hardly won a thing and know I was very privileged. Alan Shearer, one of the best strikers the game has ever seen, has only got one winners' medal to his name, so I can't complain.'

He quips: 'The captaincy didn't matter too much to me, it was bad enough looking after myself never mind the rest of the team!'

There is no doubt that a switch south of the border would have been more financially rewarding at that point, with even the man at the top driven out by a strict fiscal policy at Rangers. 'Willie Waddell held the purse strings during Jock Wallace's time in charge, there's no doubt about that. He took it seriously. I remember Colin Stein, Sandy Jardine and myself held out for more money and got a £20 rise – we thought that was unbelievable. Big Jock left to go to Leicester in 1978 because they offered him far more money than Rangers. I spoke to him about it many times and there's no doubt he felt he wasn't valued. Even in Scotland, with all the success he had, he was only the third or fourth highest paid manager in the country.'

Johnstone collected his first trophy as captain under Wallace's replacement in the 1978/79 League Cup final, in which Aberdeen defender Doug Rougvie was sent off after a clash with the Ibrox skipper. He was back up the steps again at Hampden to collect the Scottish Cup later that season after the final against Hibs had gone to a second replay. Johnstone's part was decisive, scoring twice in a 3–2 win to complete the double.

Rangers had also reached the quarter-finals of the

European Cup that year, edged out by Cologne, but the hopes of continued success at home and abroad were dashed. In 1979/80 they fell to fifth, the following season climbed back to third and remained there in 1981/82.

In the cups there was greater success for Rangers and their captain, winning the 1981 Scottish Cup with a 4–1 replay win over Dundee United and the 1981/82 League Cup with a 2–1 win over the same opponents.

At the end of the 1982/83 season Johnstone, who had been succeeded in the captaincy by Ally Dawson, bade farewell to Ibrox and moved to Chelsea in a £30,000 deal. It was very much pre-Abramovich at Stamford Bridge, with the London club finishing 19th in the Second Division the season before their latest Scottish recruit's arrival.

John Neal was the manager charged with returning the Blues to the top flight of the English game and did it in style, with Chelsea winning the league in 1983/84 on goal difference from Sheffield Wednesday. Johnstone was a bit-part player, hampered in the early stages by a hamstring injury, and was allowed to leave for a loan stint with Dundee United in October 1983.

Jim McLean had approached the club with a view to bringing the former Scotland internationalist to Tannadice on a permanent basis but Chelsea maintained he was part of their long-term plans. Instead, Neal sanctioned a one-month loan and Johnstone returned home to Tayside to fill the boots of the injured Paul Sturrock.

United were the reigning champions but were struggling to retain the title, finishing third behind Aberdeen and Celtic in the end. The introduction of Johnstone was an intriguing throw of the dice by McLean. He made his debut for the Tangerines in a League Cup tie against Morton and finished off fittingly by lining up against Rangers for the first time in his life.

'The move to Chelsea came too late for me. I could have gone to Arsenal or Spurs after the World Cup in 1978 for big money, but I was a home body and I wanted to be close to my friends and family. I played very few games for Chelsea and spent most of my time as a substitute, although we did get promoted back up to the big league in that time.

'When Jim McLean asked me to go up to Tannadice on loan I bit his hand off. All of my family were Dundee United supporters and it was a team I'd always wanted to play for. On top of that, it gave me a good opportunity to get back playing football again. It was a win-win situation. Before I went to Rangers as a kid I had trained with Dundee United but didn't like the set-up, so to get a chance later in life was fantastic.

'My last game for United was against Rangers at Ibrox. I was on the bench and Jim asked me if I wanted to go on. I told him I was bloody sure I did. I went away and did my warm-up and without thinking about it automatically sat down in the Rangers dug-out. Big Jock told me in no uncertain terms to get out. I got on for the last 15 minutes. We drew 0–0. I hardly had a chance but if I had I would have had to have been professional about it.'

Johnstone had to wait until December 1984 to make his debut for Chelsea in a First Division game against Sheffield Wednesday at Hillsborough, a match which ended in a 1–1 draw. It was more than a year since he had joined the club and he only made a handful of appearances after that.

Within a month the Londoners had decided they were willing to listen to offers. By that time Jock Wallace was back for his second spell as manager at Ibrox and he handed his former talisman a second chance too, weighing in with a £25,000 offer that was accepted.

Like Jim McLean before him, Wallace was pinning his hopes on Johnstone as a saviour. Rangers had won just four of their opening 13 games in the Premier Division and fans were beginning to turn against the boss. Prior to Johnstone's return they had lost to relegation candidates Hibs and been hammered 5–1 by Aberdeen.

The former skipper made his second debut on 2 February 1985, at Ibrox against Morton. Just as he had done in 1970, he was on the score-sheet. His goal and one from John MacDonald gave Rangers a much needed 2–1 win.

He began his Ibrox renaissance in attack but was dropped back into defence again, only missing two league games in the run-in but not being able to combat the problems that saw the side finish fourth in the table. A further eight games in the top flight in 1985/86 brought his Rangers career to a close once and for all, with Wallace moving aside to signal a change of guard as Graeme Souness prepared to take control.

'Jock asked me to come back and coach the reserves. He wanted me to play alongside them and I did that, the theory being that it's much easier to talk people through games if you're in amongst them. He said I would get a coaching job long-term, but when Graeme Souness came in it all changed.'

He pulled on the light blue No.5 jersey one final time in a 2–1 defeat at St Mirren on 19 April 1986. It was the last of 546 appearances for the club which brought 210 goals, a statistic only bettered by Ally McCoist. He won the championship three times, the Scottish Cup five times, the League Cup five times and collected that precious European medal in 1972.

The bad news for Rangers supporters is he feels he could have done even better: 'I became a utility player and in many ways they took the rise out of me. I would be playing centre-half one week, up front the next and in midfield the week after that. I never got a run in one position. I played something well over 500 games and I would say a third of those were at the back. I never took penalties or had a good run as a striker, so to be the club's second-highest scoring player of all time is something I'm proud of. I never tire of telling Ally McCoist that I would have beaten him if I'd been playing up front regularly.'

As one door closed at Ibrox another opened up across Glasgow at Firhill, home to Partick Thistle. It was an exciting time for the Jags, with Chelsea chairman Ken Bates branching out into the Scottish game by taking a 65 per cent stake in the club after a failed attempt to buy Hibs. Despite his initial claims to the contrary, the idea behind the move into Scottish football was to use Thistle as a feeder club for Chelsea to toughen up reserve and youth team players in danger of stagnating at Stamford Bridge. Billy Dodds and Colin West arrived on loan from Chelsea shortly after.

Courtesy of a £100,000 investment and additional £100,000 interest-free loan from the new owner, for the first time since 1969 there would be full-time football at Partick. Johnstone was Bates' first big-name signing, snapped up on a free transfer and appointed player coach in June 1986.

The masterplan was for the former Scotland star to work alongside manager Bertie Auld as the club attempted to rise out of the First Division, having finished eighth in the 14-team league the previous term, and make an impact in the Premier Division. The blueprint faded fast and was ripped up within a month as Auld walked out and Johnstone was thrust into his first managerial job.

He explains: 'When Bertie got wind of what I was being paid he asked for the same – and was given a straight answer by Ken Bates. He left and after joining as player-coach I was player-manager. I knew I had to get an experienced man in beside me and John Hagart agreed to come on board, having been a coach at Rangers alongside Jock Wallace and Alex Totten. I leant on his experience and really he was the manager – he certainly did most of the coaching.'

With the league reconstructed and featuring 12 teams, hopes were high that the 1986/87 season would bear fruit. Instead it was one of frustration, with the Jags again finishing eighth, but Johnstone, who turned out a handful of times for Partick, does not regard his dalliance with management as a let-down. 'When I took on the job we were second bottom and when I left, after about seven months, we had climbed two places. There were signs of improvement but

Partick were-underachieving. If I hadn't taken that job I would always have wondered "what if?" It didn't work out. I left, and it turned out to be the best thing that ever happened to me. I joined Radio Clyde and have been working in radio ever since. Since coming into the game as a 16-year-old I've only had five days out of work.'

Johnstone had been one of Scottish football's most colourful players for 17 years and his personality remained in demand when he parted company with Thistle in March 1987. He became a member of Radio Clyde's sports team and moved to Real Radio in 2011, combining his broadcast career with that as newspaper columnist in his adopted home city of Glasgow.

Unavoidably that leads him to pass judgement on the teams he played for and some of the men he played alongside. Fortunately, conflict has been a rarity. 'If you are being constructive I think everyone accepts it. Of course there are times you have to be hard on players or managers but you have to be able to support your argument. I've never had a problem with anyone in that respect and I'll keep calling things as I see them.'

## CHAPTER SIX

# DAVID SMITH

The joints are creaking, the pace has faded and the audience is smaller, but Dave Smith is still turning on the style playing the game he loves more than three decades after the Barcelona triumph. Now past his 67th birthday, the Aberdonian has to be content with parading his skills in playing field kick-abouts as a granddad rather than football star. Nevertheless, he still sets about the task with the same enthusiasm that launched him into the professional game in the 1960s. Only a few years ago he was still a regular on the five-a-side football scene in his native city, outwitting opponents 40 years his junior with ease.

It is now 49 years since Smith made his debut as a pro, starting for Aberdeen in a 1–1 draw at home to St Johnstone in January 1962. Even he could not have imagined the highs and lows which were to follow in a career that took in nine teams, three continents, two leg breaks and two European finals memorable for very different reasons.

At this point comes a qualification. While known as David to family and Dave to team-mates, football fans and the media, in fact he is just plain old 'Dad' to this particular author. Still, the research process was the same . . . only the margin for error is, at least in theory, reduced.

Playing as one of the first ever sweepers deployed by a Scottish team, he was credited as an inspirational figure in the European Cup Winners' Cup victory of 1972. As provider of two of the three goals and a key part of the rearguard action that kept the Russians of Moscow Dynamo out in the latter stages, his performance helped clinch the coveted Scottish

Football Writers' Association's player of the year trophy that year. It even brought comparisons to Franz Beckenbauer and Bobby Moore from team-mate Willie Johnston.

His post-Rangers career would take him to the hills of Hollywood and the beaches of Berwick, but throughout his love of football has remained as strong as ever. Smith is the first to admit all of that was beyond his wildest dreams when he made his first tentative steps into the professional game, following in the footsteps of elder brother Doug, who was already a fixture in the Dundee United team, and Hugh, who turned out for Forfar and Morton.

He recalls: 'I always wanted to be a footballer, like every young boy, but it was all about having fun at primary school. Charlie Forbes was the chairman of Aberdeen at that time and was also the headmaster at Middlefield, my school. I wouldn't say that gave me a head start at Pittodrie but obviously he was keen on football so we always had a school team. I went on to play with Hilton, my secondary school, and Lads' Club in Aberdeen. It was the same club Denis Law had come from and there were a lot of good players around at the time.

'It was from there that I trained with Aberdeen, as I did when I left school and went to trade school. I started working as a draughtsman virtually straight away – you couldn't sign professionally for a club until you were 17 at that stage, so I had to find something else. The way round it was to be on the ground staff, like the wonder kids were . . . although I don't remember too many of them going on to make the grade. I eventually signed when I was 17 and was into the first team pretty quickly. Tommy Pearson was the manager at that time, a real gentleman. He was a lovely man, maybe too nice to be a manager.'

Smith made two appearances for the Dons in the 1961/62 season, his debut at Pittodrie against the Saints followed by another 1–1 home draw, this time against Airdrie, just three days later. It was a fleeting introduction to a team which went on to finish 12th in the 16-team First Division, an underachievement for a club that had been crowned champions of Scotland just seven years earlier.

The following season brought a change in fortunes, with a rise to sixth in the league and saw Smith make the Aberdeen No.6 shirt his own in his first full season as a senior player. He turned out 31 times in the league and made four starts in cup competitions.

In the next two campaigns, as Aberdeen fell to ninth and 12th in the First Division, their Scotland under-23 cap missed just a solitary game in each season but bettered that in the 1965/66 campaign, his final one in the red of his home-town club, when he was among three ever-presents in league, Scottish Cup and League Cup games with 45 appearances to his credit.

The performances caught the eye of scouts in Scotland and England. After 166 games and 13 goals, the curtain was about to fall on his Pittodrie career. The only question was which stage he would be appearing on next.

Countless clubs were credited with an interest, but it came down to a three-way contest between Rangers, Everton and Tottenham Hotspur. English football, buoyed by the World Cup success of the national team that summer, was the transfer of choice for the Aberdeen board – more lucrative financially and offering little chance of seeing their old-boy coming back to haunt them.

From a playing perspective, both Spurs and Everton were attractive. Each had won the English championship in the past five years. But there was a sticking point: the player in question had his heart set on Ibrox. Smith went as far as threatening to walk away from football altogether rather than have his hand forced by the Dons board.

That doggedness paid off and in the summer of 1966, a fee of £50,000 was agreed and the next chapter was about to be opened. He explains: 'We had a decent team at Aberdeen and by that time Eddie Turnbull had come in as manager. He was the best I ever played under, tactically and as far as training was concerned. Tommy Pearson was more office based whereas Turnbull was always on the training field. But I wanted to win things, I wanted to move to Rangers. The club made it clear they wanted to sell, even if Turnbull wasn't so keen. At that time they could survive by taking advantage of their assets. Myself, Charlie Cooke and others were all moved on for big fees. Now there aren't the players and there isn't the market to make ends meet the same way, and that's what is killing clubs like Aberdeen.

'I was pushed to go to Tottenham or Everton but I told Aberdeen I wanted to stay, I was prepared to wait for the right move. When the Rangers transfer happened it went in a bit of a blur. My name was on the Aberdeen team sheet on the Friday when I got called into the manager's office and was told to go and meet the Rangers manager in Perth at 1.30 p.m. It was already twelve o'clock by then and I had to make my own way. I got there as quick as I could and it was all agreed in five minutes. I don't even think we discussed terms, I just signed on the spot. I didn't have to think twice.

'Scot Symon signed me and, like Pearson, was another true gentleman. I still remember him around Ibrox in his bowler hat, always immaculate. I went straight into the team the day after signing. We beat Hibs 1–0 at Ibrox and the atmosphere was special. It was different playing in front of tens of thousands of Rangers fans compared to what I'd been used to most weeks and that was another reason I was so keen to make the move happen.'

As debut seasons go, 1966/67 was as eventful as they come. Rangers went into the campaign as Scottish Cup holders, but it was Celtic who were champions. Nobody predicted it would be the beginning of nine-in-a-row domination by the Parkhead side. The Hoops, guided by Jock Stein, did the treble in Smith's first year at Ibrox and capped it with European Cup success in Lisbon against Inter Milan.

In response, Rangers too carved out a European run to be

proud of, in the European Cup Winners' Cup. Glentoran, Borussia Dortmund, Real Zaragoza and Slavia Sofia were all brushed aside to give the blue half of Glasgow a shot at European glory in Nuremberg. Six days earlier, Celtic had completed their mission – for Rangers there was no happy ending. Bayern Munich, courtesy of a Franz Roth goal in the second period of extra-time, edged the tightest of finals.

It was a desperately disappointing end to a season that had also seen the mighty Glasgow Rangers humbled by their lower league namesakes from Berwick in a Scottish Cup tie.

Symon's side were beaten 1–0 at Berwick and although he played in that infamous match, Smith was one of the lucky ones – he survived to play again for the club. He recalls: 'At least by getting to the European final we'd shown we weren't such a bad side. Not everyone survived that Berwick tie – Jim Forrest and George McLean never kicked a ball for Rangers again. I don't think it was right to blame two players. Yes, they missed a few chances, but everyone is guilty of that at some point.

'In some way the final of 1967 was a better occasion than Barcelona, because there was more of a special feel to it. Obviously the result wasn't right but there was a good feeling around the match. There was a big post-match banquet after the 1967 final in Nuremberg at a time when teams used to get together after European ties for a meal. That type of thing petered out in the years after. European football became run of the mill.'

Less than 18 months after tempting Smith to Ibrox, manager Scot Symon was gone. The replacement was Davie White, the coach he had brought in as his assistant in the wake of the Berwick defeat. The fact his team sat proudly at the top of the league and were unbeaten in eight games when he was dismissed in November 1967 was cold comfort for the departing boss.

The 1967/68 league was eventually lost on the final day of the season, ironically Aberdeen denying Smith the championship medal he left Pittodrie to chase when they beat Rangers 3–2 to ensure Celtic retained the title.

The following term proved fruitless, defeat in the Scottish Cup final against Celtic giving Smith his first taste of the Hampden big occasion. Fate conspired to ensure it would also be the last, as he missed the League Cup final win in 1970 due to a broken leg. He did pick up a Scottish Cup winners' medal in 1973, having played in every game apart from the final, but had to be content with a place on the bench. A championship medal also proved frustratingly elusive as Celtic continued to rule the roost in Scotland.

He spent eight full seasons at Ibrox and in that time finished runner-up to Celtic five times, third twice and fourth on one occasion. The same period saw Rangers reach four Scottish Cup finals and the League Cup final twice, but it was in Europe that Smith collected the treasured Rangers winners' medal.

Outsiders could be forgiven for thinking that being a Rangers player in the late 1960s was not easy. Nothing could be further from the truth, at least off the field: 'Nobody wants to be second, but I never had a problem with Rangers supporters or Celtic fans, who I seemed to get on with quite well. I've always found supporters from both sides of the Old Firm to be good people – it's just a shame a few idiots spoil it for the rest. On the whole you could go about your life as normal, go to the shops or out for a meal, without any hassle at all. My wife Sheila and I were always made so welcome in Glasgow. Maybe as players we didn't have the same lifestyle as those who have followed, and we didn't put ourselves in the spotlight. It was probably different for me as well because I came from outside of the city. The Glasgow boys were more wrapped up in the rivalry than those of us from elsewhere.'

Smith had the misfortune of suffering a broken leg on two occasions, fighting back from potentially career threatening injuries in both 1970, after a clash with Kilmarnock's Ross

Mathie at Rugby Park, and 1971 after a training ground challenge from Willie Henderson.

He explains: 'They healed relatively simply, although the first time, my left leg, the ankle was dislocated and my foot was left hanging the wrong way round. Effectively I had to learn to walk again. The next time it was my right leg. Both were accidental, 51 weeks apart, but I never doubted I would recover – I don't know if others did. There's no question it is hard work coming back, but you know the goal at the end of it. I think it's worse for the people around you. After the Kilmarnock game, Sheila was waiting at the top of the road to meet me from the bus in Newton Mearns and it drove right by without stopping. It was a neighbour who told her what had happened in the end and that I was in hospital.'

Those two serious injuries came at the peak of his career, keeping him out of the Rangers side and also, crucially, out of the Scotland reckoning. After he had won two caps against Holland in the 1960s, Smith's international career did not take off in the way most had anticipated. That is one of the few regrets from a career spanning three decades. The international debut came in 1966, while still an Aberdeen player, at Hampden against the Dutch masters. John Prentice was in charge of the Scots and handed Smith his familiar No.6 shirt in a side that featured future Rangers team-mates John Greig, Ronnie McKinnon, Willie Henderson and Willie Johnston. That game ended in a 3–0 defeat, but there was a rematch for Smith in his second Scotland appearance, two years later in the Olympic Stadium in Amsterdam. This time Holland were held to a 0–0 draw, with the national side managed by Bobby Brown by that time.

'I don't think there's any doubt I would have played more games for Scotland if I hadn't had the bad luck with the broken legs. It's a great honour to play for your country and I do wish I had won more caps, especially when I see very ordinary players picking up 50 caps relatively easily now. I always wanted to play at Wembley for Scotland but never got that opportunity.'

Disappointment at international level was countered by elation in Europe with his club in 1972. On his way back from injury, Smith missed the first-round ties against Rennes but came back into the side for the 3–2 win over Sporting Lisbon in the second-round first leg. He was on the bench for the second leg but was called into action after Ronnie McKinnon suffered a broken leg in Portugal. From then on he was an ever-present in the run to the final, being called upon to play Torino at their own game in Turin as part of some tactical fine-tuning by Waddell.

The manager had visited Italy previously to study the methods of Inter Milan coach Helenio Herrera and took on board the system they labelled 'catenaccio'. He turned to that for the tricky trip to face Torino and instead of playing as sweeper alongside Colin Jackson as usual, Smith swept up behind the two-man central defensive pairing of Jackson and Derek Johnstone. It worked a treat.

'It basically meant we were playing a tight 5–3–2. It was devised to frustrate the Italians and we perfected the system in training games before flying out for the quarter-final. I had faced pressure in European ties from Yugoslavia to Germany and Spain but nothing like that night in Turin.'

Rangers withstood that pressure in the main, holding out for a 1–1 draw, before winning 1–0 in Glasgow to book a semi-final spot against Bayern Munich. As one of the survivors from the disappointment of 1967, Smith was glad to set the record straight when he captained Rangers to victory against old rivals Bayern Munich. That set the tone for the final against the Russians. 'After beating Bayern in the semi-final we were expected to win, and that put us under a bit more pressure. The Bayern game was the key to the whole run and we made it count. As the years pass maybe the reality of what we achieved grows. At the time I think the final was just another game for us. We prepared at a hotel away in the middle of nowhere. We had a different manager from 1967 in Willie Waddell and a different approach. We certainly knew much more about the opposition and their style – although I don't necessarily think that's always a good thing. I'm a great believer in going out and playing your own game, letting them worry about you. Because of the trouble at the end of the final we didn't get presented with the cup on the pitch, which was a bit of an anti-climax. The parade around Ibrox made up for that a little bit but it is very difficult to recapture the moment. The time to celebrate was in the Nou Camp and we couldn't do that properly.'

The hard work and injury problems in the previous two years paid off with that victory in Barcelona, the undoubted highlight of a Rangers career which spanned seven years and more than 300 first-team appearances. The win came in the same year Smith beat Kenny Dalglish and Joe Harper to be named Scotland's player of the year. That award and the bronze marking his place in the Rangers hall of fame are the only mementoes of his playing career that still take pride of place at home.

'Funnily enough I think I played better in the year I broke my leg for the first time, in 1970. I was captain for most of that season, with John Greig out injured, and had a good year, but obviously 1972 is the one that goes down as my best because of the award. It was pleasing because I was the clear choice and any type of recognition, in any walk of life, is always nice. I did have a good season, especially in Europe, and I think the Barcelona performance clinched it. I must have been the first real sweeper to be used in Scottish football and it held things together at the back in a way that wasn't really tried in Britain.'

Those two high spots were to prove a fitting swansong, with Smith's Ibrox career beginning to wind down. He would play 29 of 34 league games in the season after Barcelona, savouring the club's centenary year in 1973, as well as nine League Cup ties and every game in the run to the Scottish Cup final in the first season under Jock Wallace. While the new manager went on to become revered in Rangers history, for Smith his reign was not an enjoyable one and the search for an escape route began soon after his appointment, ending in November 1974.

Arbroath, then playing in the top flight, now sounds an unlikely destination for a man who had been voted the nation's best player just two years earlier, but it proved a welcome opportunity, and a £30,000 transfer was completed after a proposed return to Aberdeen had broken down.

Smith reveals: 'I just couldn't play under Jock Wallace, it was as simple as that. I didn't like his style of play and didn't agree with going out to kick people off the park, which in the end was what he was asking me to do. That isn't what football should be about and I wasn't prepared to do it in the way he wanted me to. I wasn't a kid and had my own views on the way things should be done. In hindsight I could have stuck it out and stayed at Ibrox a lot longer – but you have to go with your gut feeling.'

Windswept Gayfield was to be a temporary staging post for Smith. After his debut in a 3–2 win over Hearts, he went on to make 20 league appearances for the Red Lichties as player-coach under veteran manager Albert Henderson before swapping the east coast of Scotland for more exotic shores.

First stop was the quaintly named Arcadia Shepherds in South Africa, followed by the Seattle Sounders and LA Aztecs in the flourishing North American Soccer League. He explains: 'I'd played with Kai Johansen at Rangers. He was the manager out in South Africa and took me there. Pretoria was a lovely city and totally different to anything we had been used to, although the football wasn't great. It was a completely different lifestyle, I suppose better than Scotland because of the weather. Apartheid was at its peak at that point – there were separate leagues for white and black players. Although that was difficult for outsiders like us to understand, it didn't really affect our quality of life. Maybe that sounds a selfish attitude but it's true, whether it is right or wrong. The only problems we encountered were with white South Africans who couldn't understand the family's willingness to accept black South Africans as our friends.'

After the political tensions of Africa, a more liberal way of life in America followed as Smith became one of an increasing number of British stars to cash in on a boom in the NASL. The New York Cosmos, Tampa Bay Rowdies, San Jose Earthquakes and San Diego Jaws . . . the US may still have been learning the game, but they could teach the rest of the world a thing or two about naming teams.

There was a serious side to football in America – just ask Pele, Eusebio, Franz Beckenbauer, George Best or Johan Cruyff. They all sampled the NASL for varying periods in their careers. They were all lured to the States with lucrative contracts and the promise of the American dream. Ultimately it would prove an expensive failure, with the league in its old guise folding in 1984 after a 17-year existence, as a sceptical public refused to be convinced of the benefits of soccer.

The peak was in the 1970s and Smith's year in the NASL was at the heart of that interest, with a record 34 per cent rise in spectator numbers that season. Nevertheless, gates averaged only 10,000 and did not do justice to some of the most spectacular stadiums in sport at that time. The Sounders, for example, opened the futuristic Kingdome in Smith's time at the club – an enclosed concrete arena with an Astroturf pitch and the ability to hold 58,000 fans. The stadium was demolished in 2000, but at least outlasted the league it played host to in the early days.

Smith recalls: 'The standard in America was a lot higher because of the type of players being attracted to the league – World Cup winners and the best from around the globe. I went over to Seattle at first, playing at the Kingdome which is a wonderful arena. Players like Geoff Hurst, Harry Redknapp, Mike England and Jimmy Napier were in the side at a time when the NASL was the place to be. Seattle had their full quota of overseas players, I think it was six or seven at that time, and I moved on to California soon after. It was everything you would expect of LA. George Best was in the team, Rod Stewart would come down and train with us from time to time and I remember Alice Cooper being around filming some footage for Bill Cosby's show. Looking back it was typical Hollywood. George was in good shape and looking after himself but players wanted to give him the ball at every opportunity and that cost us games.'

Even the lure of the American sunshine and the glitz and glamour of the North American Soccer League was not enough to compete with the attraction of another seaside spot: Berwick-Upon-Tweed. Berwick Rangers presented the sweeper, now in his thirties, the first step into management in 1976 and an opportunity for the family to plant roots back in Britain. Wife Sheila and daughters Amanda and Melanie were soon to be joined by a son, brother and author-in-the-making two years later.

'Living abroad was never going to be permanent and the attraction to come back home to Scotland was strong. I was all set to sign for Alex Ferguson at St Mirren when the Berwick job came up. Even when I was in the interview with Berwick I got a call from Charlie Cooke, who I'd played with at Aberdeen and who had also been out in America, to tell me not to sign anything – Paris St Germain wanted to take me to France. Although nothing was in black and white, my mind was made up and I went with Berwick over PSG. Not too many players can say that. They were the worst team in Scotland by a long way when I took over – that was the big attraction. The other options would have been easier but it seemed like a challenge. We were bottom of the Second Division, the lowest league at that point, when I took over in September 1976.'

When Smith walked through the door at Shielfield to take the helm at Berwick, he found a team yet to register a league win in 13 attempts and with home games attracting just 400 hardy souls. His arrival, with fellow Barcelona veteran Willie Mathieson on the coaching staff, brought an immediate turn-around.

As one of the first player-managers in Scottish football, he featured in 27 league games after making his debut at home against Meadowbank in October 1976. The following season he played in every single one of the club's 39 league games as they finished just five points behind champions Clyde and runners-up Raith, who tied on 53 points. Berwick were fourth, behind Dunfermline only on goal difference.

'We finished eighth in that first season in a 14-team league, the second year it was fourth and in the third we won the Second Division championship. Of everything I've done in football that gives me the most satisfaction – it was the only time the club had won anything. The fact it was the first will never be taken away, a bit like the Barcelona win. I won the Second Division player of the year award that season and was still enjoying my football. The championship meant so much to the town and it was wonderful to play such a big part in it.'

The championship winning season of 1978/79 started in inauspicious circumstances, a 6–1 defeat at Falkirk hardly serving as inspiration to the fans who were being asked to buy into Smith's vision for the future. Nevertheless, they did and turned out in force for the opening home game of the season. More than 1,000 filtered into Shielfield, more than twice the previous average home gate, to see the Wee Rangers defeat Stenhousemuir 6–1 as Smith capped the performance with a goal from the penalty spot. Gates continued to rise, peaking at 1,500, pulling in the type of revenue the club had never before experienced and adding to the proceeds of cup ties against both halves of the Old Firm in that period.

Smith was again an ever-present as Berwick pipped Dunfermline to the title by two points, with Falkirk missing out on promotion in third place. Notably the title winners' tally of 82 goals outweighed that of any other senior club that season in Scotland, an indication of Smith's attacking philosophy.

Inspiration on the pitch was matched with innovation behind the scenes, with squad numbers introduced to Scottish football and Smith retaining the lucky 13 he had worn in the US with the LA Aztecs. Shirt sponsorship was also attracted during an era in which that commercial nettle had yet to be grasped by the majority of clubs.

While the Aberdonian holds those memories dear, the appreciation was mutual – he was voted Berwick's player of the millennium in 2000. In the grand scheme of football, that award may not register on the Richter scale, but it was a gesture appreciated by the old boy honoured by the fans.

To use a well worn cliché, football can be a funny old game. 'Berwick was a great place to live, the family loved it there, but unfortunately all good things come to an end, particularly in management. There were things going on at the club that I didn't agree with and I resigned. I don't regret that and I've still got a lot of time for most of the people who were involved at that time. I'm still in touch with some of the players. The crowds shot up at that time, there was a real feel-good factor, and hopefully I'm remembered well down there.'

After parting company with Berwick during the 1980/81 season, in which the Borderers would eventually be relegated from the First Division after a nightmare campaign from start to finish, he went on to guest for Meadowbank Thistle in 11 games and also turned out for Hamilton on half a dozen occasions before calling time on his senior career. Roots were set down back in the north-east, where the football adventure had begun in the 60s, and brief player-manager posts with Huntly and Peterhead followed.

The stay may have been short, but Smith still made an impact in the Highland League and is credited by Peterhead club historians with the finest ever display in the team's colours during a 3–2 cup final defeat against Inverness Caledonian, to add to an eclectic list of tributes amassed in a long and colourful career.

Life in the paid ranks ended in the early 80s, but Smith did make a return to the game as a volunteer in the youth ranks, coaching teams his son played for at a north-east junior club. The old philosophy returned . . . defenders were encouraged to dribble from their own box, a sight familiar during Smith's own playing days – including in the red-hot atmosphere of the European Cup Winners' Cup final of 1972 – and expletives were banned, by a player never booked in his entire playing career, to be replaced with the stock curse of 'oh dear'. Often met with bemusement from opposition teams spitting and swearing their way through games following strict orders from touch line dictators, the approach, according to Smith, stemmed from his own childhood experiences.

'When I was at primary school, a Polish teacher took the team. He didn't have much of a clue about football but was really enthusiastic and just let us get on with the games. That's the way it should be for kids. A lot of the time there's far too much emphasis on coaching and making kids learn how other people think the game should be played, when really they should just be enjoying playing football. How often do you see a player beat a man now? Never, because that's stamped out at an early age. Kids are told they have to pass the ball as soon as they get it and end up petrified to try and take someone on in case they lose it. People on the touchlines can have as many coaching badges as they like, but they can't kick the ball for the players on the park.'

With all three children now grown up and having flown the nest, Smith is now retired from the licensed trade after he and his wife Sheila's stint as mine-hosts at an Angus watering hole. Based in Fife, enjoying the quiet life walking the countryside with trusty dogs Ollie and Millie and chasing after my own son Finlay and daughters Mia and Zara, as well as grandsons Tom and Zak on visits to their home in America, is the main exercise.

Having celebrated his 67th birthday in November 2010, he has just one lingering regret from a sporting career that spanned five generations before the boots were packed away once and for all after two hip operations in 2009. 'I still thought I had a few years' playing left in me, but the doctors said otherwise. I would have loved another proper run out, maybe in a reserve game, to test myself. That never happened . . . but there's always next year.'

CHAPTER SEVEN

# TOMMY McLEAN

He was young, gifted and in demand, but Tommy McLean had the foresight to look beyond the bright lights of London and rejected Chelsea to pave the way for a crack at making history with Rangers in 1972. I can say with confidence, certainty even, that no current Kilmarnock starlet would send the Chelsea manager packing if he came battering down his door. It's fair to assume that none in the future will either if Roman Abramovich travels north with an open cheque book.

McLean did, however, snub the Stamford Bridge side in favour of staying in Ayrshire, and that decision as a youngster proved to be one of the best he ever made. He was something of a prodigal son at Killie. When he did eventually move on to pastures new it was not before the Rugby Park club had made Rangers fight all the way to prise him from their grasp.

Mind you, the provincial side were battling not just to retain one man but also to keep the remnants of the club's most famous team together. The Lanarkshire-born player had burst onto the scene at Killie at a tender age and helped the club win the First Division championship in 1964/65. It was his first season and it was his club's first title.

The youthful right-winger came into the Kilmarnock team at a time when Willie Waddell had worked miracles as manager. Aside from winning the league, they had earlier in the season overturned a four-goal deficit in the Fairs Cup to beat the feared and revered Eintracht Frankfurt 5–4 on aggregate. The west coast club had also been runners-up in the league for four of the previous five seasons and regulars in the latter stages of the cup competitions, so he was justified in feeling he was on to a good thing.

To clinch the First Division trophy they needed to win against leaders Hearts at Tynecastle. The odds were stacked in the home team's favour but Killie won 2–0, McLean providing the cross for the opener and getting his professional career off to a flying start. Davie Sneddon, the scorer of that most famous of goals, described it as the perfect ball.

McLean recalls: 'Willie Waddell signed me when I was 15 for Kilmarnock from the amateur leagues and I was fortunate to be at the club during a great period in its history. I came into the side halfway through the championship season and played enough games to earn a medal. I actually won two medals in my first season, the league and the reserve league title, but I never took winning for granted. I was always a winger and the great thing was that every team played with two men wide and there were a lot of great players who came through as a result of that: the likes of Jimmy Johnstone, Willie Henderson and Alex Edwards. Every manager relied on wingers. I made my debut when I was just 16 and a half. There were one or two hard guys, from the old school, but generally I didn't get a hard time of it.'

With a reputation as a fast and intelligent flanker, his dangerous crosses and dead-ball ability made McLean an instant hit in Scottish football. He had been capped at every level, from schoolboy to under-23 and full international, by the time he was just 21. Brothers Willie and Jim were both professionals and both of them tipped junior as the best of the clan.

His international debut came in a 5–0 win over Cyprus on 11 December 1968, in a World Cup qualifier in Nicosia. The side featured future Ibrox colleagues John Greig, Ronnie McKinnon and Colin Stein. Over the next three years he lined up against Wales in a 5–3 win and 0–0 draw, Northern

Ireland in a 1–0 victory and played his final game for Scotland on 9 June 1971, in a 1–0 defeat in Copenhagen during Bobby Brown's tenure as national team coach.

He would go on to star in Europe with Rangers and win every domestic honour, but nothing he could do was enough to convince a succession of Scotland managers that he was worthy of further caps. You would forgive him for being bitter, but as a coach himself he appreciates football is all about the opinions of those who pick the team. 'At the time I felt there could have been more caps for me but I've got no regrets. To play once for your country is a dream and there was a lot of good competition for my position. I got all of my caps early in my career with Kilmarnock, which was a bit of a quirk. Usually players had to move to the likes of Rangers and Celtic to get the recognition but I was the other way round.'

His final international appearance came on the same day as he ended his association with Kilmarnock and embarked on his adventure with Rangers. The Glasgow club succeeded in 1971 where Chelsea, who had offered £70,000 for his services, had failed four years earlier.

'I had the opportunity to go to Chelsea in 1967 but I just didn't feel ready to move away from Scotland. I was still a young boy and it would have been a big thing to move to a big city like London and a club like Chelsea. Don't get me wrong: I put a lot of thought into it, but I decided in the end that it wasn't the right move for me. I was happy to stay on at Kilmarnock and continue to develop. Rangers had three offers turned down and by the time they reached an agreement I was away with Scotland. Willie Waddell didn't want to risk the Killie board changing their mind over the fee again and came over to do the deal. I was on a tour of Russia and Denmark, so the manager came across to Copenhagen to complete the transfer. When I played in the game against Denmark I was technically still a Kilmarnock player because the paperwork hadn't gone through in time.'

Waddell paid £60,000 to get his man after protracted negotiations with his old board at Rugby Park. The winger had just turned 24 and was joining a team who had finished fourth in the league but had shown signs of a revival by winning the League Cup in the 1970/71 season.

He provided competition for terracing hero Willie Henderson, who had been unchallenged in the No.7 shirt since ousting another fans' favourite, Alex Scott, six years earlier. Both Henderson and Scott had warmed the hearts of the Ibrox faithful with their brand of wing wizardry and McLean admits he lived in their considerable shadows as he settled into his new surroundings.

A heart-to-heart with coach Jock Wallace turned things around swiftly, so much so that Henderson was allowed to leave on a free transfer during the course of the run to the Barcelona final. McLean recalls: 'It was difficult going into the Rangers team to begin with. I was in Willie Henderson's place and he was a big favourite with the crowd, so it was a while before they took to me. Jock was a big help, taking me aside and telling me I was trying to please too many people. He said that I should only be worried about impressing him and Willie Waddell because they were the ones who had signed me and they had done that because of who I was, not because they wanted me to do what Willie Henderson could do. They were right – Willie was a dribbler and I was more of a passer. When I concentrated on doing what I did best it worked for me.'

The 1971/72 season started with Rangers on League Cup duty in the group stage of the competition, losing 2–0 against Celtic at Parkhead. McLean scored his first goal for the club in the next match, his debut at Ibrox, as they won 4–0 against Ayr, but the side failed to negotiate the preliminary round and their title defence was over.

The new wide-man's first league outing was in the season opener at Partick Thistle, but there was no dream start as the Light Blues fell to a 3–2 defeat. It was symptomatic of their inconsistent season, which would end with a third-place finish. McLean featured in 22 of the 34 First Division fixtures, scoring his one and only goal in a 2–0 win at home to St Johnstone. He was more prolific in the Scottish Cup, scoring in the third round against Falkirk and then grabbing a double in a 4–1 fourth-round win over St Mirren before adding his fourth of the campaign in the quarter-final replay against Motherwell as Rangers progressed to the last four. Hibs ended their hopes of reaching the final in another tie that went to a replay.

The player who had won the league in his first season at Kilmarnock did, however, prove to be a lucky charm in Europe during the famous march to success in Barcelona. He played in seven of the nine ties in that campaign, missing out on the second leg of the first-round showdown with Rennes and the first leg of the second-round contest with Sporting Lisbon. He played an integral part in the build-up to Alex MacDonald's match-winning goal in the second leg of the quarter-final against Torino and there was another industrious performance in the final with his customary forays down the right wing and some menacing shots at the Moscow Dynamo goal.

Those seven games have provided McLean with some of the fondest memories of his career: 'In the beginning it was just a team getting together for a couple of years, but what that team achieved was amazing and has never been given full credit. We beat top quality teams from the best football countries in Europe and in the entire history of Rangers that has never been matched. It wasn't just in one-off games we were beating these sides. Over two legs against Rennes, Sporting Lisbon, Torino and Bayern Munich we proved we were better than them and they were all fantastic sides. The build-up was difficult. There was a long gap between our last league game and the final and one of our two friendlies in between was against Inverness Clachnacuddin from the Highland League, not an ideal warm-up to a major

European final by any means. We were a very fit team, but the long lay-off before the game had an impact: by the end of the final we were out on our feet. I honestly think if the Russians had got an equaliser they would have gone on to win it, but we held out.'

The Barcelona final was played in front of 35,000 supporters at the Nou Camp, the large majority wearing Rangers colours. It was an altogether different story in McLean's next cup final. More than 122,000 were crammed into Hampden Park for the 1973 Scottish Cup decider, but the scale of the occasion did not daunt McLean. With the game balanced at 2–2 he whipped in the pinpoint cross that led to Derek Johnstone's header being knocked home by Tom Forsyth after striking the post. The only medal McLean needed to complete his domestic set was the League Cup and that would follow.

First, he and Rangers had league business to attend to and in the 1975 season the right-winger missed just one game on his way to collecting a championship medal to match the one he had earned with Kilmarnock a decade earlier. He scored 14 goals in the 33 fixtures in which he featured, including a hat-trick against Dumbarton.

A turning point in that league-winning season was the 3–0 New Year derby win over Celtic. McLean teed up Derek Johnstone for the first and scored the second himself before Derek Parlane wrapped up the points and put Rangers well on their way to securing the flag.

In the treble-winning season of 1975/76 he again missed just a single league game and was a key man in the League Cup run which ended with a 1–0 victory over Celtic and the Scottish Cup sortie that climaxed with a 3–1 win over Hearts, McLean's free-kick against the Jambos setting up Derek Johnstone for the opener after just 42 seconds.

He made an equally important contribution to the 1978 treble, playing in 31 of 36 Premier Division games on the way to the title and scoring a vital double in the League Cup quarter-final against Dunfermline en route to the 2–1 win over Celtic in the final. The Scottish Cup was taken back to Ibrox with a 2–1 victory against Aberdeen as the champagne flowed.

'There were a lot of good times and I gathered a lot of medals. So many stayed together for five or six great years and that meant the spirit was fantastic. We grew up together, on and off the park. We played for each other. We were the team that stopped Celtic's run of championship wins, which was so important to the supporters. To play a part in that was great.'

He remained a key man when John Greig replaced Jock Wallace at the tiller in the summer of 1978, on the eve of a season that saw Rangers claim a double thanks to a 2–1 win over Aberdeen in the League Cup final and 3–2 win over Hibs in the second replay of the Scottish Cup showpiece.

The same year saw Rangers threaten to repeat the European success they had savoured earlier in the decade and McLean was once again at the centre of it as his side eased past Juventus and then PSV Eindhoven in the European Cup to set up a quarter-final date with Cologne. They fell to a 1–0 defeat in Germany and, despite McLean's goal and promptings in the 1–1 draw at Ibrox, fell out of the competition.

The winger was always a hard taskmaster, just ask Peter McCloy. The keeper tipped a penalty round the post in the 1979 European Cup Winners' Cup tie against Valencia in Spain to be met with McLean asking: 'Why did ye no haud it, big man?' A joke at the time, but in later life a queue of players would testify that, although small in stature at 5ft 5in, McLean was not a man, or manager, to be messed with.

Over the next two seasons, 1979/80 and 1980/81, McLean remained a regular but success was proving harder to come by for a team that had grown old together. In the league in those two years they finished fifth and then third. In the knock-out tournaments there was slightly more cheer.

McLean was restricted to a place on the bench in the 4–1

Scottish Cup final replay win over Dundee United in 1981, having played in the initial 0–0 draw, and missed out on the 2–1 win over the same opponents in the 1981/82 League Cup final. He made fleeting contributions to that season and retired from playing after coming on from the bench in the final game of the campaign. 'I was playing First Division football at 16 and finished when I was 33, so I had a good innings. Seventeen years is a long time at the top level and it was the right time for me to call it a day.'

McLean had made 452 appearances for Rangers, on top of well over 200 for Kilmarnock, and his ties with the club were not severed. He was retained by Greig and appointed assistant manager as his former captain tried in vain to turn around the fortunes of the ailing giant. Greig resigned a year later after the strain began to tell and he suffered from health problems. It was a revealing time for his right-hand man.

'John had started me in coaching early, going in at night to take the S-form youngsters for training sessions at Ibrox while I was still playing. Eventually I became his assistant and that gave me a good insight to the pressures of a job at that level. I've heard people criticise John Greig and Willie Miller for walking straight into top management jobs at big clubs, but you can't blame them – there are some opportunities you just can't turn your back on.'

It seemed written in the stars that McLean would eventually become a manager in his own right, with his brothers Willie and Jim, at Ayr and Dundee United, having already trodden that path. In fact, he was a reluctant coach: 'I was always a keen student of the game but, having seen what Jim and Willie had to put up with, I'd decided at one point I wouldn't follow them into management. That changed over time and I had a good grounding at Morton and then Motherwell.'

McLean, who had a two-week spell as caretaker manager after Greig's resignation, was relieved of his Ibrox duties late in 1983 after Jock Wallace had returned to fill the vacant seat.

Having cut his teeth in coaching at Rangers, McLean walked straight into the manager's job at Morton. The Cappielow side were part-time and playing in the First Division. Under McLean, who had replaced former Gers team-mate Alex Miller following his departure to St Mirren, they climbed the table and won the championship by three points from Dumbarton. The Greenock side were destined for the big time and the Premier Division, but their young manager would not be going with them.

Motherwell, in his native Lanarkshire, had been relegated from the top flight, rock bottom and 12 points adrift of safety. Manager Bobby Watson, another Rangers old-boy, had resigned on the final day of the season and McLean was the man they wanted to fill the vacancy. He accepted the post with the full-time side, becoming their ninth manager in only 11 years, and gambled on his ability to be able to help them bounce back to the Premier Division.

The rookie coach came up trumps as he guided his new club to the First Division championship. Clydebank were two points short of the league leaders but made the step up alongside them. McLean's instincts about swapping colours proved spot-on, with Morton enduring a torrid time in the Premier Division after their promotion. The Greenock side won just five games in 36 and fell straight back through the trapdoor with just 12 points.

'Morton were a part-time club and it was totally different to be dealing with players who were only training a couple of nights a week and even then would call off at the last minute through work or other commitments. We had a good bunch though and did well, winning the championship. Motherwell were going in the opposite direction but I thought there was potential. When I went to the club it was virtually bankrupt, there wasn't a penny, and I knew money wouldn't be laid on a plate. Instead we worked hard to bring through young players: Chris McCart, Fraser Wishart, Tom Boyd and Phillip O'Donnell among them. We got straight back up, winning the championship and that is one of my proudest achievements. If we hadn't got up, we would have had to sell the good young players and would have gone part-time. Some clubs never recover from that.'

Until then the Steelmen had been a yo-yo club. Under McLean they found new stability and grew stronger season after season. Upon their return to the elite league in 1985/86 they found ninth place was enough to keep them up as the leagues were reconstructed. The following year they gained another place and held that in 1987/88. In the next campaign 'Well dropped to ninth but again scraped to safety before regrouping and finishing sixth, their highest under McLean up to that point, in 1990. They retained that place the following term, but it is the Scottish Cup for which the 1990/91 season will always be remembered by Motherwell fans.

They lifted the famous trophy after one of the most entertaining finals in the history of the competition. To get to that stage they overcame Aberdeen 1–0 in the third round and dumped Falkirk 4–2 at the next hurdle. A tense 5–4 penalty shoot-out victory over Morton, after the replay had ended locked at 1–1, took them through the quarter-finals and Celtic were shocked 4–2 in the semi-final to set up a showdown with brother Jim and Dundee United at Hampden.

For the siblings it was a day riddled with emotion as 57,000 supporters turned out, a remarkable attendance for a game devoid of Old Firm pulling power. McLean recalls: 'It was a difficult time for Jim and I because our father had died in the build-up to the game. There was obviously great sadness, but I think the final was a fitting memorial to him. It was always difficult going in against Jim, whether it was in a cup final or league game. Whoever won would still feel for the brother who had lost.'

It was Tommy who came out on top in the 1991 clash, but

only just. The final went to extra-time as it flowed from end to end. The late Phil O'Donnell, who later became the club's most valuable asset when he moved to Celtic in a record £1.75 million deal, got the decisive goal but every player was a hero. Ian Angus, Iain Ferguson and Steve Kirk were the other men to cancel out the United goals from Dave Bowman, Darren Jackson and Michael O'Neill.

Motherwell remained in the Premier Division throughout McLean's tenure, beating relegation by finishing tenth in the 12-team league in 1991/92 before gaining ground and finishing eighth in 1993. Any fears the club was stagnating were dispelled in stunning fashion in the 1993/94 season. In the league Motherwell emerged as genuine, if unlikely, title contenders. Rangers won the championship in the end on 58 points, with Aberdeen three points further back and the Fir Park side just one point off the Dons. It took the club into the UEFA Cup – but also signalled the end of the manager's decade in charge.

In 1987 he had been appointed to the board of directors, again following in the footsteps of his brother Jim, who became chairman at Dundee United, but by the summer of 1994 there was a split over the direction the club was taking. He resigned from the board in May 1994, and within weeks stepped down as manager.

There are no hard feelings, only affection for the club he spent ten happy years at: 'Obviously, winning the cup was the highlight, it meant so much to the people of the town, but getting them back into the Premier League and, eventually, Europe was just as important in the long term. As a director I was in total control of signings and the football side. I was given a budget and stuck to it. I knew there was no point going asking for more and appreciated the club had to live within its means. I enjoyed that side of it, the responsibility, and it was another learning curve. It's easy to get caught up in wanting to put the best team on the park and forget about the responsibility to secure the future of the club. I had ten years at Motherwell and it was time for a change. My relationship with those who ran the club, particularly John Chapman, was superb. He fully supported me in everything I wanted to do while I realised there had to be a Motherwell after the man.'

Those claims are borne out in fact. Motherwell had stability and redeveloped their ground comprehensively during the 1980s and early 1990s. Valuable revenue was raised by the sale of several players McLean had introduced to the fray, including captain Tom Boyd, who moved on to Chelsea for £800,000 in 1991 before returning to Scotland to lead Celtic. Chris McCart, another to fall from the 'Well conveyor belt of that period, had a long period on the Fir Park coaching staff before switching to Celtic's youth system.

Before the month was out, McLean was back in football and in one of Scottish football's biggest jobs. Hearts had finished seventh in the Premier League, making a mockery of the belief they could be a genuine third force in the domestic game behind the Old Firm.

Sandy Clark, after a year in the hot seat, had departed and McLean was the man the new boardroom regime saw as capable of landing the club's first honour in 32 years. The former Motherwell manager saw it as a chance to wake a sleeping giant. In truth, however, Hearts remained a selling club, with star players like Alan McLaren coveted by clubs such as Rangers and the directors unable to resist the lure of the guaranteed income a sale generated. 'When I went to Tynecastle, Chris Robinson had just taken over. There was a lot of potential and it was a good opportunity, but a lot of promises were made that simply were never fulfilled. It was another false dawn for Hearts.'

He left Tynecastle in May 1995, after seeing his side finish sixth but also within an ace of repeating the cup Midas touch he had displayed at Motherwell. Hearts brushed aside Clydebank, Rangers and Dundee United in the Scottish Cup before stuttering at the semi-final stage and losing 1–0

The proud squad with the European trophy. *Back row, from left* – Willie Waddell, Jock Wallace, Colin Stein, Alfie Conn, Derek Johnstone, Peter McCloy, Dave Smith, Sandy Jardine, Willie Mathieson and Tommy Craig. *Front row, from left* – Tommy McLean, John Greig, Alex MacDonald and Willie Johnston.

The young and care free Alfie Conn in Old Firm action against Celtic, beating George Connolly to the ball.

The smiling Alex MacDonald was a vital cog in the Rangers machine throughout the 1970s.

Willie 'Bud' Johnston was one of the most talented players of his generation.

Alex MacDonald, Graham Fyfe and Colin Stein look on as Willie Henderson's strike loops into the Sporting Lisbon net over keeper Damas during the run to the final.

Action from Rangers v Sporting Lisbon.

Enjoying a spot of retail therapy during the trip to Italy to face Torino, from left, are – Bobby Watson, John Greig, Peter McCloy, Dave Smith and Willie Johnston.

Bayern Munich captain Franz Beckenbauer shakes hands with his Rangers counterpart before the 1972 semi-final. David Smith deputised for John Greig as skipper.

Alex MacDonald in action during the semi-final against Bayern Munich.

Derek Parlane is congratulated by Tommy McLean after his goal against Bayern Munich at Ibrox.

The imposing Nou Camp Stadium in Barcelona as it appeared in 1972.

The Bears in Barcelona as they make their voices heard on the terraces of the Nou Camp.

The Rangers bench look on anxiously as the Russians from Moscow are edged out in the final showdown.

Willie Johnston beats two Russian defenders to the ball to score his first and Rangers' second in the final.

Willie Johnston scores his second of the night to put his side 3-0 ahead.

Alex MacDonald and Colin Stein celebrate with goalscorer Willie Johnston in front of the delirious Rangers fans.

Overjoyed Rangers supporters spill onto the pitch in Barcelona after their side's historic win.

Cup final hero Colin Stein is mobbed by Rangers fans on the Nou Camp pitch.

Colin Stein holds the trophy aloft in the Nou Camp bath.

Ibrox chairman John Lawrence with the European Cup Winners' Cup.

Relaxing by the pool-side at the team hotel near Barcelona are, from left – John Greig, Derek Johnstone, Jim Denny, Derek Parlane, Bobby Watson and Willie Mathieson.

Star man Willie Johnston is all smiles at the team hotel on the outskirts of Barcelona.

The victorious squad rejoice with their hands on the European prize.

Dave Smith and his wife Sheila share a unique piece of duty-free silverware with John Greig and his wife Jeanette.

*Right*. One of the iconic images of 1972 as captain John Greig holds the European Cup Winners' Cup aloft to give Bears at the Spanish city's airport a glimpse of the prize.

*Below*. Familiar faces reunited in 1992 for the 20th anniversary celebrations in Glasgow.

to Airdrie, managed by McLean's old team-mate, Alex MacDonald.

McLean, who was replaced by Jim Jefferies, spent a year on the sidelines before the briefest managerial stint in Scottish football. He was paraded at Stark's Park by Raith Rovers on 3 September 1996 as their new manager and took charge of the Fifers in a 4–1 defeat against Aberdeen. Working without a contract at a club enveloped by off-field uncertainty, within a week he had moved to Tannadice to work for brother Jim and succeed Billy Kirkwood as boss of Dundee United. It was a whirlwind affair, although Raith were compensated financially by United for the loss of their manager.

McLean did not flinch at the prospect of following orders from his new chairman: 'It was a good experience. When I took over we were bottom of the league but we came back to finish third, getting back into Europe, and went something like 20 games undefeated. Unfortunately, when things weren't going well the same people who had been singing our praises started falling back on the old "Brothers Grimm" stuff and I felt I had to resign for the good of the club. The fact we were brothers kept getting thrown up, even when it wasn't relevant.'

It was indeed a dream start for McLean on Tayside, becoming the first manager ever to win a hat-trick of consecutive manager of the month awards. He steered the club into Europe for the first time in three years and reached the last four of both cup competitions in the 1996/97 season.

The following campaign proved to be his last as United fell to seventh in the ten-team top flight, having also been beaten by Celtic in both the Scottish Cup and League Cup. The UEFA Cup campaign had been ended by Turkish side Trabzonspor, who had won 1–0 at home before being held 1–1 at Tannadice. Paul Sturrock was lured from St Johnstone to fill the void but could not improve the club's fortunes.

McLean was actually enticed back to Dundee United by Alex Smith, who served as manager from 2000 to 2002. Smith valued his experience and handed the former boss a place on the coaching staff: 'I went back for a while during Alex's time, coaching the youngsters, and went to Rangers in a similar capacity.'

After Rangers opened the £14 million training base at Murray Park they looked towards their former winger to head up the youth development programme alongside Dick Advocaat's recruit, Jan Derks. McLean's own contribution was stifled, but he remains philosophical about his short stay at the complex: 'The plan was for me to replace Jan Derks and head up the youth system, but when Alex McLeish came in he wanted his own people in place. It was disappointing but these things happen in football and life moves on. Although I enjoy working with young players, I'm in my element with a senior team and I would love to get back to working at that level.'

Proof positive that what goes around comes around in football, since it was McLeish who replaced McLean at Motherwell in his first managerial role. Once voted one of the country's top 50 managers of all time, McLean used his break from football to spend precious time at home in the central belt with wife Beth and daughter Lorna after a lifetime in football. His golf skills have also been sharpened, but it is the training field and not the fairways that he now craves.

'I always said I would like to get back into management, although I wasn't prepared to dive in at the first offer to come my way. I still feel I have a lot to offer, although a lot of clubs are going down the road of going for inexperienced coaches who have just finished playing. There's a place for that, I've been there myself, but there has to be a balance. Before, there were experienced managers, the likes of Terry Christie and Alex Smith, who were bringing through players in the lower leagues, but now there are younger coaches who tend to fall back on more experienced players to get them through. That is stifling the young talent. I am a better manager now than I was when I was at Motherwell because of the experiences I have had since then.'

CHAPTER EIGHT

# ALFIE CONN

He is every football quiz writer's dream. Which player won medals with both Rangers and Celtic? Which son followed his father into the Scotland team? Which player took the mickey out of the notoriously brutal Leeds United team of the 1970s? The answer to all three, of course, is Alfie Conn. His career took him from Rangers to Tottenham, from Celtic to Pittsburgh and back to the Scottish Premier League, but wherever he travelled, headlines were sure to follow. Conn, a family man now living and working in Lanarkshire, did not court controversy but it seemed attracted to him.

His decision to pull on the green and white hoops of Celtic just five years after collecting a European Cup Winners' Cup medal in the blue of Rangers in 1972 provoked outcry among football followers in Glasgow – indeed, it still does. Conn saw it simply as a job, nothing more sinister than that. His spur of the moment decision to sit on the ball in the heat of battle in a vital Spurs v Leeds game had the Yorkshire team's fans baying for blood. To Conn, it was just about giving his side's faithful something to cheer.

In 15 years as a professional he was always willing to go his own way and even before football came calling, he refused to be pigeon holed. Football and rugby have never been comfortable bed fellows, yet he embraced both sports as a schoolboy, despite coming from a family rich in football heritage thanks to the exploits of his father, Alfie senior, with Hearts and Scotland. Even today, Conn remains a fan of the oval ball game so often loathed by the football fraternity. 'Where we stayed, in Prestonpans, it was a rugby district.

We even had to go to the head teacher just to get a football team together for the school, which we did eventually. I played rugby and I loved it, it's a fantastic contact sport. I had rugby trials with the south of Scotland district team but I enjoyed football as well.'

Alfie senior signed for Hearts in 1944 and spent 14 years at Tynecastle, turning out 361 times for the Jambos and going down in club folklore. His son was six by the time he moved on to Raith, the club where he also served as manager in the early 1960s. He was capped by Scotland against Austria in 1956, paving the way for a family double to be completed by Alfie junior 19 years later when he took his international bow.

Despite that football tradition, there was no pressure to follow in his father's footsteps. While his peers clamoured for a chance to make it as a player, Conn refused to be rushed as his football career began to take off and resisted the influence the chasing pack began to exert. 'My father never really pushed me one way or the other, he just wanted me to enjoy whatever I chose to do. I did train with Hearts, under John Harvey, who had been my father's trainer, and Hibs. Eventually Hearts gave me an ultimatum to sign with them or stop training – I stopped training and went across to Hibs.'

Conn lit up English football in his spell with Tottenham, but it could have been in the white of Leeds United that he made his mark if the Elland Road side had held him to his first professional contract. As a 15-year-old, Conn had committed himself to football and accepted an apprenticeship with Leeds. It was 1967 and the English side were a force to be reckoned with, fourth in the top flight the previous season, led by manager Don Revie and boasting the likes of Billy Bremner, Eddie Gray, Norman Hunter, Jack Charlton and Peter Lorimer on the park. The teenager travelled south to sign the contract and arrived back home in Scotland to walk into the jaws of a dilemma. Rangers wanted him at

Ibrox and he wanted to go: only the small matter of the Leeds contract, with the ink barely dry, complicated matters. Revie, who was revered as one of football's strong characters, showed the other, more compassionate, side of his nature when he ripped up the paperwork to enable his young signing to move to the west coast and join a club who were European finalists that year.

The 1967 European Cup Winners' Cup final came too soon for Conn, but he would get his chance five years later in Barcelona. 'When we got home from Leeds, Scot Symon, the Rangers manager, and a director were waiting at the house. My dad had to phone Don Revie to ask him to cancel my contract. He did it because it was the right thing to do, which is a measure of the type of man Revie was. I owed him a debt of gratitude for doing that for me.'

Rangers had shown determination to trump Leeds and lure Conn to Govan. That eagerness was maintained once the new recruit had joined the staff and he waited only a year for his senior debut as his side dumped Irish outfit Dundalk 3–0 in the Fairs Cup on 13 November 1968, away from home. 'I made my debut when I had just turned 16, coming on as a substitute for Alex Ferguson. At that age you are far too young to feel the pressure, you just go out and play the game. Even as I got older, I still approached it the same way.'

He left Rangers at the tender age of 22, but by that time Conn had already packed in what some players fail to achieve in a lifetime. He served under Scot Symon, Davie White, Willie Waddell and Jock Wallace in a six-year period and collected his first winners' medal as an 18-year-old when he helped the Light Blues to a 1–0 win over Celtic in the 1970 League Cup final.

In the league the men from Ibrox could not overcome their city rivals but there was no inferiority complex, with Conn insisting: 'In a one-off game we were as good as anyone. Over a course of a season we just didn't match Celtic's consistency. There were some great individuals in the side by 1972, but what really set the team apart was the way the individuals came together as a unit. Everyone could play the game. Somebody like Derek Johnstone is a prime example. He was comfortable in defence, midfield or attack.'

It was as part of that unit that Conn enjoyed his finest hour as the club's one and only European honour was claimed. The 20-year-old belied his youth in the final after being drafted into the side late, playing in the centre of the park alongside Alex MacDonald against the experienced Russians of Moscow Dynamo and surviving some heavy-handed treatment to help the team to the all important 3–2 victory.

He had featured in four of the nine ties in that victorious campaign and had the gold medal to prove it, although he believes the triumph is in danger of being overlooked as the years pass. Conn protests: 'People keep talking about what Rangers have done since then, about winning nine in a row, but what is overlooked is the fact the club spent millions to achieve that, to beat the best in Scotland, but still couldn't live with the best in Europe. What the 1972 team did had never been achieved before at Rangers, not even by the great teams with the likes of Jimmy Millar and Ralph Brand or Jim Baxter and Willie Henderson, and will never be done again. We beat the best with 11 home-grown players, just as Celtic had done previously. Rennes were a leading French side, Sporting Lisbon were packed with internationals, Torino were a top quality Italian side at that time, as hard as that is to believe now, while Bayern Munich had more than half of the fantastic German national side playing for them. Moscow Dynamo were basically the Russian international side in club form. In comparison to the type of money spent chasing European success in the last ten or fifteen years, it cost buttons to put that side together. If you were good enough you were old enough – now it seems if you are good enough you still won't get a game because there will be an expensive signing ahead of you in the queue. We were part of Rangers history, it had never happened before and probably never will again. Nobody is looking for anything from Rangers . . . except to remember what we achieved for the club.'

In 1973 he completed a hat-trick of cup honours when he lined up at Hampden again, this time in the Scottish Cup final, to help the Ibrox men to a 3–2 victory over Celtic in front of 122,714 fans. The only domestic medal missing was a league winners' gong as the Hoops dominated the championship during his period with Rangers. Conn would have to wait until he was a Parkhead player to complete the set.

Two years can be a long time in football. In that period after the Barcelona cup final, Conn's value rose and he became an asset Rangers were willing to cash in on. There was also a new man at the helm in Jock Wallace, so it was fair to expect change, but Conn does not believe he was the man responsible for his departure, which was the latest strike in the dismantling of the 1972 team.

Willie Waddell had remained as general manager and it was he who pulled the strings in the transfer saga that unfolded. Having been used sparingly in the 1973/74 season, playing in just 11 of the 34 league fixtures, Conn was resigned to a departure once the campaign had ended.

He could be comforted by the fact that two exiled Scots had noted his ability and were prepared to back that interest with hard cash, with the youthful midfielder set to break the previous club record sale of £100,000 paid by Coventry for Colin Stein in 1972. The two clubs circling were Manchester United, aiming to bounce back from relegation from the English First Division under Tommy Docherty's leadership, and Bill Nicholson's Tottenham Hotspur, who had finished the previous season in eleventh as Leeds ran out champions.

Both clubs had a track record of fostering Scottish players and on paper it was a difficult choice – made easier by the simple fact that Conn was given no option. Indeed, he knew nothing of the approach from Spurs until he found himself flying to the capital for signing talks. The prospect of a move to Manchester appealed to him, but Rangers held the cards and Spurs were the only club they were willing to deal with. Tottenham paid £140,000 to secure the services of Conn in July 1974.

'I didn't want to go – I was forced out of Rangers. Willie Waddell had resigned after winning in Barcelona, putting the pressure quite cleverly on Jock Wallace, but as far as I'm concerned he was still in control at the top. For me, that was half the problem. I don't think the Barcelona team ever played together again after that match. Colin Stein was sold, Willie Johnston was sold, I was sold and Dave Smith and Willie Mathieson were sold within a couple of years.

'When I was about to leave, I had met Tommy Docherty along with the journalist Ken Gallacher, who was a good friend of mine, and agreed terms with Manchester United. Then I got a phone call from Rangers to tell me to go to Glasgow airport. I thought I was going to Manchester, but instead I was put on a flight to London to meet Bill Nicholson. I was just glad to get away from Ibrox in the end. I would have been happy to go to Old Trafford but Willie Waddell didn't get on with Tommy Docherty and wouldn't sell me to him. According to Bill Nicholson, they had been watching me for three years, since we had played a friendly down at Tottenham and I'd made an impression.'

Conn would prove to be Nicholson's final signing, the manager making way for former Arsenal defender Terry Neill. The new man in charge was not known for a love of the type of flamboyant play the new boy had been brought to White Hart Lane to provide. A cartilage operation delayed his Spurs career, making his debut more than a month into the 1974/75 season as a substitute in a 4–0 League Cup defeat at home to Middlesbrough as Nicholson's reign drew to a close. It was a bad season for a flair player to try and make an impact, with the club struggling at the foot of the table and led by a manager determined to scrap and battle clear of the relegation zone. Still, Conn found the opportunity to turn himself into a cult hero among the north London side's fans, thanks in no small part to the type of debut every player dreams of but few turn into reality.

He made his first start in January 1975, at St James' Park against Newcastle United. If any of the travelling fans had wondered what Conn would bring to the party, they were left in no doubt by the time the referee blew for full-time. The 22-year-old had bagged a hat-trick as Spurs emerged 5–2 winners. 'Obviously I'd played at Rangers, a big club, but it was still impressive looking round the dressing room at Spurs where there were players like Pat Jennings, Mike England, Cyril Knowles, Martin Chivers and Ralph Coates. I loved it down south and had Bill Nicholson stayed on I doubt I would have come back to Scotland. Not long after I moved to London, Bill left. That was near enough the end of it for me. When a new manager comes in he's got his own ideas and it was just a clash of personalities with Terry Neill – we didn't get on at all and he had his own way of looking at things.

'After he left, Bill was never off the phone encouraging me and telling me to keep my head up. He said that I'd got the talent and would break through. I did get a break, against Newcastle, and didn't do myself any harm, especially with the fans, by scoring a hat-trick in that first game. I played less than 40 games but even now I still get letters from Spurs fans. Scottish players, like Alan Gilzean and Dave Mackay, had always been favourites at White Hart Lane and I was another who liked to play to the crowd.'

Until that blistering debut, Conn had been languishing in the reserves and it later transpired that Jennings and Knowles, two of the senior professionals, had gone knocking on their manager's door to persuade him that the Scottish import was too good for the second string. To his credit, Neill took note and acted on their advice. It was a decision that proved crucial to their top-flight survival.

Spurs beat the drop by a single point in Conn's first season and a win against European Cup finalists Leeds was the result needed to do that. It was a tall order, but Conn stepped up to the mark once again. He turned in a sublime two-goal contribution in a 4–2 win against the highly fancied Yorkshiremen.

It was in that game, in front of a capacity crowd at the Lane, that he showcased his audacity by sitting on the ball in the heat of battle. It is a moment still talked about by the Spurs fans who witnessed it – their treasured equivalent to Jim Baxter's impromptu keepy-up session at Wembley for Scotland. In fact, in more recent times Tottenham followers could be found on an internet forum debating whether Conn or the 1990s darling of the terraces, David Ginola, all £2 million of him, was the more skilful player.

The Scot admits: 'It was just one of those things – I don't think I even realised I had done it. We needed to beat Leeds to stay up and it was worth so much money to the club. You can talk about pressure in cup finals, but a game like that is when there's real pressure. We were 3–0 up and I sat on the ball on the spur of the moment. Straight afterwards, Billy Bremner collared me and said: "Wait until you see what you have just done." Sure enough, Peter Lorimer hit a screamer into the top corner and we ended up hanging on for a 3–2 win. Afterwards, I went into the Leeds dressing room and apologised. I think they took it the right way in the end.'

Conn, an internationalist at youth and under-23 level, was a Tottenham player by the time he was given his first Scotland cap. Just a month after his 23rd birthday he got the call from Willie Ormond, as part of the squad for the 1975 home international championship. Ormond gave Conn both of his two caps, coming within the space of four days but still providing a taste of the highs and lows of life as a Scotland player.

His debut came as a substitute in a 3–0 win over Northern

Ireland at Hampden in a team featuring the likes of Bruce Rioch, Kenny Dalglish and Gordon McQueen. Goals from Dalglish, Ted MacDougall and Derek Parlane clinched victory. The newcomer did enough in his appearance from the bench to merit a starting place for the following game against England at Wembley. It was not a fairytale homecoming for the adopted Londoner, with the hosts cantering to a 5–1 win.

Despite winning over the Scotland manager and Spurs fans, the Kirkcaldy-born player found it much tougher to curry favour with Neill and Keith Burkinshaw, his successor in the White Hart Lane hot seat. Neill had left for Arsenal at the start of the 1975/76 season, but the approach from the new manager remained the same and Conn was regarded as a luxury player.

His career in England was hampered by a serious Achilles injury, which kept him sidelined for nine months, and the club opted to recoup the bulk of the investment they had made in 1974. The price tag of £120,000 did not frighten potential buyers. It did, however, prompt fans to bombard the Tottenham offices with pleas for the player to be removed from the transfer list. In total, he started 35 games and made three appearances from the bench, scoring six goals in the process, but the time in London was far more eventful than those bare statistics could ever tell. According to the legions of Spurs fans, who 30 years on have still been known to chant Conn's name, it was also far more memorable.

Today, agents are at the hub of every major transfer, but in the 1970s the profession was yet to take off. Instead, journalists often played the role of go-between and instigator. The late Ken Gallacher, one of Scotland's most respected football writers during a prolific career, had built up a strong relationship with Conn while covering events at Ibrox. Gallacher had been part of the press pack in Barcelona as Rangers beat Moscow Dynamo and wrote a book on the subject in the aftermath. He had come close to orchestrating a move to Manchester United when Conn left Scotland and would succeed in pulling together an even more dramatic transfer when it was time for him to return. Not only did he report on the biggest Scottish sports story of a generation, he created it.

In 1976 Celtic were regrouping after seeing their dominance smashed by Rangers, who won the league in 1975 and the treble the following year. They paid £60,000 to take Conn back north during the course of the 1976/77 season, a move the player feels served the dual purpose of bolstering the Parkhead squad and gaining an off-field victory against their fierce city rivals. 'I phoned Ken and told him Spurs had put me up for sale. There was interest in England but I knew they would cut the transfer fee in half if I went to a club in Scotland instead. My wife Susan and I were settled in London and had a lot of fantastic friends, so if I was going to uproot the family it would only be to go back home to Glasgow. Ken phoned Ibrox and Parkhead to alert them to my availability. It was as much a surprise to me as it was to anyone when Celtic were the club who followed it up. In hindsight I shouldn't have been surprised. I had played under Jock Stein for Scotland's under-23 side. He was an unbelievable manager and someone I always enjoyed playing for. He was also a persuasive fellow – he would say little things you wouldn't necessarily pick up right away, but they would always make sense in the end. I thought about it long and hard, but the simple fact was my old club hadn't come in for me. I was the first since the war to play for both teams, and it was big news. It was hard for me and hard for my family, but I had a mortgage and bills to pay.'

When Conn walked through the front door at Parkhead on 1 March 1977, he joined a Celtic team on course to regain the Scottish crown they had surrendered two years earlier. The Hoops sat proudly at the top of the Premier League, seven points clear after 22 games and with a match in hand over challengers Rangers.

He made his debut on 5 March in a 2–0 defeat at Pittodrie against Aberdeen as a substitute for Pat McCluskey and four days later capped his first start with the opening goal in a 2–1 home win over Partick Thistle. From then on, Conn was a permanent fixture in the Celtic side that season and took part in his first Old Firm bout fighting from the green corner just 19 days after signing. It was a 2–2 draw at Ibrox, Conn denied a goal only by the post. Celtic won the league comfortably, nine points clear of Rangers, and Conn made 14 appearances after joining late in the campaign to earn his first championship medal. He also joined in time for two crucial Scottish Cup outings, playing in the 2–0 semi-final win over Dundee United and the 1–0 Old Firm victory in the final to match the winners' medal he had collected with the Light Blues in 1973.

The 1977/78 campaign was an anti-climax, Celtic suffering their poorest season in 13 years as they fell to fifth in the final standings. It was a transitional period for the Hoops, with talisman Kenny Dalglish leaving for Liverpool in preseason in a £440,000 transfer and the inspirational Danny McGrain missing the bulk of the season after Pat Stanton had also been sidelined with what proved to be a career-ending injury.

It would also prove to be Jock Stein's Celtic farewell. Conn added 17 appearances before Billy McNeill returned from Aberdeen to take the helm. It proved to be a successful appointment for the Parkhead club, who once again claimed the league title in 1978/79. Six-figure sums were spent before that campaign to recruit Murdo MacLeod and Davie Provan, but Conn stood his ground and was a first-choice pick as McNeill's reign got underway with a 2–1 win at Morton. At the half way point, Celtic were in sixth place but mounted a late charge to the summit. By the time Celtic won the league with a last game of the season 4–2 win over Rangers, Conn's career at the club had ended.

He played his last game in a 1–0 win over Aberdeen at Parkhead in March 1979, scoring the match-winning goal to sign off in style after a further 23 appearances that term. Even now the repercussions of his time at Parkhead can still be felt on the streets of Glasgow, but there are no regrets. 'I got a lot of grief at the time – I came behind Adolf Hitler in a popularity contest, that's how bad it was. It can still be difficult now. It was 30 years ago but I still get pulled up for it, getting called a turncoat and all the rest of it. Half the people making the comments wouldn't even have been born when I played for Celtic – it must have been passed down from father to son. I went to Celtic to play football and left with two championship medals and a Scottish Cup medal, so from that perspective I couldn't complain. I played in the north London derby for Spurs against Arsenal, but it was Chelsea who were our biggest rivals – there was a real hatred in that fixture. Yet it still didn't come close to the Old Firm. Nothing can.'

A move to Derby County fell through when manager Tommy Docherty left for QPR and instead America beckoned. After the goldfish-bowl environment of Old Firm life, Conn's next football stop was as far removed as he could get. He left Celtic in May 1979 to sign for Pittsburgh Spirit in the Major Indoor Soccer League of America. The North American Soccer League, as already mentioned, had attracted Pele, George Best, Franz Beckenbauer and Johan Cruyff at its peak and the MISL, founded in 1978, was designed to take advantage of the interest the outdoor league had created. It presented Conn with an opportunity to sample life on the other side of the Atlantic, swapping Parkhead's terraces for the more modern surroundings of the 17,000 capacity Mellon Arena where the Spirit played their home games and he insists: 'I thoroughly enjoyed it. I played outdoor over there as well but the six-a-side league was something totally different and a great experience.'

The New York Arrows were the undisputed indoor kings

of the time, crowned champions in Conn's season in the States and only overtaken by the wonderfully named San Diego Soccers and their eight championships before the league folded in 1992. Conn also soaked up some sun in the NASL while on the roster of the San Jose Earthquakes in 1980 before returning to sign for Hearts in the summer of that year.

Conn returned home to Scotland and Edinburgh to sign for the club at which his dad had made his name almost four decades earlier but he himself had rejected as a teenager. Aged 28 by that time, Conn was seen by the Jambos manager Bobby Moncur as the type of experienced player he needed to bolster a side preparing for their return to the Premier League after winning the First Division championship.

It was not a happy return to the top flight for the club, with relegation the end result. Conn made his debut for the Gorgie side in a 3–2 defeat against Partick on 30 July 1980, and his final appearance on 10 January the following year in a 2–0 home defeat at the hands of Aberdeen. In between he turned out 21 times for Hearts before returning to England for a second stint south of the border.

Blackpool, managed by Allan Brown and playing in the old Third Division, proved to be a temporary staging post as he played three games for the Bloomfield Road side before rejecting a permanent switch in favour of staying in Scotland. 'When I came back home to Hearts it wasn't a good time for the club. I never even stayed the season, going down to Blackpool at the tail end. They wanted me to stay long-term but I wasn't interested in uprooting the family again.'

Fir Park in Motherwell proved to be the latest and final port of call in an extraordinary football journey for Conn. The Lanarkshire side, like the Hearts team he had left behind the previous season, were faced with the task of escaping from the tough First Division. Both clubs ended the season achieving that aim, but it was 'Well who had the upper hand.

They took top spot on 19 September 1981, and remained on top of the pile until the final ball had been kicked on 15 May the following year, a 1–0 win at Tynecastle confirming the Steelmen's status as worthy champions. Conn played in that match, joining the celebrations of a club who had not toasted title success since the Second Division win of 1969, and collected his third league winners' medal.

After making his debut in the second game of the season, a 1–0 win over Queen's Park, Conn went on to make 22 league appearances and chipped in with two goals as Ally MacLeod's men marched to victory. Jock Wallace was in charge for the club's Premier League return in 1981/82, which saw Motherwell cling to the safety of seventh place, but for Conn it was not to be a lengthy reunion with his former Rangers boss. He started the season in the 'Well team in a campaign that saw the new guard break through in the shape of Gary McAllister and Brian McClair, but by the end of the first quarter he had suffered a knee injury.

His career was brought to an end after an eventful 15 years as a first-team player. 'It was Jock who had to tell me my playing days were over. He called me in to go over the surgeon's report after an operation on my knee. The advice was that I either stopped playing or ended up a cripple. In a lot of ways, it was easier to be told that than maybe trying to come back again and again. You see that happening time and time again.'

The family remained in the Glasgow area, where son Steven is a policeman and daughter Samantha works as a nursery teacher. Conn, who worked in the licensed trade before retiring, stepped away from the senior game and had a clean break from the professional ranks. His love of the game remained strong, even guiding Coatbridge to the Scottish Amateur Cup title in the 1980s. He does not venture back to his old haunts of Ibrox or Parkhead often but still appreciates the finer things in the sport . . . it is just a case of knowing where to look for them. 'I go back now and again, but to be honest I always got more pleasure and enjoyment from watching my son playing amateur football. Then you've got 22 men playing the game because they love it, which is what it should be about. It's easy to lose sight of that.'

CHAPTER NINE

# COLIN STEIN

Colin Stein is still a champion. Almost four decades after winning the European Cup Winners' Cup, Scotland's first six-figure signing is still no stranger to trophy presentations. In fact, if you ask the good people of Linlithgow Bowling Club they would probably tell you they wished he was still playing football and not proving an insurmountable obstacle on the green of their town. Stein, a no-nonsense centre forward who gave as good as he got, has been bowls champion at the club countless times and the bad news for his rivals is he plans to keep treading the lawn for a few years yet. He quips: 'I can just about manage to get from one end of the green to the other, so I'll carry on.'

For those who worshipped Stein from the terraces and roared him on, the thought of the Lothian-born football star in the more tranquil surroundings of his home bowling club will paint an unlikely picture. When you consider that he left football behind because the weekly threats and abuse became too much of an annoyance to deal with, it is not such a surprise. 'I've lost count of the number of people who told me they were going to break my legs. I just thought I didn't need that week in and week out.'

The imposing striker called time on his career in 1978, by which time he had served 13 years in the English and Scottish leagues and bagged more goals than he could even attempt to recount. He had two spells at Rangers and in his first boasted a scoring ratio of more than a goal in every other game. He had the ability to turn pressure into goals at just the right moment, including in the European final of

1972, when he helped Rangers on their way to victory with the opening strike.

For Scotland he boasted the same type of form and returned nine goals in just 21 appearances. Not bad for a player who started life as a defender and can thank a twist of fortune for the switch in position that made him a star. 'I was a left back when I started with Armadale Juniors as a teenager. We needed somebody to play up front in one game. I volunteered and scored a hat-trick. That became my position.'

It was another well-timed hat-trick that earned Stein his first break in the senior game, joining Hibernian from the junior ranks in 1965 as an 18-year-old. 'We played a cup final at Easter Road with Armadale and I scored a hat-trick. I was supposed to go to Partick Thistle the next day, but Bob Shankly signed me there and then. It was a case of being in the right place at the right time.'

Stein joined the Edinburgh side in the aftermath of Jock Stein's resignation, the manager leaving to move west and take charge of Celtic. His successor at Hibs was Bob Shankly, who made the switch from Dundee. He was traditional in his approach and fostered an attacking style well suited to Colin Stein's natural poaching instincts.

In the 1965/66 season Shankly led his new side to sixth place, went one better the following term and reached the heady heights of third spot in 1967/68. That third season was the one in which Stein made his big impact. Peter Cormack was the top dog at the club at that point, leading scorer in Stein's first two seasons on the books at Leith, having taken on the mantle from Neil Martin following his switch to Sunderland.

Soon, the new kid on the block proved he had what it took to be proclaimed as the new goal king of Hibs, being leading scorer with 29 goals in all competitions in the 1967/68 season. It was in that season that the bustling striker sampled the type of European drama he would experience at Rangers in the years to come. After squeezing past Porto in the first round of the Fairs Cup, the Hibees went head to head with Italian cracks Napoli. Stein scored in the away leg, but it was not a happy tie for the Scottish side, who fell to a 4–1 defeat. The return was sensational, with the men in green firing five without reply and Stein rounding off the scoring with an unstoppable shot past legendary keeper Dino Zoff.

The next round saw Hibs paired with Don Revie's Leeds United. Stein was carried off after a typically hefty Leeds tackle as his side fell to a 1–0 defeat at Elland Road but was fit for the English side's trip north and gained his revenge with a cute lob to level the tie early on. Leeds went on to win with a Jack Charlton goal in the closing stages, but Stein had proved he could mix it with the best in the business. 'Hibs already had Peter Cormack and a lot of other good players when I joined the club but I took my chance when it came and scored plenty of goals. I gave them good service.'

Those European performances and his domestic exploits made the striker, still only 21, a man in demand. Despite Shankly's determination to hold on to his prize asset, in the end Hibs gave up the fight in October 1968 when the big guns of Everton and Rangers set their sights on Stein. Everton, champions of England in the past decade, had finished the 1967/68 campaign in fifth position and saw him as the key to their attempts to break the Manchester dominance which had seen City claim the title and United finish runners-up. They also had to match city rivals Liverpool, who had finished two places better off than the Toffee Men. Rangers, on the other hand, had a city battle of their own to take care of as Celtic continued to pull the strings in the Scottish First Division. Davie White had taken over from Scot Symon in November 1967 – the year Symon had led Rangers to the European Cup Winners' Cup.

It took White the best part of a year to land the big signing he craved to show he meant business, and Stein was that man. A Rangers fan as a boy, the Hibs striker was happy to spearhead what White hoped would be a revolution and switched to Ibrox in a record-breaking £100,000 deal in October 1968. The sale was later credited as the reason behind Shankly's resignation from his manager's post at Hibs less than a year later. White, in contrast, was just getting into his stride and willing to pay top dollar for the cream of Scottish talent, as he proved soon after Stein's arrival with the recruitment of another of the rising stars in the shape of £50,000 midfielder Alex MacDonald.

Stein recalls: 'I was called to meet Harry Catterick, the long-serving Everton manager at the Caledonian Hotel in Edinburgh. I was engaged to my wife Linda by then and they even sent for her to try and persuade me. I was very close to signing for Everton. The Hibs chairman had said I would never sign for another club in Scotland – but then £100,000 is a lot of money. I was a Rangers supporter as a boy and it was the chance I was waiting for. When they came in with that offer I don't think it was one Hibs could refuse.'

It truly was a lot of money. Rangers could have bought an entire village and ferried its residents around in the lap of luxury for the same money they spent on Stein, with the average house price in Britain at the time £4,000 and Jaguar's newly introduced XJ6 a snip at £2,200. The fee eclipsed anything the club had paid before, not just breaking the previous record but absolutely shattering it. Two years earlier Dave Smith had cost £40,000 from Aberdeen and Alex Smith commanded a £50,000 fee from Dunfermline Athletic at the same time. A certain Alex Ferguson had set Rangers back £65,000 in 1967 and MacDonald earned St Johnstone £50,000 when he made the switch from Perth to Glasgow the following year. The legendary Jim Baxter was valued at £72,500 when he was sold to Sunderland in 1967, yet Davie White had to increase that figure by more than a quarter to prise Stein away from Hibs. The club did not repeat the six-figure spending spree until Davie Cooper was recruited from Clydebank in the summer of 1977 and the magic figure wasn't broken until Gregor Stevens moved from Leicester in a £150,000 deal two years later. The arrival of Graeme Souness, backed by new owner David Murray, would rewrite the record books when it came to expenditure in the years that followed.

It represented a massive investment for the Light Blues and they were entitled to expect a substantial return. What they got must even have made the bank manager break out into a smile. Stein made his debut for his new club on 2 November 1968, at the notoriously weather-beaten Gayfield Park against Arbroath. Rangers were 2–1 up against the plucky Angus minnows when Stein took control, completing a quick-fire hat-trick within the space of just four minutes to announce his arrival to the travelling support inside the packed ground.

The script, as so often happens, could not have been written any better as Stein's next game was against Hibs at Ibrox. In front of a crowd of 66,000 he demolished his former club with another stunning treble in a 6–1 win. He went into his third match as a Ranger with the improbable opportunity of making it a hat-trick of hat-tricks, Irish side Dundalk providing the cannon fodder this time in the Fairs Cup. In the end, he notched a double and was denied a third by the woodwork as his tally rose to eight goals in three games. All of a sudden the £100,000 fee seemed like the bargain of the century.

Stein was no stranger to high scoring, having grabbed three trebles in the space of six months in his final season at Hibs. The statistics meant little to the new golden boy: winning the approval of the Ibrox faithful meant much more. 'I was sent off in my last game against Rangers as a Hibs player after an incident involving Alex Ferguson at Ibrox. I had the entire Rangers support calling me all of the names under the sun . . . a few weeks later I was being treated like a god by them. A lot of players have found it difficult to get the Rangers supporters on their side – even Ally McCoist and

Mark Hateley struggled – but the best way for a striker to do that is to score goals. Once you do that, and have them on your side, it is a fantastic feeling. Obviously one of the hat-tricks was against Hibs, who had Thomson Allan in goal. Thomson was actually my best man and we went out after the game. He stayed pretty quiet that night.'

In the four years between his debut and crowning glory in Barcelona, Stein endeared himself to the Ibrox faithful with his rugged style and deadly shot. Chants of 'We don't need Eusebio because we've got Colin Stein' replaced the abuse previously meted out to him at Ibrox when he had visited as a Hibs player, with the Edinburgh club's traditional links with Celtic and Ireland ensuring that the cross-coast rivalry was intense.

His hopes of a trophy-winning start to his inaugural season as a Rangers player were dashed when the new goal-scoring king was hit with a six-week suspension by the SFA for retaliation in a 6–0 win against Clyde, a game in which he had already bagged a hat-trick. He was forced out of the league run-in, as Celtic moved on and won the championship, and sidelined for the 1969 Scottish Cup final as Celtic ran out 4–0 winners.

Stein, as Scotland's big-money man, found himself being targeted on the field as well as off it and quickly learned he had to look after number one. 'I think the price tag bothered the players I was up against more than it did me. They were always reminding me about it. So were the opposition fans, but I always thought if they were shouting about me then I must have been doing something right.'

Despite the disappointment of finishing his first campaign empty handed, he would only have to wait a matter of months to claim his first medal, playing in the following term's Old Firm triumph in the League Cup final as Derek Johnstone claimed the winner in a 1–0 victory. Stein scored a double in the opening game of the 1970/71 cup winning campaign, a 4–1 win over Dunfermline at Ibrox. He was on target against the Fifers again in the return leg of that tie at East End Park and also hit the net in the group stage against Motherwell before Rangers moved past Hibs and Cowdenbeath in the knock-out stages to set up the final showdown with Celtic.

The Hoops proved frustrating opposition to his league dream, with Rangers finishing second and five points adrift of their fierce rivals in the first season and then second, fourth and third in the next three. For Stein, unlike most Old Firm players in any era, the chance to redress the balance would come in the very early days of a rare second spell in the cauldron of Glasgow football.

Stein's immediate impact in Glasgow after his switch from Easter Road caught the imagination of his new supporters, but his form even before the transfer had convinced Scotland manager Bobby Brown of his worth. 'I'd played for the Scottish League select but it was still a surprise to get the Scotland call. I think it is always a surprise to get that first cap. Every boy dreams of playing for their country and I was fortunate to get that chance early on in my career. I was proud to play for Scotland.'

At the age of 21, the Hibs striker made his first Scotland appearance in a 1–0 win over Denmark at the Idraetspark stadium in Copenhagen in an international friendly on 16 October 1968. He wore the dark blue No.9 jersey in a team captained by Billy Bremner. Stein went on to win 20 further caps and scored nine goals for the national side. His first strike came within two months of taking his bow on the big stage in a 5–0 win over Cyprus in a World Cup qualifier in Nicosia.

It was against the same opponents that Stein made his biggest mark as a Scotland player, torturing the Cypriots when they arrived at Hampden for the return leg in 1969 as he hit the net four times in the space of just 39 minutes in an 8–0 win. That performance also makes him the last to have scored three or more goals for Scotland and Stein holds another international record as the last player to score in five consecutive matches. His rich vein of international form came in 1969, when he bagged goals against Wales, Northern Ireland, England, Cyprus and then the Republic of Ireland. Kenny Miller has come closest to matching that, with three consecutive goals in three appearances in 2005. Stein says: 'It's unbelievable that in more than 30 years my record still hasn't been matched. It won't bother me when it does go because I want to see Scotland do well. I could actually have made it five because we got a penalty in that match against Cyprus – but Tommy Gemmell was our penalty taker and grabbed the ball off me.'

After being given his break by Brown, Stein played his final match for his country at Wembley in May 1973, in Willie Ormond's Scotland side. By that stage he was a Coventry City player but his knowledge of the English scene was not enough to prevent a 1–0 defeat in front of a baying crowd of 95,000 underneath the famous old twin towers.

In all, Stein played on the winning side for Scotland six times, drew five of his international matches and lost ten. The home international championship dominated his career with the national side and Stein helped Scotland to a rare success in the 1970 series as Bobby Brown's side finished tied for the title with England and Wales on four points from three games. They were unbeaten in 270 minutes of the traditionally hard-fought competition after holding the English to a 0–0 draw at Hampden, Wales to the same score and defeating Northern Ireland in Belfast. The previous year he became one of the select band of Scots to have scored at Wembley, albeit in a 4–1 defeat.

By the time Stein's international days drew to a close, Willie Ormond was pinning his goal-scoring hopes on the likes of Kenny Dalglish and the emerging talent of Joe Jordan, who took his Scotland bow the week before Stein bade farewell to the Tartan Army. With Denis Law still on the scene, Scotland had an embarrassment of riches in attack.

What would Rangers give for a Colin Stein in today's football climate? More than the club could possibly afford.

The forward's first European sojourn with Rangers can be deemed a success, ending at the semi-final stage as Newcastle ran out 2–0 aggregate winners in the 1968/69 Fairs Cup. Having scored his double against Dundalk early in the competition, he popped up with the winner in a 2–1 second-leg victory over DWS Amsterdam to cap a 4–1 aggregate win and earn a place in the quarter-finals. He was on target again against Athletic Bilbao as Rangers claimed a 4–3 win over two legs but Newcastle presented a hurdle too high in the final four of the competition.

It was not until 1971/72 that Rangers came good again on the European stage and Stein played a full part, starting all nine of the games in the cup-winning campaign. He weighed in with a double against Sporting Lisbon, both at home in the 3–2 win, and away, in the 4–3 defeat, before adding his fifth of the competition in the final against Moscow Dynamo. Those goals made him the leading scorer for Rangers in the tournament, one ahead of Willie Johnston in the final standings. Like the other ten who helped Rangers to victory in the European Cup Winners' Cup final in 1972, Stein holds the memories close to his heart.

It was a defining moment for him, as he was at the peak of his powers and central to the historic victory in Barcelona. The most valuable of his five strikes in that tournament was the opener to settle the nerves in the final against the Russians. His clinical strike from Dave Smith's incisive pass was fit to grace the occasion, but Stein does not possess the type of arrogance it is all too easy to assume prolific goalscorers must have.

'There were a lot of good players round about me and when you are playing in a good team you will always get chances. You still have to take those chances, and confidence is a big factor for any centre forward. If you don't have confidence, one touch can turn into two touches and the chance is gone. It's difficult to coach a striker because so much of it is about instinct. You can try and teach somebody to make the right runs, to be in the right place at the right time, but you can't turn them into a finisher. Willie Waddell had Dave Smith playing sweeper before it had been heard of in Scotland, with Colin Jackson and Derek Johnstone there to attack the ball. We built from the back and it worked very well.'

The European experience covered the whole spectrum of emotions. Like his colleagues, Stein felt the 'huge disappointment' of not being presented with the cup in the stadium, but there is pride in his voice when he says: 'We played a lot of good teams and came out on top. The bulk of the Bayern team went on to win the World Cup just two years later. Nobody can take that away from us.'

The memory of that final, and Stein's contribution, lives on not just in Scotland. When Anatoli Baidachny arrived in Glasgow as manager of the Belarusian national team to play Scotland in a World Cup qualifier in 2005, the former Moscow Dynamo player took a matter of minutes to tell waiting journalists that Walter Smith's men had to recreate the Rangers spirit of 1972. He sang the praises of the team that had beaten him and his Dynamo colleagues, singling out Colin Stein for the way he led the line in Barcelona.

The euphoria of the win in Europe had barely subsided by the time Stein was packing his boots and preparing for a new life in England. He was sold to Coventry City in a deal worth £140,000 when the £50,000 valuation of Quinton Young, who was transferred from the Midlands club to Rangers as part of the package, was taken into account.

It was just three months into the 1972/73 season after he had made two starts and one substitute's appearance under new manager Jock Wallace, the last coming from the bench in a 2–1 defeat at Kilmarnock, in the Scottish First Division.

'We won in Barcelona in May and by October I was gone, sent to Coventry quite literally. I didn't want to leave but I took some good memories from my time in England. Coventry had not a bad side at the time, guys like big Tommy Hutchison and Willie Carr, and I was captain of the team. It was a good club and playing in a different league was a great experience.'

Like Rangers before them, Coventry were willing to put their finances on the line to secure the services of Stein. The £140,000 represented a club record, matched by the outlay for his new striking partner Tommy Hutchison at the same time. He moved to a side who were going through a period of transition, with management duo Joe Mercer and Gordon Milne still in their honeymoon period having taken over from Noel Cantwell in March that year.

Despite reaching the heady height of sixth in England's top flight under Cantwell, staying in that league was the name of the game for the Milne and Mercer partnership. The Scotland internationalist first appeared for the Sky Blues away to Crystal Palace in a 1–0 win and soon made the No.9 shirt his own. His first goal for his new side came in the next game, a 3–2 win over Manchester City at Highfield Road, and he went on, despite joining after the season had begun, to climb to second in the end-of-season scoring charts with 12 league and cup goals.

In Stein's first season south of the border they achieved the aim of consolidation, finishing 19th in the 22-team division, topped by the mighty Liverpool. He weighed in with five goals in 28 league appearances the following term, in 1973/74, and helped Coventry climb three places in a year Leeds were crowned champions and Manchester United were relegated.

He was again Gordon Milne's main striker as the 1974/75 campaign kicked off. Despite leaving two-thirds of the way through the season to return to Rangers, Stein, with seven league and cup goals, still finished second top scorer at Coventry, just one strike behind Dundee-born Brian Alderson. The club also maintained its progress, gaining another two places in the league, despite their main man being recalled by Rangers.

In March 1975 Stein returned to Scotland in an £80,000 deal after a two-and-a-half-year absence from Ibrox. In that time the club had won the Scottish Cup, but the striker came back in time to celebrate the big one, the end of Celtic's nine-in-a-row domination. The old hero was reunited with his old terracing backers in a 1–0 win over St Johnstone in Glasgow and helped the side to another two wins before notching his first goal since his homecoming, waiting until the most opportune of moments to do so. On 29 March the Light Blues travelled to Stein's old stamping ground at Easter Road needing a single point against Hibs to secure the title with four games to spare. More than 38,000 packed into the Edinburgh ground and saw Ally McLeod give Hibs an early lead. Sandy Jardine missed from the spot before Stein, in the 61st minute, rose above the home defence to bullet home a Bobby McKean cross with his head and spark amazing scenes of celebration among the Rangers fans, who had waited since 1964 to herald their team as the best in the land.

Stein scored another two goals in the remaining games of that historic season – the last before the introduction of the Premier League – to take his tally to three strikes in eight games. That contribution was not enough to win over his manager, who declined to award his signing a championship medal. Stein has seen and done it all in football, but that experience still riles him. 'It was nice to score the goal to win the league – but it would have been even nicer to have got a medal. It upset me at the time and still does. I even offered to pay to have my own medal struck, but Jock Wallace said no. A lot of water has passed under the bridge since then, but it still amazes me that I had such trouble persuading a club like Rangers that I deserved one. Maybe they felt the league was already won by the time I came back but I still played in eight of the games, with only one defeat, and feel I played my part.'

The 1975/76 season was a treble-winning campaign for Rangers but Stein was restricted to a cameo role, with six league appearances including the 2–1 Old Firm victory in front of 69,000 as the flag was unfurled at Ibrox on the opening day. He also got the chance to collect a medal – and not even Wallace could dispute it this time. Rangers cruised through the group stage of the League Cup, with Stein scoring in the opening game against Airdrie. They went on an unbeaten run of six ties, and brushed aside Queen of the South and then Montrose in the quarter and semi-finals to book a final appearance against Celtic. Stein wore the No.8 jersey as Rangers clinched the first of three trophies that season with a 1–0 win against the Hoops at Hampden courtesy of an Alex MacDonald goal in the 67th minute.

In 1976/77 the one-time record signing's contribution was restricted to a handful of league appearances and by October 1977 Rangers were prepared to allow Stein to move on and join Kilmarnock. The west coast side were seeking to escape the lower reaches of the First Division under Willie Fernie and Davie Sneddon, Fernie's successor that season, and offered an escape route on loan. Stein's impact was immediate, scoring in a 2–2 draw against Dumbarton on his debut at Rugby Park. He was third in the scoring charts for Killie in his solitary season with the Ayrshire club, returning eight league goals in 23 starts as they moved from 12th place in the league when he joined to sixth by the time his loan deal expired in May. Morton and Hearts won promotion to the Premier League and Stein was faced with the choice of seeking a fresh challenge or calling time on his career. He opted for the latter, in a shrewd act of self-preservation.

'When I came back from Coventry, I wasn't the same player. I'd had a couple of hamstring injuries while I was at City and my pace had suffered. That had been a big part of my game. I eventually stopped playing when I was 30. I could have kept going, but it is a downward spiral when you leave Rangers and you end up becoming a target for madmen. Fine, if that's what they enjoy, but I didn't have to stand there and take it. It might have been different outside of Scotland and I could have gone to play in Australia, but it didn't appeal to me.'

Instead he swapped the rough and tumble of Scottish football for the more forgiving surroundings of the country's bowling greens. 'My wife is from Linlithgow and that became home to us. The only time we've been away was while we were in Coventry. I've been champion of the bowling club and enjoy the game. I'm a joiner by trade and that keeps me busy, too busy at times. Our daughter Nicola and son Martin have given us wonderful grandkids to be proud of and we enjoy that side of life.'

The difference is, not too many kids can say their granddad could give Eusebio a run for his money. Now that is something to shout about in the playground.

CHAPTER TEN

# ALEX MACDONALD

Vladimir Romanov, backed up by the might of his £270 million Lithuanian business empire, breezed into Heart of Midlothian Football Club in 2005 with the lofty ambition of dislodging Rangers and Celtic from the seat of power in Scottish football.

Ideas above his station? Well, not quite. Hearts have been close to fulfilling that particular master plan even before the new owner and his litas arrived at Tynecastle. The answer back then lay much closer to home in the shape of Alex MacDonald, the manager who took Hearts to within seven minutes of the Premier League crown in 1986 – a mere 420 seconds from emulating Sir Alex Ferguson and Jim McLean's achievement of knocking the Old Firm down from their perch.

Hearts fell agonisingly at the last hurdle on that occasion. Still, MacDonald could console himself with recognition as Scotland's manager of the year. Scant reward at the time, but as the years pass and the pain subsides the place in the history books remains. Like his Barca Bears team-mate Tommy McLean, MacDonald was voted among the top 50 managers the country has ever produced in a poll of the nation's football fans. Not a bad achievement, when you consider the thousands who have tried their hand.

It is now 25 years since that award and seven since his last managerial post, with Airdrie, yet MacDonald is young enough to be patrolling the touch lines of Scotland's leagues. After the highs of cup finals and European adventures, don't expect him to be digging out his CV for one last tilt, though. No, that itch has been scratched. The suggestion of a return to the dug-out is greeted with a knowing laugh. 'It's like a Kays catalogue of players now: you put a couple of quid down now and pay later or you can send them back if you don't like them. I don't need that. It's okay if you've got £20 million in the bank and can cut your cloth to suit yourself, but how many clubs can give their manager that luxury? You end up cutting your cloth to suit somebody else.'

MacDonald combines his day job as general manager with a Glasgow firm with match-day duties as part of the hospitality team at Ibrox, the best of both worlds for the fan turned player turned fan again. He still approaches life with the same zest as he applied on the football field, glad to be kept busy with an increasingly congested programme of Rangers games and able to let work and pleasure collide at Ibrox once again. He was quick to seize upon my own optimism in trying to catch up with him on the night Rangers were on Champions League duty on home turf. Interview postponed. I should have known better than to expect this particular former player to have been camped indoors when his beloved Rangers were in action a short drive from his home on the north side of the city. He has reverted to type, having grown up as a devoted Gers supporter and become one of the privileged few lucky enough to have experienced life on the other side of the track.

'Coming from Glasgow, every game I played for Rangers was like a cup final for me – and games against Celtic, that was it. I got to do what the other 400 boys at school wanted to do, that was my job. It doesn't get much better than that.'

Turning out in the light blue of Rangers was a dream come true, but MacDonald served his apprenticeship in the blue of St Johnstone before winning the dream ticket to Ibrox. Plucked from the amateur leagues by the Perth side as a raw teenager, the Glaswegian quickly carved out a reputation as one to watch.

He remained based in his home city despite signing for Saints, making the daily trip north by train to link up with a squad who were well established in Scotland's top flight, where they remained during his three seasons with the club. St Johnstone, playing out of Muirton Park – like so many Scottish grounds now relegated to life as a retail park – benefited from strong management and in the midfielder's last full season at the team were within an ace of securing a place in the Scottish Cup final. In the end, it took a semi-final replay for Dunfermline to get the better of their Tayside opponents.

On a personal level, MacDonald was voted player of the year at St Johnstone in 1967 and was second in the scoring charts with 14 goals in his penultimate season. That sparked interest from Celtic, Sheffield Wednesday, Spurs, Sheffield United, Derby County, Middlesbrough and Fulham . . . but Rangers was the destination of choice, and the Ibrox side were the quickest to move when Saints chose to cash in on their most valuable asset.

'I had three years at St Johnstone playing under Bobby Brown and Willie Ormond, two Scotland managers. Alex Ferguson was there at the same time. I had started out playing amateur football with Glasgow United and was picked up by the St Johnstone scouting network at the time. There was a rule back then that stopped you playing junior football if you turned professional first, so the way round it was to get me signed with Luncarty Juniors in the first place.'

He did enough in 36 months as a Saint to tempt Rangers and new manager Davie White to open the chequebook during the 1968/69 season to bring him home, quite literally, to Ibrox in a £50,000 deal.

'When I signed for St Johnstone I lived with my granny in Govanhill, so I decided to buy a flat there. I still remember coming home from training one day with Ian McPhee to find the fire brigade camped in the street. Ian joked it would be funny if they were at my house – and they were. My good lady and I ended up at her uncle's place opposite Ibrox, so I'd walk past the ground every day on my way to get the subway to Queen Street for the train on to Perth. After I signed for Rangers I was thinking: Do I really go in here?'

Rangers had paid big money for a 20-year-old with less than 36 months under his belt as a professional. The weight of that hefty price tag, and the self-imposed pressure derived from his feelings for his new club, took its toll on MacDonald as he made his first steps towards becoming a hero among Rangers fans. 'The first two years were really hard for me. I was just a boy from Kinning Park and now I was there as a Rangers player. I must have been one of the fittest players at the club but I was totally and utterly shattered during that time, just getting through on adrenaline. Looking back, it was just sheer nerves. It took me a couple of years to settle down from that. After then, it really blossomed for me.'

Equally, it took Rangers and their new recruit two years to break Celtic's stranglehold on the Scottish game. He picked up the first of his 12 winners' medals as part of the team that won the Old Firm final of the 1970 League Cup. It was success, but not the league championship that he and the Ibrox faithful craved. Jock Stein's Celtic were proving a tough nut to crack and that hurt for a youthful midfielder who had no way of knowing that the tide would turn in his favour in later years.

'By the time I signed for Rangers, Celtic were going through their nine-in-a-row – it was hard to take. I was 21, nine-in-a-row was what I wanted to do with Rangers not watch Celtic do it. I wouldn't say there was a big gulf between the two sides, a lot of the difference was tactical. Quite often we would set out our stall to play a certain way and keep Celtic at bay . . . then Jock Stein would switch Jimmy Johnstone to the other wing and it would all be up in the air again.

'Every person you met – your gran, the postman, the petrol pump attendant – would pull you up if you lost and ask what had gone wrong. You had to learn how to disappear, to run on the blind side as I put it. You would end up going out to fill the car up with petrol at three in the morning just to avoid all of that. Of course the other side is the adulation you get when things go well. Every cloud, and all that.'

MacDonald was one of White's first significant signings but barely had a chance to repay the manager's faith in him before Willie Waddell took the helm. Jock Wallace and John Greig followed in the hot seat, each fostering a thirst for knowledge that would ultimately lead to the midfielder becoming a manager in his own right. Even in his twenties, the seeds were being sown as he soaked up the moves in a chess-like battle between Rangers and Celtic.

'Davie White was a great tactician but he had a tough time. He didn't have the same recognition or reputation as some of the guys in the team. He hadn't played in European finals or the World Cup, he'd come from Clyde. He came to Rangers and tried to stamp his style on the side. Tactically he was a good manager, but maybe it was the wrong job at the wrong time for him. Every manager had a different way. With Jock Wallace it was more rough and ready: you were told the way things would be done. Willie Waddell was the man for me. He changed me from the laid-back midfielder nutmegging his way through games to the push-and-run player I became, in the mould of Alan Ball and guys like that.

'I didn't realise how important the push-and-run style would become in football, but Waddell was ahead of me on that. In later games against Celtic I was told to man-mark wee Jimmy Johnstone, which was a real experience. In fact, I took a lot from that into my management with me, learning how to cope with different teams and different players.'

After League Cup success in 1970, MacDonald waited more than two years for his next taste of glory as he helped Rangers to victory in the European Cup Winners' Cup final in Barcelona. He scored the match-winning goal against Rennes in the first round and repeated that against Torino in the quarter-final.

His all-action style was put in sharp focus in the final against Moscow Dynamo as he snapped into early tackles to leave the Russians in no doubt that they had a game on their hands. The memory of the emotions he experienced as Rangers finally got their hands on European silverware will never die . . . but as for the game, it was just another 90-minute shift for the No.10.

'I've played in Europe more times than I can count, but I couldn't talk you through any one particular game. I roomed with Sandy Jardine and he'd be saying after the game: what about that player or how about that pass? I'd be saying: who? It wasn't that I didn't pay attention, more that it was always a blur for me. I had a job to do and I went out and did it. I'd be turning backwards and forwards a hundred times in a game, never stopping.'

Of course there are always exceptions to any rule. One game, one glorious afternoon, will always stick in the memory. After all, he's reminded about it often enough. To set the scene, it was 10 October at Hampden Park as Rangers went head to head with Celtic in the 1975 League Cup final.

Three days earlier Rangers had fallen to a 2–0 defeat at the hands of St Etienne in France in the European Cup. Their cup-final opponents were also drained after European action against Boavista of Portugal in the days leading up to the Hampden showdown and both showed signs of fatigue. True to form, MacDonald battled on and popped up in the 67th minute, with the game deadlocked at 0–0, to dive and head home a dramatic winning goal from Quinton Young's cross. It was the bright spark in the match and saw Rangers take the trophy back to Ibrox.

'It was a boyhood dream come true for me. It's impossible to explain the adrenaline rush from something like that. You would do anything to get that result, to score that goal.

Football is fun and it is simple. You train hard, you rest hard and you play hard. As long as you can look yourself in the mirror and say you've given your all after every game, you've done your bit. As a manager I wanted players in my team that I could hang my hat on – as a player, I hope I was that type. I think I was.'

On top of the 1975 League Cup success, MacDonald was an integral part of the side that savoured that winning feeling with increasing regularity. The Scottish Cup was claimed in 1973, the league title in 1975 to stop the Celtic juggernaut after nine consecutive championships and unforgettable domestic trebles in 1976 and 1978. His haul by the time his Rangers career drew to a close in 1980 included three league winners' medals, four Scottish Cup badges and four matching League Cup winners' medals. Add into the lot the treasured European prize, and it amounts to serious reward for 12 years of service.

Yet MacDonald has just one Scotland cap to add to that treasure trove. A mainstay of a Rangers side regularly picking up trophies in the current era would expect to cruise to the Hampden hall of fame before their 30th birthday, but in the 1970s international recognition was harder to come by. Maurice Ross, never more than a fringe player at Ibrox before his switch to Sheffield Wednesday in 2005, had 13 caps to his name before moving to England – but just 60 appearances for Rangers in the five years after his millennium debut.

In contrast, MacDonald was one of the first names on the team sheet for a succession of Ibrox managers, but was given one solitary chance to shine for Scotland. You work it out. He was 28 when his old St Johnstone manager Willie Ormond gave him his international debut in a 1–0 win over Switzerland at Hampden in 1976, a stage he graced so often at club level. Motherwell's Willie Pettigrew, a fellow international rookie, was the match-winner but the team was not devoid of experience and featured Kenny Dalglish and MacDonald's club colleagues Tom Forsyth and Derek Johnstone. Archie Gemmill and Joe Jordan were the men in possession of the jersey when the competitive action began later in 1976 and proved impossible to shift, an indication of the battle for places during a period in which Scotland were spoilt for choice.

For MacDonald, club commitments ensured he had no time to dwell on his Scotland prospects and the rewards were plentiful. Having lived through the pain of Celtic's nine-in-a-row as a fan and as a player, he donned the No.10 shirt for his side's moment in the sun.

A 1–1 draw at Easter Road against Hibs in 1975 clinched the title he had craved since signing for his boyhood heroes almost seven years earlier. If that 1974/75 season was sweet, the following campaign was football heaven for MacDonald and his team-mates. Rangers became the first ever champions of the Premier Division, maintaining an incredible unbeaten run throughout the season, and of course MacDonald was the individual hero in the League Cup success against Celtic.

The Scottish Cup followed to cap an amazing season for Jock Wallace's side, sweeping Hearts aside 3–1 in a game that again saw the midfield general rise to the big occasion with a goal to add to Derek Johnstone's double. It had been 12 long years since Rangers had swept the boards. In contrast, the 1976/77 campaign saw Rangers finish empty handed – but the winning habit returned in 1977/78. A 2–1 extra-time win over Celtic in the League Cup final and last-day league title success with victory over Motherwell set the Light Blues up for another tilt at the treble. Aberdeen were the hurdle to be overcome and MacDonald's canny knack of finding the back of the net at Hampden again proved valuable, opening the scoring in the final against the Dons before Johnstone added a second in a 2–1 win to set the champagne flowing again. MacDonald had played in 46 of the 49 games in the '78 treble-winning season.

The following season saw John Greig take charge of the team following Wallace's departure, but it was business as usual for MacDonald. He put his name on the score-sheet in the League Cup final at Hampden as Colin Jackson completed the job to give Greig his first trophy as boss with a 2–1 win over Aberdeen. Celtic went on to reclaim the league, but the Scottish Cup stayed at Ibrox courtesy of a 3–2 extra-time win over Hibs in a final that required two replays.

In August 1980 the curtain fell on an illustrious Ibrox career. Although MacDonald played the club's games in the 1979/80 term, a bid of £30,000 from Hearts was accepted as the club revamped the squad to try and keep pace with Celtic and the emerging threat posed by the New Firm of Aberdeen and Dundee United.

Rangers had finished third, behind champions Celtic and runners-up Aberdeen, and at 32 MacDonald was allowed to move on. He admits: 'It shook me, it was a real wrench to leave Rangers. I could have gone to any team in the Premier League then but there was something about Hearts, something special about Tynecastle. There was a feeling of tradition and history about the place, like there was at Ibrox . . . or maybe it was just the décor.'

Under manager Bobby Moncur, Hearts had just been promoted to the Premier League as champions of the First Division and passed city rivals Hibs on the way as the Easter Road side dropped through the relegation trapdoor. MacDonald made his debut at Partick on 9 August 1980, in a 3–2 defeat and went on to make 34 appearances in his first season, a tally only John Brough and Willie Gibson could beat. His efforts could not prevent his new club from finishing bottom of the pile as the Edinburgh merry-go-round continued, with the Hibees celebrating promotion back to the top flight as First Division champions.

Still, the green shoots of recovery were already sprouting at Tynecastle with Dave Bowman and Gary Mackay, two future internationalists, among the emerging talents making their debuts alongside the veteran schemer MacDonald in his first year with the Jambos. He had a potential get-out in that first season, but his hesitation in leaving Hearts proved pivotal in his future in the game. 'After moving to Hearts, I had a phone call from Alex Ferguson, asking if I would sign for Aberdeen. It was at the time Gordon Strachan had picked up an injury. I said I would go away and think about it – and went away and got injured myself. I ended up in hospital, but there was a good luck story in there somewhere because I ended up with the Hearts job.'

MacDonald remained with Hearts as a key player in the 1981/82 season, when the club just missed out on promotion, and took control of team affairs after Tony Ford's dismissal during that term. MacDonald went down in Hearts history as one of the most successful managers the club has ever seen, yet it almost never happened.

He had his arm twisted to take on the challenge at Tynecastle, and it really was a challenge. The club was then led by controversial chairman Wallace Mercer, who was determined to win promotion back to the top flight to appease an increasingly restless set of supporters. Under Ford, a disappointing run saw the team's ambitions of promotion founder. The fans took their protests to the street, and the manager's position became untenable. Hearts did not look far for a replacement, charging MacDonald with restoring them to their rightful position in the upper tier of Scottish football.

After taking temporary charge, he was installed on a permanent basis as manager in the summer of 1982. When he took over the hot seat, the club was at its lowest ebb, languishing in the First Division with attendances down from the 1970s average of 13,000 to just 5,000. The economic picture was worrying. The only way to improve fortunes off the pitch was for a rapid improvement on the field, and the board's faith in the unproven boss would be repaid.

'I spent two years as a player before I was asked to become player-manager. I rejected it straight away. I had too much respect for the club and didn't want to do them any harm. I was always asking why didn't we do this or why didn't we do that. It wasn't disrespect to Tony Ford, who I took over from, but out of curiosity and enthusiasm. Les Porteous was in the background at the club, but he must have seen something in me. I'm glad I was persuaded to take it on because I had some great experiences in management.'

Old Ibrox room-mate Sandy Jardine was a crucial signing, coming on board as a player and assistant manager. Jardine went on to be promoted to the position of co-manager in November 1986 and held that post for two years. MacDonald says: 'It was an experience for Sandy and I to be able to do something where we could put our own ideas across to a group of players: their eating habits, drinking habits, sleeping habits. We looked at every aspect. Sandy managed to entice sprint and fitness specialists on the coaching side and that helped us enormously with what we wanted to do. Sandy played until he was 40 and I played to 37 – mind you, I was picking the team, so maybe that explains why I stayed in it so long!'

The results were instant. In the duo's first season in charge the Tynecastle side claimed second place in the First Division and, more importantly, won promotion back to the Premier League. Any fears that the return could be short-lived were soon dismissed as Hearts announced their arrival back in the big time with a confident opening to their league programme in the 1983/84 season.

That term ended with a fifth-place finish and the bonus of European football in the shape of a UEFA Cup place. League form the following season remained consistent as Hearts finished seventh, but cup performances offered greater encouragement. In the UEFA Cup, Paris St Germain accounted for Hearts with a 6–2 aggregate win, although the Jambos did hold the French aces to a 2–2 draw at Tynecastle after a disappointing away tie. In domestic competition, MacDonald led his side to the quarter-final of the Scottish Cup, only edged out by Aberdeen after a replay, and the semi-final of the League Cup where Dundee United proved too strong. That was only a hint of what would follow.

'We were fortunate to have a group of Hearts-minded players like Dave Bowman and Gary Mackay, who were desperate to play for the club. John Robertson was coming through at the right time for us and we also had players at an age where they wanted to enjoy the game, Sandy and Willie Johnston. There were also plenty who had a point to prove, John Colquhoun being one of them after leaving Celtic.'

The 1985/86 season has a well-thumbed place in Scottish football's folklore. It was the best of times and the worst of times for Hearts supporters, their players and a management team who would learn all about the highs and lows of their chosen career in the months that followed.

The season started with a 1–1 draw with Celtic at Tynecastle, John Colquhoun scoring his first competitive goal for Hearts against his old club. As it panned out, the two clubs would not be separated over the course of the enthralling ten months of football that followed. Hearts did not lose a single home game and only six on the road as they matched the big-hitting Hoops blow for blow in what became the closest championship race in the history of the competition. On 3 May 1986, Hearts made the trip to Dens Park to face Dundee and needed a single point to claim the title. Ravaged by illness, they hung on for 83 minutes until Albert Kidd smashed a double for the Tayside outfit to rob their Edinburgh visitors of the point they so desperately needed.

While Hearts toiled on the east coast, events on the other side of the country took an equally dramatic twist. Even in defeat, Hearts could have claimed the league flag if St Mirren had resisted Celtic at Love Street. In the end, Billy McNeill's side hammered the Buddies 5–0 to win the league on goal difference, the two sides level on 50 points after 36 games but with the Parkhead team two goals better off. A heart-breaking end to a marathon effort.

The misery was compounded exactly a week later when Aberdeen swept to a 3–0 victory in the Scottish Cup final against Hearts. It left MacDonald empty handed, save for the Scottish manager of the year award bestowed upon him in recognition of the job he had done in reviving his club. In four years, Hearts had been transformed from First Division also-rans to Premier League challengers.

The Tynecastle faithful were certainly convinced by MacDonald's abilities, with gates rising to average almost 17,000 and a three-fold improvement on the season before his appointment. Indeed, more supporters were turning out in Gorgie than they had done since the early 1960s. On the park, Hearts were in good shape, with internationalists like Henry Smith, Craig Levein, Gary Mackay, John Robertson and John Colquhoun forming a formidable spine. Sandy Jardine was enjoying a renaissance, missing just one of the 44 games that season.

MacDonald admits: 'Losing out on the league title in 1986 was heavy. It was a case of a bad day just when we didn't want it. In the run-up, maybe six weeks before, quite a few teams were hit by a virus that was doing the rounds. We avoided it until that day – big Craig Levein was ill and didn't make it, Brian Whittaker and Kenny Black phoned in on the morning ill. In the end we told them to come in and we'd make a decision. They ended up playing part of the match each. Roddy Macdonald came in and was magnificent for us – I was 40 at the time, if I'd been a year younger I would have played myself. It was horrendous and just proved the point that, in football, around every corner there's a slap in the face. I've never seen so many grown men cry. It even took me three attempts to go into the dressing room to say my piece after the match because I was choked. They were so unlucky, but I had to go in and remind them they had the little matter of a cup final against Aberdeen to get their heads straight for.'

MacDonald became a victim of his own success in many respects. Having taken over a struggling First Division team, the bar had suddenly been raised. Expectations were weighty, among fans and the board. In 1987 his side finished fifth but once again they finished runners-up to Celtic in 1988. The following season sixth place in the league caused flutters among the hierarchy and, just months into the 1989/90 season, the manager was shown the door. The board's sacking of Jardine late in 1988 – he had been promoted to co-manager in 1986 – was an early warning sign for MacDonald.

When it was time for the top man to go, the board claimed they wanted a new person to take the club to the next stage and Joe Jordan was appointed as the successor. Shell-shocked players were outspoken in their criticism of the club's decision to dispense with the manager, none more so than star striker John Robertson. As a manager in his own right, Robertson learnt all about the fickle nature of the coaching business when he too was dethroned less than a year after taking charge of Hearts in 2004.

MacDonald had a nine-month break from the game before Airdrie offered him a route back into football, and another roller-coaster ride. The Diamonds had just been promoted to the Premier League in 1991 when boss Jimmy Bone announced he was quitting to accept a lucrative offer from FC Dynamo in Zambia.

Within hours of that news, Airdrie had tracked down the former Hearts boss, interviewed him and confirmed his appointment. It marked the start of an eight-year association with the Lanarkshire side. The board were certain they had the right man and he wasted no time in endearing himself to the fans, guiding his new charges to the safety of seventh place in their first season back in the top flight and to a dream appearance in the Scottish Cup final. They were edged out 2–1 by Rangers, but because the Ibrox side had already been crowned champions the Broomfield underdogs could still celebrate a place in the European Cup Winners' Cup.

MacDonald had taken them into Europe for the first, and last, time in the club's history. Although Airdrie went out in the first round of a tournament that he had won as a player, they could still hold their heads up high after losing 1–0 to the experienced Sparta Prague at home and 2–1 away.

That early high spot in the 1992/93 season preceded the low of relegation to the First Division, where the club remained during his tenure. It was a battle to escape the First Division, with the club finishing runners-up once, third once, fourth three times and eighth on one occasion during the six years that followed. The rigours of the league were broken by some dramatic cup runs, Airdrie being defeated 1–0 by Celtic in the 1995 Scottish Cup final and winning the Scottish Football League's challenge cup with a 3–2 win over Dundee in the same season.

He worked on a tight budget. 'Experience taught me that spending vast amounts of money on players, and average players at that, is no guarantee of success – something the majority of Scottish clubs have learned at their cost over the years. There were always players out there who could be had for fairly modest outlays and I proved that over and over again at Tynecastle and with Airdrie.

'At Hearts I wheeled and dealed to bring in players like John Colquhoun, Dave McPherson and Craig Levein for next to nothing because I didn't have a big budget to work with, and no one would argue that they didn't improve Hearts as a side. It was the same at Airdrie. Management isn't about spending money, it's about instilling your own personal pride in a group of players who want to play for the jersey.'

Airdrie represented an entirely different challenge for MacDonald, but he can still look back on his achievements with pride. The Diamonds became renowned for their strong-arm tactics, making up in attitude and application what they lacked in big names and bumper pay packets. It was the perfect illustration of MacDonald's philosophy that the beautiful game should also be a simple game.

'Managers don't complicate things – I think it is people outside the game who make it complicated. What managers do is understand the pressure, understand that it falls on one man and one man alone. Mind you, I don't think that really hit me until I was in the dug-out at Airdrie. At Hearts you would go into the dressing room or out on the training park and say this or that, and it was done. At Airdrie it took longer to get the point across because it was a different group of players. But, with time, we got there. I don't see so much of them now because they are all managers themselves now, but we used to get together quite regularly for a few drinks and to talk about the good days we had.'

With Airdrie's board chasing the ultimately fatal dream of life at the newly constructed Shyberry stadium, with a capacity far outweighing the average gates, their long-serving manager walked away in 1999 when it became clear his contract would not be renewed. Broomfield, the club's spiritual home, had been sold in 1994 and it took five years for the move to the new ground to materialise. In between, a financially draining and morale-sapping temporary stay at Clyde's home in Cumbernauld only served to complicate MacDonald's job. The constraints he had been forced to work under became clear once he had left, with the club going into liquidation in 2000 and being eventually killed off in 2002. The Diamonds emerged from the ashes as Airdrie United, with former player Sandy Stewart at the helm. MacDonald was quick to offer his support to the new club, quipping that Airdrie United is much easier to spell than Airdrieonians in any case. Support is one thing, but the tracksuit is remaining locked in the cupboard. 'I've got my grandkids and a job to keep me busy. I get to catch up with my old pals at Ibrox every second week – life's good.'

CHAPTER ELEVEN

# WILLIE JOHNSTON

If the mark of a player is how well you are remembered by the paying public then Willie Johnston is at the top of the pile. From Ibrox to West Bromwich and Vancouver to Tynecastle, the supporters still talk about him. Whether it was sitting on the ball in the heat of battle or taking time out to take a swig from a fan's beer can, Johnston's antics have gone down in football folklore.

He was an entertainer, pure and simple. Even now, he lights up when he talks about the incidents that made him one of a rare breed. Softly spoken and typically relaxed, he breaks into a laugh as he speaks about pulling off the type of tricks that would make the Largs coaching mafia grimace and gets exasperated when it's pointed out that he makes it all sound so easy: 'It is easy,' he retorts, 'football's the easiest game in the world. Good players make it look that way but some players, and managers, make it difficult.'

While researching Johnston's career in Canada, with the Vancouver Whitecaps, I stumbled across a fan who still to this day regales fellow soccer fanatics with the anecdote of the day the winger, whom he described as 'that rowdy Scot', jogged over to take a corner, spotted a beer can on the front rail of the stand and took time out to refresh himself with its contents. George Best had been credited with that act, his reputation preceding him, but it was in fact the winger known as Bud, not Bestie, who was responsible.

The rowdy Scot breaks into a chuckle again and admits: 'Yes, I did that. It was a bit of fun.' That's Johnston's only bugbear with the game today, that his type are a thing of the past. 'The entertainment has gone out of the game because people are told not to do it, it's coached out of them. I'd do things like trapping the ball by sitting on it, flicking it over people, putting it through their legs – it was what the people who paid their money enjoyed seeing. Now all that is gone. I remember when Robert Pires was absolutely crucified when he made a mess of the short penalty routine with Arsenal, but he should have been applauded. At least he had the guts and the imagination to try it.'

Johnston has been described so often as a flawed genius because of his lengthy disciplinary record, but nobody, not even referees, could question his lightning pace over 40 yards, or his ability to go past men at will and cross with frightening accuracy. Johnston shot to stardom at home and abroad as a tricky winger but he started life as a forward. When he was shunted out wide he thought it would be for a game or two – it turned out to be for a couple of decades.

He sampled the high life as one of Scotland's best known and most notorious players, but never lost sight of his roots on the east coast, having sampled enough of life as a working man to know he didn't want to go back to it: 'I was an apprentice miner at the pits in Fife, not for long but it felt like a long time to me. It was a hard way to earn a living. I was qualified to work beneath the surface but didn't. I was one of the lucky ones to stay on the top side. It was hard work.'

Johnston had attended the same Fife school as future Rangers colleague Willie Mathieson and caught the attention of scouts on both sides of the border when turning out for Lochore Welfare. When he eventually had to make a choice on his future in the game, he opted to turn his back on the lure of England's glamorous First Division.

'I was all set to go to Manchester United as a 15-year-old. I spent two weeks at Old Trafford and they wanted me to sign, but I was just a boy who'd never been out of Fife, except to visit my grandparents in Glasgow, and I didn't fancy it.'

United had finished 15th in the 1961/62 season, and in the

same year Rangers won both domestic cups. The previous year they had been crowned champions and reached the final of the European Cup Winners' Cup. Johnston chose Ibrox over Old Trafford, eventually becoming a Scot Symon signing rather than one of Matt Busby's babes. He joined the Glasgow club in April 1964, and stardom was just around the corner.

He made his debut in the 1964/65 season in a team featuring the likes of Willie Henderson and Jim Baxter. By the time he collected his first medal, Johnston already had his name etched alongside theirs on the roll-call of Ibrox entertainers. The reluctant winger.

'I was an inside forward, a striker, but Rangers saw I could run and gave me my debut wide left. Everyone wants to be scoring goals and at first I thought they just put me out there to get a bit of experience before moving me back through the middle – I was wrong on that score. I always wanted to be involved, and the problem with playing wide is you're relying on too many people to pass you the ball. Through the middle you can make things happen yourself.'

That was a niggle throughout his career. He even got down on his hands and knees during a Hearts cup tie against Inverness Caledonian to beg for the ball from team-mates as the Maroons coasted to victory and he patrolled a lonely beat out wide.

Johnston's first experience of a cup final victory came in the League Cup showdown with Celtic at Hampden on 24 October 1964. The rookie lined up at No.11 in front of more than 91,000 baying fans packed inside the national stadium. After a deadlocked first half, the game burst into life after the break and a Jim Forrest double gave Rangers a 2–1 victory.

It was cold comfort in the grand scheme of things, with the Light Blues slumping to fifth in the league race but the youngster made it two medals from two seasons in the 1965/66 Scottish Cup. Again it was Celtic who provided the opposition and this time the resistance was stiffer. They held out 0–0 in the final to force a replay which Rangers won courtesy of a single, albeit dramatic, long-range goal from Danish defender Kai Johansen. This time Johnston, still only 19, was playing to an audience of 98,000 and he loved it.

'Clubs gave young boys a chance then. I always said I was a good player at 17, better at 18, very good when I was 19 and over the hill by 21. I played a lot early on and I was still just a kid, still growing up. We didn't have anyone telling us what to do or helping us learn from our mistakes: you were left to go over it yourself in your own mind after every game. Maybe better coaching would have made us better players, but on the other hand we were able to go out and express ourselves. Once you cross the white line you're on your own anyway.'

In that Scottish Cup-winning year Rangers finished second, and in the six campaigns from then until his departure in 1972 were runners-up to Celtic four times, fourth in 1971 and third the following year. Johnston did not feel as though he was living in the shadow of the green and white machine, so well oiled by Jock Stein. 'Of course we were under pressure, we knew that if we had two or three bad games we'd be out. It happened to so many players over the years whether the club was winning trophies or not. It wasn't a difficult time to be a Rangers player – we were reaching European finals, matching the best of them. I'm not saying we were the most consistent team in the world, but we certainly had people who could play the game. I've always maintained that the difference was Celtic had a good conductor. If Jock Stein had been at Rangers, with the players we had, I'm certain it would have been the other way round. He had good players at Parkhead and turned them into a winning team.'

Johnston had first-hand experience of the Jock Stein way of working. He was handed his Scotland debut by the Celtic boss in a World Cup qualifying tie against Poland on 13

October 1965, at the age of 18. Scotland, led by goal-scoring captain Billy McNeill, fell to a 2–1 defeat despite the efforts of the debutant and his new international team-mates such as Denis Law, Billy Bremner and Alan Gilzean. The Glasgow-born winger was no stranger to representative honours even before then, being an internationalist at youth level and with the under-23 team. He also turned out for the Scottish League select.

Scotland were roared on by 107,000 members of the Tartan Army against Poland, and it was another chance for Johnston to sample the big-game atmosphere. Indeed, he believes it was that type of scene that brought the best out of the Rangers team of that era.

'We always enjoyed playing against Celtic because we knew we would get a hard game and we could rise to the occasion. It was in some of the other fixtures over the course of a season that we sometimes struggled. In Europe it was the same: we enjoyed the big games and could compete.'

The first proof of that theory came in the 1966/67 European Cup Winners' Cup campaign. Johnston featured in six of the nine ties on the way to the final against Bayern Munich in Nuremberg, scoring against Glentoran in the first round and also turning out against Borussia Dortmund in the second round. He missed the next stage, as Real Zaragoza were overcome, after suffering a broken ankle in the miserable Scottish Cup defeat at Berwick, but was back in time for the semi-final second-leg victory against Slavia Sofia and booked his place in the team for the showpiece game against Bayern. Of course it ended in heartbreak, with a 1–0 defeat, but it provided Johnston with the inspiration to make his European dream come true five years later.

In between, there was a crucial role to play in the next domestic honour to be landed on the Ibrox sideboard. Johnston took his familiar place on the wing for the 1970 League Cup final and was the provider for one of the most famous goals in the club's history, dashing down the flank to cross for 16-year-old Derek Johnstone to head home a *Roy of the Rovers* winning goal. Playing wide as a creator did not curb his goal-scoring instinct, and he was leading scorer along with record signing Colin Stein in the 1970/71 season with 11 goals in the league alone. Aside from the goal, the League Cup final also brought Johnston's controversial nature to the fore. Celtic fans, just as much as their Rangers counterparts, still talk about the audacity of the winger they loved to hate – sitting on the ball at one point during that fiery encounter.

It was his last Scottish trophy with the club, but not his final victory in a final. That was reserved for Spanish soil and done in style as the European Cup Winners' Cup was, at the third time of asking, won by Rangers. Johnston missed only the first leg of the second-round clash with Sporting Lisbon in that glorious campaign. In the first round his 68th-minute goal in Rennes was cancelled out by the French side, but a 1–0 win at Ibrox took them through to face the Portuguese stars. With that tie negotiated, courtesy of the away goal rule after a 6–6 aggregate draw, Johnston was the hero against Torino in the Communale Stadium as he pounced on a Willie Mathieson cross that the Italian keeper had spilled to hammer home the opener after 12 minutes. Once again the opposition came back to claim a 1–1 draw, but once again a 1–0 win at Ibrox completed the job when Alex MacDonald tucked away Johnston's header inside the box. After another 1–1 draw on foreign soil in the semi-final first leg, this time against Bayern Munich, the winger was provider again in the second leg with a corner for Derek Parlane to score the second in the all-important 2–0 win. He was in imperious form against the Germans and was voted by continental journalists as one of the best three attacking players in European competition that season, the only Scot recognised by the foreign writers.

And so to the final. Johnston's two-goal contribution was a dream even for him and it made up his mind that his time in Scotland was drawing to a close. He explains: 'I came back in and said: "That's it, that's me finished." Everyone was asking why and I said: "How can I possibly follow that? I'm getting out." I was hit with a ten-week suspension by the SFA just after, so that made sure of it.'

His goals, a first-half header and composed finish from Peter McCloy's long clearance early in the second, are among the defining images of that famous night. Just don't try and tell him that. 'I think I've seen the goals once. If they are being shown I just turn my back. Mind you, I get reminded about it often enough. To me it's just history. I'm proud of it, but I'm more interested in the here and now. To be honest, I remember more about the build-up than the game itself.'

It proved to be the final game of Johnston's first stint at Rangers. He would return in the 1980s, but a move across the border was beckoning and, after two previous failed bids, it was West Bromwich Albion who got their man for a cross-border record fee of £138,000. He had signed in Scot Symon's reign and played under Davie White and Willie Waddell, leaving just after Jock Wallace had taken control.

Waddell, who had become general manager, wanted to keep hold of his enigmatic wide-man and offered him a mammoth six-year contract. It was to no avail, the latest brush with the SFA disciplinary chiefs having convinced Johnston the time was right to move on. The relationship between the unpredictable player and his strait-laced manager could be strained at times, but there was a mutual respect. 'I must have been up the marble stairs to his office more than any other player. He always had the last word but never held a grudge. He was a great help to me, having played as a winger himself.'

Don Howe, the West Brom coach more noted for his love of discipline and organisation than of flair and passion, is credited with the main role in the pursuit of the Rangers star man but his prey was not as convinced. 'I think the chairman wanted me more than the manager . . . under Don Howe I became the best left back in England I think – he played me that deep. I was an overlapping full-back before they had been invented. Eventually I got a chance to make an impression and they took to me down there. I had always fancied playing in England or abroad, and in the end I did both. West Brom was a fantastic experience for me and I met a lot of good people. I'm still in touch with quite a few from my time down there.'

He moved to the Hawthorns in December 1972, and went on to play 22 games in his first season. Johnston, the club's most expensive player, was not surprisingly thrust straight into action. He made his debut in the English game on 9 December 1972 in front of 32,000 fans at his new home ground. Liverpool were the guests, with the imported winger wearing No.11 and helping his side to a 1–1 draw.

Despite endearing himself to the fans, the campaign ended with the Baggies bottom of the First Division and relegated. A period of consolidation followed, eighth in the Second Division the following year and sixth after that, before they bounced back with promotion in the 1975/76 season. Johnston was a virtual ever-present up to that point and played a key role as West Brom clinched third place to make the step back up to the top flight, playing 39 games and scoring six goals. His side finished just three points behind champions Sunderland in a thrilling climax to the season.

The new, more powerful, West Brom became a force to be reckoned with in the First Division and finished seventh in their first season back among the elite of the game, with Liverpool crowned champions. Johnston was one of the orchestrators behind their success, continuing to thrill the Hawthorns faithful with his repertoire, which included his favourite method of controlling the ball: sitting on it. They climbed to sixth in 1977/78 as their favourite Scottish son's days at the club drew to a close. He played seven games the following season, when his side scaled the table to reach third place, before he moved on to Vancouver in a £100,000 deal.

The exciting trio of Laurie Cunningham, Cyrille Regis and Brandon Batson were tagged the Three Degrees as they took English football by storm and blazed a trail for a new, pioneering generation of black football players. Johnston was part of the supporting cast in their honeymoon period and eventually made way for Cunningham.

The Ibrox old-boy made 261 appearances for the Baggies, grabbing 18 goals. He bade farewell to the Hawthorns on 14 March 1979, when he came on as a substitute in a 0–0 draw with Chelsea. By that time, Cunningham had taken possession of the No.11 shirt. Johnston's successor, who went on to earn a move to Real Madrid, but was tragically killed in a car crash in 1989, was recently voted by Baggies fans as the best winger ever to grace the Hawthorns, with Johnston next on the list.

The switch to Vancouver brought to an end an enjoyable and eventful time for the winger. 'I played under more managers at West Brom than I probably did in the rest of my career. Ron Atkinson was one, a law to himself. He was a character, something else. We had some great players, guys like Bryan Robson coming through and Laurie Cunningham, Cyrille Regis, John Osbourne . . . too many to mention. West Brom is a great club and I still look out for their results.'

He had a point about the managers, though, with his first boss, Don Howe, lasting until 1975 before a succession of men took charge. First was Johnny Giles, for two years, and then came a six-month tenure for Ronnie Allen. John Wile was next to steer the ship, for all of a month, before Ron Atkinson arrived to such great acclaim.

There had been few dull moments at the Hawthorns and Johnston swapped one fast-moving environment for another when he joined a host of British exiles in the North American

Soccer League in March 1979, after rejecting an offer from Queen's Park Rangers to stay in England. It was not just the Brits who cashed in, with Dutch star Johan Cruyff coming out of retirement that year to sign a reputed $700,000 per year contract with the LA Aztecs.

Johnston was lured to Canada by the Whitecaps and arrived to play a pivotal role in the best year in the history of the franchise. The league was booming, having secured a broadcast contract with national station ABC, and a US-wide audience tuned in to see Johnston end the domination the New York Cosmos, bankrolled by Warner Brothers and boasting Franz Beckenbauer and Brazil's Carlos Alberto among their number, had previously enjoyed. In the 1979 Soccer Bowl it came down to the Whitecaps and the Cosmos in the play-offs. A sell-out crowd of almost 33,000 at the Canadian side's Empire Stadium saw Johnston score in a 2–0 win before he grabbed another strike in New York as they were held to a 2–2 draw and beaten in a shoot-out. A mini-game decided the series and the Whitecaps shocked the favourites to win and book a place in the Bowl final. A crowd of 50,000 saw Vancouver beat Tampa Bay 2–1 to win the nation's most coveted soccer prize.

Canada's adopted Scot added: 'I'm still welcome in Vancouver – winning the Soccer Bowl made sure of that. I loved it out there, playing with guys like Alan Ball and all the rest. It was a great standard.'

The Whitecaps folded in 1984 when the NASL faded away, but have since reformed, with supporters still holding former stars close to their hearts. He turned out for the Whitecaps in 1979, 1980 and 1982. His time holds great memories for the club, who even flew him back to Canada in 2001 to allow the fans' hero to unveil a new playing kit, designed to hark back to the club's glory days, to his adoring public. He was one of the first names on the team sheet when Whitecaps fans picked their all-time best team, alongside the likes of Peter Lorimer and Peter Beardsley.

Of course, by the time he arrived in North America to sample the highs of life as a champion, he had already endured the lows in South America at the 1978 World Cup in Argentina. It seems that no reference to Willie Johnston has been made in the 27 years since then without mention of the failed drug test that ended his international career. It cannot be ignored, as the man himself acknowledges, but in truth it was just one chapter in an incident-packed life on the world's football fields.

The controversy came after Ally MacLeod's team had started their finals campaign with a morale-crushing 3–1 defeat at the hands of unfancied Peru. Johnston failed a doping test after the game, having taken Reactivan. His pleas that the decongestant was taken to combat a cold, as it was designed to do, fell on deaf ears and he was told by the SFA that he would never play for his country again. Reactivan was found to contain fencamfamin, which was on a list of 400 banned stimulants compiled by FIFA. He says the news he had played his last game in dark blue hit him 'like a blast from a shotgun' and he was not prepared for his treatment at the hands of the Scottish game's rulers. 'The SFA's reaction was what hurt the most. They told me I wouldn't play for Scotland again, then bundled me in a car to the airport. I went from Buenos Aires to Rio, to Lisbon and then home. It was a terrible journey, made worse by the way they washed their hands of me.'

In many ways his career and past achievements were brushed aside in an instant and even today it's a subject that continues to rear its head. Former team-mates, just as much as the media pack, are among those to keep the saga alive as the 30th anniversary of the incident looms. 'I get it every week of my life. I took two tablets and then played the worst game of my life, so I don't follow the argument they were performance-enhancing. I know I didn't do anything wrong. It is part of my past but it seems to have been built up and built up over the years. I don't shy away from it, but it's sad when other people try and use it for their own ends, particularly people who were team-mates. At least I have always told the truth.'

The match against Peru was the last of 22 caps Johnston won between his debut in 1965 and that day on 3 June 1978. Despite his claims that he had a nightmare of a game, the official FIFA report from the 1978 World Cup in fact hailed the attacking threat Johnston provided as one of the few shining lights for Scotland on a bleak day.

In all, he played in a winning Scotland side ten times, losing just seven times, and conquered England at Wembley in 1977 as part of the side that beat the Auld Enemy 2–1 in the home international championship. The same year he was red-carded in a 1–1 draw with Argentina, not the first or last time he would take an early bath.

Most famously he was sent packing during a game for West Brom in 1976 when he playfully kicked referee Derek Lloyd, two minutes from time. He jokes: 'The referee kept getting in my way. I was beating defenders and then having to beat him, so I chased him and gave him a kick up the backside.' For his comic gesture, the flying Scotsman was handed a five-game ban for bringing the game into disrepute. In 1972, at Rangers, he was banned for 67 days by the SFA after another sending off, and in a 22-month period at Ibrox before that he was sent off five times.

By the time he received the 19th red card of his career, while at Hearts in 1983, he was staunchly defended by his club as they claimed Johnston was an easy target for the country's referees, judged on his past conduct. The Tynecastle directors even threatened to go to the courts to fight on behalf of their player.

Johnston's path to Hearts had taken him via Canada, England and Glasgow. He returned to Britain from his stint in the NASL for a loan spell with Birmingham City in the 1979/80 season. He was 32 by that point but still turning on the style.

Birmingham were in the Second Division when Johnston flew in to take on his familiar No.11 shirt. He made his debut in a 0–0 draw away to Preston on 6 October 1979, and played week in and week out over the course of a five-month loan spell with the Midlands club. The Blues went on to win promotion that term, finishing third in the championship behind Leicester and Sunderland.

His form and fitness at St Andrew's tempted former Ibrox team-mate John Greig, the Rangers manager, to dip into the coffers and come up with a £40,000 fee to buy him from Vancouver and put him back in light blue. Greig had no doubts about the transfer in August 1970, and said at the time: 'Rangers are always looking for good forwards and Willie comes into that category. He will give wide scope to our first-team pool.'

Johnston renewed his acquaintance with the Rangers support, after an eight-year absence, when he helped the team to a 4–0 win over Partick Thistle at Ibrox in the second league game of the 1980/81 season. It was as if he had never been away, making 21 Premier League starts and six appearances from the bench. Rangers finished third in the league, went out of the League Cup in the third round but beat Dundee United 4–1 in a Scottish Cup final replay, a game which the now veteran winger missed out on after playing in the 0–0 draw in the initial final three days earlier.

He made a further eight appearances the following term, but was allowed to move on at the end of that 1981/82 season in search of regular football after 393 games and 125 goals for the club. It was another former Rangers team-mate who stepped in, Alex MacDonald adding Johnston to his pool at Hearts in September 1982, in a typically shrewd piece of business.

He took his bow for Hearts on 22 September 1982, against St Mirren at Tynecastle. His new team won 2–1 and the latest chapter in the Johnston story had opened. He made 28 starts in his debut season in Edinburgh as his new team won promotion from the First Division as runners-up to champions St Johnstone, and were restored to their place in the top flight.

MacDonald used him from the bench 31 times in the 1983/84 campaign, throwing him in from the start six times but preferring to keep him fresh for late shows, as the Jambos consolidated with a fifth-place finish in the Premier League. Even as a Hearts player he continued to haunt old Glasgow foes Celtic, firing home a dramatic goal at the end of the Tynecastle side's first season back in the Premier League to finish off their evaporating championship hopes as they were held to a 1–1 draw in Edinburgh. The result also secured a return to the European stage for the Jambos, gaining entry to the UEFA Cup.

In the next season he made seven starts and 16 cameos from the bench before seeing out the last month at East Fife, close to his childhood home. His final game for Hearts was on 20 February 1985, in a 1–0 Scottish Cup win at home to Brechin. He went on to play three games for the Methil men in the First Division, as they kept their place in the league, to round off a career which had spanned three decades and taken in six clubs.

By that stage Johnston was approaching his 39th birthday and packed his well-travelled boots away and concentrated on family life with wife Margaret, son Dean, daughter Stephanie and their grandchildren. 'My ankles are killing me. I suffer badly from arthritis in both of them. When I take the dog for a walk I stop myself from getting a taxi back – and I've only gone 300 yards.'

When he stopped playing he severed his ties with the game, save for taking his place in the stands to watch the occasional match. 'I never entertained the thought of turning to coaching or management long term. I was only interested in playing the game and the minute I stopped enjoying it I walked away. I looked after myself and played until I was 38, so I'd had my time.'

Instead, a new career in the licensed trade beckoned and Johnston spent many years behind the counter at his Port Brae Bar in Kirkcaldy. But reruns of those Barcelona goals on the big screen were seldom, if ever, seen. This hero is a modest one.

CHAPTER TWELVE

# COLIN JACKSON

As a member of the illustrious 500 club, that most exclusive of Ibrox groups, Colin Jackson walked away from his beloved Rangers with a treasure chest packed full of medals and a memory bank piled high with the cherished recollections of a career to rival the finest ever to grace the Scottish game. The towering defender won every domestic honour, represented his country with distinction and did it all in his own impeccable style.

Yet the story of the man known as Bomber inevitably starts not with one of the 506 matches he featured in, rather with a game he did not play in – that game. It is, of course, a well-worn tale of woe but one worth recounting in the interests of completeness. Jackson should have been one of the chosen eleven and would have been, had it not been for one of the most unfortunate injuries in Rangers' history.

On the eve of the final he pulled out of a tackle on Tommy McLean in training, aggravating an old ankle injury in the process, and was out of the biggest game of his career. Jackson was a defender never known to shirk a challenge, but he knew the importance of ensuring that the squad emerged from final preparations unscathed and would have done nothing to jeopardise that. The crushing irony was that in attempting to protect a team-mate he ended up injuring himself.

There was no coming back, no fairytale recovery. While the injury itself was not serious it was severe enough for him to miss that most memorable of 90 minutes. He worked his way back to full fitness in time for the following season, making his comeback four games into the 1972/73 campaign in a League Cup tie against St Mirren, but there must surely have been mental scars far worse than the physical pain to heal. To his eternal credit, Bomber put his personal pain to one side and threw himself back into first-team action with the same passion that had made him a certainty to start in Barcelona in the first place.

The loss of Jackson on the eve of the 1972 final presented Willie Waddell with a major headache. Up until that point, the defender had missed only one of the previous eight ties, the home win over Sporting Lisbon, and had starred against Bayern Munich when he went head to head with German superstar Gerd Muller over two legs. It was the Scot, not the World Cup winner, who came out on top on those occasions. In any company Jackson did not look out of place, with his athleticism matched by his reading of the game and ability to make match-saving tackles.

He had all the attributes of a top-class European defender and was on course to claim a continental medal to bear testament to those talents when the injury struck on Spanish soil. To fall at the final hurdle was a devastating blow for the player and his manager, who pulled Derek Johnstone back to take over the No.5 jersey vacated by Jackson. He even had to fight for a bonus, having been offered just £100 for his efforts in the European campaign compared to the £2,000 awarded to the eleven who played in the final. He eventually succeeded in fighting his corner and persuading Waddell to increase that to £500.

The Barcelona heartache was one of the very few lows in a Rangers career peppered liberally with highs. For Jackson, the chance to pull on the light blue shirt was a dream come true.

As a schoolboy growing up in Aberdeen, the city which became home to the family despite his London birth, he switched allegiance from the Dons to the Gers as an eight-year-old. From that point on he was a Bear through and through. What separated Jackson from the majority of Ibrox fanatics was that his talent won him the opportunity to live out his childhood fantasy.

He was a 15-year-old schoolboy centre-half when Scot Symon took time out from first-team commitments to make a trip to the north-east in the spring of 1962 to complete the formalities of tying the Granite City prospect to the red bricks of Ibrox.

Jackson, a pupil at Ruthrieston school in the heart of the city, had been a star for the Aberdeen secondary school select that thrived during his time in the side, playing in the Scottish Schools' Cup final in the same week that he clinched his future with Rangers. He was already a strapping young player and had won the vote of Symon's scouting team. He signed provisionally and travelled south during school holidays to train at Ibrox and get a taste for the life that awaited him among the stars he had idolised.

The teenager had harboured ambitions of becoming an architect, but put those thoughts to one side when his football moved up a gear. After signing for Rangers he was allowed to continue to turn out for Sunnybank A in the Aberdeen youth leagues, which had fostered the talents of Denis Law, Ron Yeats and Rangers' own Dave Smith just years earlier. The Sunnybank juvenile side was a feeder to the club's famed junior team, which had lifted the Scottish Junior Cup in 1954 during an incredibly vibrant period in the city's footballing history at grass roots level.

Jackson did not linger long enough to sample the junior game, instead being quickly taken west to fall under the Rangers wing. Still only 16, he was called up full-time in 1963 and moved into digs in Hamilton. He made an immediate impression with the senior players on the staff and was pushed along the club's conveyor belt of talent, which during that era included a third team competing in the reserve league.

Part of his football education involved training with the

first team three days a week, learning the tricks of the trade from Jim Baxter and John Greig amongst others and carving out a reputation for himself as one of the country's finest young defenders. He grew three inches within his first year on the books, to stand 6ft tall, and developed into a powerful stopper who had a physique to match his defensive qualities.

Outside of football the Aberdeen lad's education also continued as he was given dispensation to begin architectural studies. An intelligent player on the park, Jackson had a mature approach to life off the pitch and was keen to have a fallback position if his football ambitions faltered.

In reality there was never any danger of that happening. After a year plying his trade in the third team he was promoted to the Rangers reserves when Doug Baillie vacated the defensive berth by moving on to Third Lanark.

A year playing for the second string completed his apprenticeship and by the autumn of 1965 the 18-year-old was deemed ready for first-team action. Then disaster struck. In his final reserve outing before his top-team debut, Jackson suffered an injury that shattered his hopes of making the breakthrough. It was only a minor problem, a twisted ankle suffered during a match against the Celtic reserves, but it was enough to delay his introduction. By the time he had shaken off that knock the window of opportunity had closed, for a few months at least.

Jackson finally made his entrance on the big stage in January 1966 when he deputised for Ronnie McKinnon in a New Year's day fixture against Partick Thistle at Ibrox. The new boy did well, helping to shut out the Jags as his side cantered to a 4–0 victory.

It was the only match McKinnon missed that term and the only opportunity for Jackson to make an impact in domestic competition. He also took his bow in continental competition, again stepping in for the injured McKinnon when the team travelled to Spain to tackle Real Zaragoza in the European Cup Winners' Cup quarter-final second leg. The match ended in a 2–0 defeat but he had played his part in the run to that season's final. By serving his apprenticeship under the immaculate McKinnon, the heir apparent had the best possible start in life in the professional game. The two men provided decades of service between them in the best Rangers style.

Jackson had his appetite whetted by Symon that term but found his progress stalled under new boss Davie White. It was the appointment of Willie Waddell during the 1969/70 season that acted as a catalyst for him to become a true Rangers legend. Waddell watched the youngster blossom in the final three matches of the league card, when he was introduced as McKinnon's deputy once again and looked sure-footed, composed and mature throughout.

From the second match of the 1970/71 campaign, a League Cup tie at Motherwell, he was pitched in at left-half and never looked back. Having gone from reserve defender to first choice for the No.6 jersey, he played 50 consecutive games through to the Scottish Cup final replay defeat against Celtic on the last day of an eventful tour of duty.

During the course of his maiden year as a first-team regular, Jackson collected his first winners' medal as a star performer in the back line which shut out Celtic in the League Cup final at Hampden. Derek Johnstone stole the show with his match-winning goal, but Jackson in his own assured manner also used it as an opportunity to highlight his credentials as an emerging star.

Not only was he a football asset, the youngster was also developing a reputation as an Ibrox pin-up and was a budding male model during the height of his football fame. Modelling was not the bread and butter, though: Jackson never lost sight of his main aim of cementing his place in the Rangers team and he devoted the bulk of his working life in football to fulfilling that aim.

When Waddell reshuffled his defence in the 1971/72 season, there was still a place for Jackson. He took over as centre-half in the wake of McKinnon's leg break and a solid unit emerged, with Dave Smith sweeping behind him to offer insurance and confidence. In addition, there were the outlets of Sandy Jardine and Willie Mathieson on either side.

That familiar back four, with the security of John Greig in front, was the bedrock of the run through the latter stages of the European Cup Winners' Cup to the final in Barcelona.

The pain of missing the Nou Camp showdown was a test of character for the popular big defender and the months in the aftermath were similarly difficult. After returning to the fold early in 1972/73, injury saw him drop out of the side. Derek Johnstone, the able stop-gap in Spain months earlier, returned to the defence and his partnership with Smith remained intact throughout the first year of Jock Wallace's tenure. It left Jackson, back to full fitness, kicking his heels and feeling frustrated.

On the brink of turning his back on the Rangers dream he held so dear, Jackson knuckled down and displayed the type of resilience that would become crucial in the years ahead.

A partnership with new recruit Tom Forsyth quickly developed and the pair formed the backbone of Wallace's league-winning heroes in 1974/75, with Jackson missing just a single game. He was 29 when he first got his hands on the championship prize and ready to hit the peaks.

His talents had begun to reach a far wider audience, with Scotland manager Willie Ormond sharing Wallace's appreciation of his ability. It was Ormond who gave Jackson his international debut in a friendly game against Sweden in Gothenburg in April 1975, just a few short weeks after the club celebrations that followed the title glory. It proved to be a memorable month for Jackson, who lined up in the dark blue of his country alongside colleagues Stewart Kennedy, Sandy Jardine, Derek Parlane and Derek Johnstone.

That match against the Scandinavians ended in a 1–1 draw and proved to be the start of a remarkable sequence. In 13 months he collected all eight of his caps and emerged from that period with an unbeaten record, something very few Scotland players can boast of.

In glorious hindsight, that period of just over a year proved to be the making of Colin Jackson. In that short burst he won his first league title and followed it up at club level with the momentous treble success with Rangers in the 1975/76 campaign. He also hoovered up a glut of Scotland honours as a mainstay of Ormond's team. Life could not have been any better.

After his debut for the national team, he was back on duty for his country a month later in a 1–0 friendly victory over Portugal at Hampden. Days later he added Scotland goal-scorer to his pen picture when he netted against Wales in Cardiff as Scotland battled back from a two-goal deficit to earn a share of the spoils in the 1975 home international series. Before the year was out he had added a further two caps with appearances in the European Championship qualifiers against Denmark, which ended in a 3–1 win at Hampden, and Romania, a 1–1 draw on home soil in Glasgow.

Scotland had assembled an impressive array of talent during that golden era, a point highlighted by the domination of the 1976 home international series. With Forsyth and Jackson at the heart of his side, Ormond led his men to a memorable run of results against their British rivals.

It began with a 3–1 win against the Welsh at the national stadium, was followed by a 3–0 rout against Northern Ireland and rounded off in the best possible manner with a 2–1 win over England at a packed Hampden Park. There were 85,000 crammed into the old ground to watch as goals from Don Masson and Kenny Dalglish confirmed Scotland's place at the top of the UK tree.

That Auld Enemy encounter proved to be Jackson's swan-song in dark blue. No player wants to step out of that arena, but if there was a way to bow out then defeating the stars of the English game was as fitting as any.

For all the highs of the 1975/76 successes with club and country, it followed that there had to be a low around the corner. The barren 1976/77 season provided that grounding experience and Rangers, under the steely figure of Wallace, bounced back in style with the treble of 1977/78. Jackson missed only two games as his collection of precious metal grew and grew.

That triple crown brought the curtain down on Jock Wallace's time as manager and the John Greig era began – the fifth manager Jackson had served under. The trophy count continued to rise and the League Cup final victory over Aberdeen at the tail-end of the 1978/79 term provided Jackson with a rare moment of goal-scoring limelight as he popped up with the winner against the Dons of his home town in front of 60,000 at Hampden. His injury-time goal, a typically decisive header, gave Rangers a 2–1 win and sent the Bears home happy. There was even more champagne two months later when the Scottish Cup was taken back to the south side of the city with a 3–2 replay win over Hibs.

Jackson missed the Scottish Cup win against Dundee United in 1981 but was back in the side for the 2–1 win against the same team in the League Cup showdown the following season. It proved to be the last in a long line of honours for Jackson – five League Cups, three league championships and a pair of Scottish Cup winners' medals.

His Ibrox farewell was in a Premier Division match against Partick Thistle as the difficult 1981/82 season drew to a close. Fittingly it ended in victory, with a 4–1 win giving Jackson the satisfaction of leaving the ground that had become his home as man and boy on a good note.

His final appearances in Rangers colours were not as enjoyable, with a 4–0 league defeat at Pittodrie on the final day of that campaign followed by a 4–1 loss to Alex Ferguson's Dons team at Hampden in the Scottish Cup final.

Jackson had long maintained that he did not envisage a future in coaching or management and when the time came to reach the crossroads at the end of his time in Govan he stayed true to that principle.

Even at the age of 35 he found himself in demand as a player. He was snapped up by Morton manager Benny Rooney in the summer of 1982 and, after two months playing Premier Division football for the Greenock side, went on to play for Partick Thistle under Peter Cormack in the First Division later that season. Even as a veteran he had lost none of his influence and provided a cool, composed and calming presence at Firhill during his single season in Maryhill.

Having retired from the game, Jackson was tempted back onto the field with Morton in 1984, at the grand old age of 38, when former Rangers team-mate Tommy McLean issued an SOS in his search for experienced defensive cover as he embarked on the first steps in his managerial career. Naturally, it was a short-term measure, with Jackson going on to carve out a long career in the financial services industry after turning from football to business. In recent years he has been back on the Rangers staff as a match-day host at Ibrox, where his popularity with supporters of all generations has been put to good use.

CHAPTER THIRTEEN

# THE EXTRA MAN

Colin Jackson was the twelfth man, but the roll of honour does not stop there. The thirteenth, fourteenth . . . and so the list goes on. Eleven men won the cup for Rangers at the Nou Camp, but they did not reach the final alone, with Jackson among a total of 17 players used en route to the date with destiny in Spain.

Jackson and the other five players who missed out on the final each played a part, some large and some small, and deserve to share in the recognition. Equally, the fans who roared their side to victory in Barcelona could just as equally lay claim to the title of twelfth man, with estimates ranging from 25,000 to 30,000 blues in the crowd of 35,000.

The army of Scottish supporters gave their heroes the type of backing they had become accustomed to during a run in the competition that saw them play in front of a grand total of 425,000 people over the course of those nine matches. They descended on Barcelona by air and by road, mobbing the team coach as it snaked its way through the city streets on its way to the stadium, and celebrating into the night after watching them defeat the Russian opponents.

The following day, 20,000 turned out at a rain-soaked Ibrox to salute the men who had done the nation proud, watching the triumphant players as they paraded the trophy from the back of a flat-bed lorry as it crawled around the track. It was the first chance many had to see the cup, after the post-match troubles in Spain. The rain couldn't dampen the spirits and the occasion also gave the support crew, including some of the six players who had missed out on the final despite contributing in the earlier rounds, the chance to celebrate. The unlucky sextet were Colin Jackson, Ronnie McKinnon, Andy Penman, Jim Denny, Graham Fyfe and Willie Henderson.

Nobody made a greater sacrifice in the quest to land the club's first European honour than Ronnie McKinnon, who was at the heart of the defence in all four of the opening games against Rennes and Sporting Lisbon. It was in Portugal that McKinnon's season ended, on the turf of the Jose Alvalade Stadium. After a 3–2 win at Ibrox the return leg on the continent was poised at 2–2 when, in the 72nd minute, McKinnon crumbled to the ground with a broken leg after a bad challenge. His team-mates heard the horrifying crack as the bone snapped, but the referee played on for what seemed like an eternity before the Rangers stalwart could be stretchered from the field and taken to hospital. There, he received confirmation of the news he already knew – his season, together with his European dream, was over.

McKinnon was born in Greenfield Street in Govan and educated at Govan High, so there was only one team he was likely to sign for. Despite being courted by Newcastle United and other English sides, he joined his local club at Ibrox in 1958 as an 18-year-old. He made his debut against Falkirk in the 1961/62 season, stepping in for Jim Baxter at left-half and kept his place in the eleven as the year progressed. He collected his first medal in the Scottish Cup final of his debut campaign, as Rangers beat St Mirren 2–0 at Hampden in front of 126,930 fans with goals from Ralph Brand and Davie Wilson. Willie Henderson and John Greig were fellow newcomers to the cup-final stage, and all three went on to become key players for the Light Blues.

For McKinnon, it was the first of nine trophy wins, and he went on to become a bedrock of the league-winning sides in 1963 and 1964 – the glorious treble-winning season. In all, he won two league championships, the Scottish Cup four times and the League Cup three times. He enjoyed his finest hour in the League Cup, captaining Rangers in the 1970 final win against Celtic, a 1–0 win at Hampden, in the absence of regular skipper John Greig.

With a full set of domestic honours in the bag, only a European medal eluded him. His first taste of football at the game's top table came in the 1962/63 European Cup Winners' Cup in a 4–0 first-round first-leg win over Seville on home soil. Spurs ended Rangers' involvement in the next round and the following season it was Malmo, of Sweden, who put McKinnon and his team-mates out of the European Cup in the opening round. The 1964/65 campaign was longer lasting but equally frustrating as the club lost to Inter Milan. In 1966/67, McKinnon missed just one tie out of the nine up to and including the final of the European Cup Winners' Cup against Bayern Munich. He wore the No.5 jersey as usual against Bayern, sharing in the heartbreak of the 1–0 defeat in extra-time.

It would prove to be his last opportunity to claim a European medal, although he did play in the quarter-final of the Fairs Cup in 1967/68 and the semi-final of the same competition the following season. It was a case of so near yet so far in the continental game for McKinnon, whose experience and presence would have been valuable to Rangers in the Barcelona final had he not been robbed of the opportunity to play.

He made 482 appearances for the club and at the peak of his powers won international honours. He made his debut for Scotland in a home international against Wales in 1965 as the national team hammered the men from Cardiff 4–1 with goals from John Greig, Willie Henderson and a Bobby Murdoch double. Jock Stein was the man who gave McKinnon his first cap and Bobby Brown was at the helm by the time the centre-half made his final appearance in the dark blue of his country in 1971 as Scotland fell to a 1–0 friendly defeat against the USSR in Moscow.

In between, he made 28 appearances and scored one goal,

the winner in a 3–2 victory against Wales at Hampden in a European Championship qualifier in 1967. It was the same year in which McKinnon played for Scotland, and won, against world champions England. Those highlights came before the horrific double leg fracture in Portugal, which effectively ended his top-class career.

McKinnon was handed a free transfer by Jock Wallace in 1973, not playing a single game after the injury in Lisbon, and moved to South Africa with Durban United. It was initially on a three-month contract, but McKinnon set up home there and stayed for more than three decades before returning to Scotland. His father hailed from Skye and his mother from Lewis, where McKinnon now lives.

While McKinnon suffered his injury heartbreak early on, Colin Jackson was left stricken at the eleventh hour. For team-mate Willie Henderson, the omission from the European celebrations was painful for very different reasons. After playing a key role early in the competition, he found himself out in the cold as the juggernaut thundered down the road to continental glory.

The second-round clash with Sporting Lisbon was one of the most dramatic in the European history of Rangers and Henderson was right in the middle of that drama. He scored both at Ibrox and in Portugal against Lisbon as the sides played out a 6–6 aggregate draw, notoriously settled by the away goal rule well after the last ball had been kicked, when Rangers thought they were out of the competition. Henderson's two goals proved vital to his team's progress but were to be his final contribution to the run, although he had previously played in the home leg against Rennes.

If his goal in the first leg, a bullet of a shot from the corner of the box, was valuable then his strike in the second leg was priceless. It came in the tenth minute of extra-time, with the tie on a knife-edge at 5–5. It should have been enough to clinch a nerve-shredding victory, but a late penalty, after Colin Jackson had handled inside the box, let Sporting level it. The goals in Portugal were among his final efforts with the club he had grown up at.

The Ballieston-born winger joined Rangers straight from school in 1960 and was only 17 when Scot Symon thrust him into first-team action, having played alongside fellow teenager John Greig in the all-conquering reserve side in 1961/62.

That was the same season in which both made the breakthrough to the top team, the year in which Dundee won the championship but Rangers collected the cup double. Henderson's precocious talent persuaded Rangers to part with Ibrox hero Alex Scott, who was sold to Everton as the rookie took over his No.7 shirt.

Henderson had already won over the club's support with his own brand of wing trickery and by the time the league and cup double of 1963 and the treble of 1964 were won he was a key man.

Those championship celebrations would be his last, with Celtic ruling the roost for the rest of his stint in Govan. Between the 1964/65 season and his departure in 1972, Rangers did enjoy success in the knock-out competitions with a further Scottish Cup victory and triumph in the League Cup twice. Henderson had started under Scot Symon and Davie White, but the arrival of Willie Waddell spelled a tougher challenge for him.

Waddell came to Ibrox extolling the virtues of quiet living and dedication. He wanted his players to lead by example on and off the pitch. The approach was at odds with that of free spirits like Jim Baxter and Henderson, who both went to the extreme of shaving off moustaches before meeting their new boss for the first time.

The winger had played in all nine of the 1966/67 European Cup Winners' Cup ties, scoring the winner in the semi-final second leg against Slavia Sofia, but under the new management never reached the climax of the next run to the final in 1972. He had a fall-out with Waddell before the showdown with Dynamo and was sold to Sheffield Wednesday the same year, spending two seasons in Yorkshire before moving on to sample life overseas with Hong Kong Rangers in 1974. He returned briefly to Scottish league football with Airdrie in the 1978/79 season, but played only a handful of games before retiring.

Henderson joined a select club of players to have scored on their debut when he hit the back of the net in his first outing for the national team, a 3–2 win over Wales in Cardiff in 1962. He was just 18 when Ian McColl gave him his big break with Scotland. Henderson went on to be capped 29 times, scoring five goals for his country. In later life he was a hotelier and also found a new passion as an in-demand after-dinner speaker, with tales of his career with Rangers and Scotland to fall back on.

Derek Parlane, like Willie Henderson, was a goal-scoring hero who missed out on the final. He made his European debut in the cauldron of a packed Ibrox stadium as Bayern Munich arrived in Glasgow for the second leg of the semi-final. The tie was delicately balanced at 1–1 but Willie Waddell had to make changes for the crucial second leg after John Greig picked up a knock in a domestic game just four days before the Germans touched down on Scottish soil. Parlane was thrown in at the deep end to cover in midfield. Within seconds of the kick-off, Sandy Jardine stunned Bayern with the opener. Twenty-three minutes later, Parlane hammered a Willie Johnston corner past Sepp Maier to book a place in the Nou Camp final. It was his only contribution to the European effort, but it was worth so much to the club.

Having started out across the city with Queen's Park, Parlane was only 18 when he helped Rangers on their way to Barcelona. The son of former Rangers player Jimmy Parlane, he was in his introductory season at Ibrox. The appearance against Bayern Munich was one of only eight in total for the teenager in 1971/72, but it did not take him long to make an impression, emerging as the successor to Colin Stein on an illustrious list of players to have worn the coveted No.9 jersey.

By the time the 1972/73 season was under way he was the main striker and was on the score-sheet as his side claimed the 1973 Scottish Cup with a 3–2 win over Celtic. He retained that role as the club won the championship in 1975, missing just three games and scoring 17 goals, and was there for the two trebles in 1976 and 1978.

When the latter of the clean sweeps was won, Parlane was being used from the bench by Jock Wallace as the manager relied on the twin-pronged attack of Derek Johnstone and Gordon Smith. He enjoyed a revival under new manager John Greig in the 1978/79 season, helping the club to the cup double, but his opportunities were restricted after that. In 1979, after more than 200 league appearances and 80 goals for the Ibrox side, he moved south to begin a four-year association with Leeds United after clinching a £160,000 transfer.

In 1983 he moved across England to Manchester City, scoring an impressive 20 goals in just 48 league outings over two seasons, before joining Swansea City in the 1984/85 campaign. The following term he sampled continental football with Racing Jet in Belgium before winding down his career with Rochdale, Airdrie and Macclesfield in the late 1980s.

He won all 12 of his Scotland caps as a Rangers player. His first appearance for the national side came just days after his 20th birthday in 1973 in a 2–0 defeat in Wales, Willie Ormond pinning his hopes on the young attacker. His one and only goal for Scotland came two years later in a 3–0 win over Northern Ireland at Hampden.

The late Andy Penman was involved in the early stages of the 1971/72 trophy trail, playing in the first round against Rennes in France, a 1–1 draw, and in the first leg of the second round against Sporting Lisbon as his side secured a crucial 3–2 win. By the time the final rolled around, Penman was the favourite for the midfield vacancy created by the reshuffle to deal with Colin Jackson's absence.

The fans, the media and even the players thought he had been given the nod. It was only at the pre-match meal in Spain that Waddell revealed that the youthful Alfie Conn had pipped his more experienced team-mate to the No.8 jersey. By that stage Penman's career at Ibrox was drawing to a close.

He had been a schoolboy star in his native Fife and, after returning to Scotland homesick after joining Everton at 15, went on to become an integral part of Dundee's championship-winning team of 1962, the only time the Dens Park side has taken the country's top honour.

Capped once by Scotland in 1966, he made his debut for Dundee as a 15-year-old in 1958 and his form for the Dark Blues over the next nine years prompted Rangers to part with £35,000 and striker George McLean to take Penman's midfield guile to Glasgow. He became a reliable member of the squad, making 16 appearances in his final season and having a hand in the run to the final in Barcelona, before moving back to the east coast with Arbroath in 1973, by which point he had been diagnosed with diabetes. The illness did not stop him playing the game he loved, and he turned out at Gayfield for three seasons before spending a further three seasons in the Highland League as a player-coach with Inverness Caledonian. Penman died in 1994, aged 51.

Graham Fyfe played in just one of the nine ties, but he was treated to a classic as he lined up at No.10 in the first leg of the Lisbon tie in front of 50,000 people at Ibrox. The 3–2 win, courtesy of a Colin Stein double and a Willie Henderson strike, was the end result of an enthralling encounter. The dalliance with the European Cup Winners' Cup was typical of Fyfe's season as he tried to force his way into Willie Waddell's plans.

The Motherwell-born striker was only 20 when the final was played and flitted between the first team and the reserves, turning out 16 times for the second string and finishing third in their scoring chart with seven goals.

At first-team level he made 14 appearances, netting six goals along the way. He joined the club as a teenager and had a canny knack of scoring on the rare occasions he was given the chance to shine, with 22 goals in just 64 league appearances before his departure for Hibs in 1976. He spent a season at Easter Road before two campaigns with Dumbarton and also went on to sample the game in America with Pittsburgh Spirit.

The most fleeting contribution to the team effort came from one of the Ibrox young guns, right back Jim Denny. He came on from the bench in the opening game against Rennes only eight months into his career with the club. His European debut was one of 15 first-team appearances in his first full season. Signed from junior side Yoker Athletic as a youngster, Denny made his first senior appearance in light blue in front of 103,000 fans at Hampden in the 2–1 defeat against Celtic in the Scottish Cup final replay in 1971.

His versatility proved valuable, turning out at full-back as well as in midfield and attack. The Paisley-born player was loyal to the cause, spending eight years in Glasgow, but struggled to establish himself under Willie Waddell or Jock Wallace. He started 30 games and made seven appearances as a substitute in the league before moving to Hearts in a £15,000 deal late in the summer of 1979. He was a regular at Tynecastle, making 37 starts in his first season and 21 in the second, but was allowed to move on to Stirling Albion in 1981 after Bobby Moncur had replaced Willie Ormond at Hearts. He stayed for a year with Stirling before returning to the junior ranks with Irvine Vics.

The management team of Willie Wallace and Jock Wallace were the other key contributors to the Barcelona triumph, not to mention physiotherapist Tom Craig who had to work overtime in the run-up to the final. Waddell, who died in 1992 at the age of 71, was the mastermind and his position as the only manager in the club's history to win a European trophy is likely to remain unchallenged – as so many of his former players have testified to.

His tag of Mr Rangers was fitting, having served as a player then manager, administrator and director. His association began as a 15-year-old when he signed in 1936. Within two years the speedy winger was a fixture in the team, thanks in part to his ability to find the net – he scored on his debut against Arsenal. War interrupted his playing career, but Waddell bounced back to help his side add the 1947, 1949 and 1953 championships to the pre-war title he had contributed to. He also won the Scottish Cup twice and was capped 17 times by Scotland, scoring six goals to add to the 153 he netted for Rangers in 601 appearances.

He was given a free transfer by Scot Symon in 1956 and opted to retire rather than pull on the shirt of another club, returning to football in the 1957/58 season as manager of Kilmarnock after a year of working on the other side of the fence as a journalist. He spent eight seasons at Rugby Park and made steady progress with spectacular results. He turned a part-time side into a full-time outfit challenging Scotland's establishment, runners-up in both the league and the Scottish Cup in 1960. The following season they were second best in the championship and the League Cup, a record repeated in 1962/63.

Next time out they went one better – Waddell turned Killie into the nation's champions, for the one and only time in their history. Midway through that glorious term he had announced his intention to stand down at the end of the season and he kept to his word, moving back into journalism after leading his men to the league crown. As he joined his players in their celebrations, he said: 'This is the one thing I wanted more than anything else and it was my last chance as a manager to lift a major honour.'

That was one of the rare occasions Waddell was totally wide of the mark in football. In fact, his finest hour was still to come. When he quit as Kilmarnock manager he fell back on the writing trade in which he had served an apprenticeship while still a player at Rangers. His appointment to the *Daily Express* in 1965 became front-page news as he was confirmed as Scottish football's most intriguing football columnist.

He watched from the press box as Celtic launched their nine-in-a-row charge and could only pass judgement from the sidelines as Scot Symon was edged out of the club to make way for Davie White. Waddell was a staunch supporter of Symon and his ideology, a man steeped in the traditions of his club, but became one of the fiercest critics of White and his side.

He admitted Symon's exit had brought tears to his eyes, little realising that it was a move that paved the way for his own return to Ibrox. When White's reign ended in November 1969, as Rangers crashed out of Europe after defeat at the hands of Polish side Gornik, Waddell was scathing in his assessment. The fans agreed, with thousands demonstrating against their manager.

The board acted, White was dismissed and the media rumour-mill went into overdrive as Eddie Turnbull, of Aberdeen, was installed as the favourite for the hottest seat in Scottish football. In fact it was Waddell, on 3 December 1969, who took charge after being persuaded to return to the front line.

He was only the fifth manager in the history of the club and promised to uphold the virtues Rangers had built previous success upon: hard work, dedication and team spirit. He had turned down approaches from clubs in England and abroad, as well as overtures from the Scottish Football Association when they were seeking a new national team manager, but the chance to lead the Light Blues was one he could not resist.

Waddell won his first game, 2-1 away to Hearts, and over the course of his two-and-a-half-year tenure lost 32 of 131 games. Jock Wallace was recruited in a revamp of the coaching staff, becoming Waddell's right-hand man, and a new focus on fitness and conditioning is credited with making Rangers the fittest team of their generation. Many of the squad from that era played into their late thirties at the highest level. Waddell's transfer dealings included the recruitment of Peter McCloy and the departure of Jim Baxter and Willie Henderson.

His first trophy came in his first year, with the 1970 League Cup brought back to Ibrox, and the European Cup Winners' Cup became his second and his last. Waddell announced his resignation as manager on the back of the success in Barcelona, with nobody at the press conference on 7 June 1972 expecting the bombshell the Rangers boss was about to drop. He outlined his plan to take over as general manager to enable his coaching protégé, Jock Wallace, to complete the journey they had begun together. While Wallace was in charge of team affairs, Waddell remained in control of the purse strings and at the heart of transfer dealings and contract talks.

Nobody doubted the influence he still exerted, despite his absence from the training ground and dressing room, but he also made an impact in football's corridors of power. He succeeded in having the two-year European ban, in the wake of the pitch invasion in Barcelona, reduced to one year and helped to compensate for that suspension by working to create the European Super Cup, which paired Rangers with the European Cup winners Ajax in a gala two-leg event.

Waddell, after witnessing the horrific Ibrox disaster, was also the instigator behind stadium redevelopment as his general manager's role turned into that of managing director and vice-chairman. He stepped down from the dual role in 1979 but kept his place on the board and saw his dream realised when the new-look stadium was opened in 1981. In the decade after the disaster, he had created an all-seated modern ground that was the envy of every British club. In 1984 he resigned from active board duty, although he retained the title of honorary director and was a regular visitor to Ibrox until his death.

Jock Wallace's relationship with Rangers was more turbulent but laden with success. As a schoolboy he dreamt of running out at Ibrox for the home team, but that never happened. Instead he achieved the next best thing, taking possession of the home dug-out at the famous old ground when he took over from Willie Waddell in 1972.

It was a long and winding path that took him to the inner sanctum of his boyhood heroes. In the club's official handbook on the eve of his first season, Wallace wrote: 'I've been a Rangers fan since I was an eight-year-old. Indeed, I can recall walking the 12 miles back home to Wallyford from Tynecastle after watching Rangers and Hearts in action. But I didn't mind – as long as Rangers had won. I still feel the same way about Rangers winning.'

He served his football apprenticeship as a goalkeeper with Workington, Ashton-under-Lyne, Berwick Rangers, West Brom, Bedford, Hereford and Airdrie. It was a far cry from the Old Firm pressures he would encounter as boss at Ibrox, but he got a taste of the big occasion when he led Berwick, as player-manager, in their shock 1–0 Scottish Cup win over Rangers in 1967. He was assistant manager at Hearts when Willie Waddell invited him to become his right-hand man following his appointment in 1969.

Wallace, nicknamed Jungle Fighter after a stint of army service in Malaya, was a key ally for the new manager in his quest to improve fitness and conditioning. His gruelling training regime and run-until-you-drop sessions on the Gullane sands became the stuff of legend. He did enough in his two and a half years on the coaching staff to convince Waddell he had found his successor and took over in June 1972. Wallace was single-minded in his approach, selling the fans' favourite Colin Stein and the enigmatic Alfie Conn as the post-Barcelona clear-out began.

He won his first trophy in the final game of his first season in charge with a 3–2 win over Celtic in the 1973 Scottish Cup final. There was no repeat in the 1973/74 season as Rangers finished the campaign empty handed but it all fell into place the next term as the championship was claimed for the first time since 1964. Trebles in 1976 and 1978 were claimed before Wallace stunned Scottish football by resigning in the aftermath of that second clean sweep.

Although never publicly discussed, a dispute over terms was believed to be at the root of the decision. That reasoning appeared justified when Wallace moved to the more lucrative English leagues with Leicester City. He led the Midlands club to the Second Division championship and brought Gary Lineker to the fore, although the Foxes were relegated from the top flight the following term.

In 1982 he returned to Scotland to take charge of Motherwell, who had just been promoted to the Premier League under Ally MacLeod, and consolidated their place in the league before Rangers came calling again. Wallace took over for his second spell in charge in November 1983, after John Greig parted company with the club. He was no means first choice, with Alex Ferguson and Jim McLean rejecting advances from the Ibrox board, but that did not deter him.

He won the League Cup in the season of his return and again in 1984/85, but the following campaign was fruitless and Wallace departed to make way for Graeme Souness.

It did not mark the end of his managerial career: he was tempted to Spain by Seville in 1987 and made a huge impact. In a recent *Guardian* newspaper article Jaime Bogus Figmento, of the Spanish sports paper *Los Cojones*, paid homage to the role Wallace and Ted McMinn, the player he took from Ibrox to the continent with him, played in their brief sojourn to foreign shores. Figmento wrote: 'The Seville orange is a bitter fruit, but the Scots turned it into a delicious conserve, at once sweet and tangy, that is a fixture of breakfast tables across the globe. So it was too that Wallace and McMinn took the unpalatable and sour football of our region and with their tartan magic transformed it into something delectable and desired the world over. Before they came we were inhibited, defensive, obdurate, dull. With their relaxed, easy-going Calvinist attitudes they put us in touch with our emotions and taught us how to embrace joy.' His one-year spell in Spain was followed by the briefest of reunions with English football at Colchester in 1989. Wallace died in 1996 at the age of 61.

After the final magnum of champagne had been drained and the euphoria began to subside, Willie Waddell claimed everyone connected with the triumph in Barcelona would go down as an immortal in Ibrox folklore. As clichéd and impossible as that may sound, maybe, just maybe, he had a point. Nobody lives forever, but the memories and the joy of that May night, and the players who made it possible, will stand the test of time.

CHAPTER FOURTEEN

# THE BEARS IN BARCA

More than 100 planes, in excess of 200 buses and countless cars travelled the highways, byways and skies to transport the blue legions to Catalonia in 1972. The phenomenal operation to take the Ibrox loyal across the continent took planning, expertise and, in so many cases, huge slices of good fortune. For every charter flight planned with military precision there was another haphazard adventure taking place as the Rangers supporters found any means possible to ensure they were able to say: 'I was there.'

Barcelona may be a short hop for today's seasoned travellers, but in the 1970s the Spanish excursion was a trip into the unknown for most in the Scottish party. The modern package holiday was still in its infancy in the early part of the decade, but suddenly Scottish travel operators had a huge demand to cater for.

The operation swung into action. Charter planes, all 110 of them, were commandeered for the match. Dixon Travel, the club's official travel provider throughout the 1970s, 80s and 90s, were charged with ensuring the safe arrival of the players, officials and media as well as organising a succession of flights for supporters to follow in the trail of their heroes.

It was the type of aerial operation never before mounted by Rangers and Glasgow's travel agents, part of the plan to take the biggest travelling support ever to head from Scotland to foreign shores for a sporting event. After the heartbreak of losing two previous European finals, the opportunity to make it third time lucky captured the imagination and the invitation to arrive in style was quickly seized upon as the various possibilities for making the enticing journey began to fall into place.

The thousands of fans who managed to secure seats on those planes were the lucky ones. A short hop to the airport, a few libations to ease the journey, a couple of hours in the air and then the doors were thrown open to a waft of warm Spanish air. That was the way to travel, quickly and in style.

But for every supporter who secured the easiest of passages there were another ten who endured a more arduous trek to find their way to the Nou Camp by road, rail and by sea, leaving days in advance to make it on time for the date with destiny. Ferries from Dover to Calais, Southampton to Le Havre and almost every other combination of British and European ports imaginable were awash with red, white and blue as the Bears marched towards Barcelona with a mix of hope and expectation.

Some of the most devoted followers snaked their way down from the tip of Scotland, through England and then on through France and into Spain. Car loads from as far north as the Highlands faced days on the road tackling a relentless round trip of more than 2,000 miles on the unforgiving roads of the 1970s, with no time to pause and enjoy the scenery along the way as they battled on to keep to schedule and pitch up in Barcelona in time for the big game. The idea of 'pitching up' is apt, since many of the Rangers supporters opted to steer clear of the expensive Barcelona hotels and instead unfurled their tents to set up camp in and around the city. Of course, some chose not to sleep at all as the party spirit took over and the memories of the gruelling and lengthy journeys were quickly forgotten in favour of revelling in the present.

Time was not the only investment. Cold, hard-earned cash was the other sacrifice. The routes were many and varied, as were the price tags, but as a rule of thumb there would be no change from £30 for a basic coach trip package. In today's money that's somewhere north of £600 and when you consider the fact that many of the travelling blue army were still in their teens the scale of the financial commitment becomes clear.

Entry prices for the Nou Camp equated to less than £1, or under £20 when converted to current value. For those who were fortunate enough to make it to Spain there were significant returns on that modest outlay.

Ronnie Gault is one of the fans who staked his time and money on Willie Waddell's side and he came up trumps on what was his maiden voyage as a travelling fan. Gault, an offshore worker and member of the Inverness True Blues in his home city, remembers the adventure as though it was yesterday.

He was part of the contingent who made their way to the Nou Camp by train and by boat. He was based in England at the time but soon found himself in the thick of the action as the followers made their way from all corners of Britain and beyond to form a convoy heading towards Spain.

Gault recalls: 'The supporters who flew in 1972 were far outnumbered by those who went by road or rail. I was living in London at the time and decided to make the journey through to Spain for the final, travelling with a few fellow Rangers supporters that I worked with at the time. I had gone down to London in 1969 from Inverness, returning in the 1970s after working abroad for a spell.

'I was in my early 20s and although I'd been abroad on holiday I had never been to watch Rangers in Europe. Initially when I went down to London I made a point of getting round various grounds and watching the local teams play, but football isn't the same if you're not watching your own team. After that I made a point of going back to Glasgow at least once a month to go to the games at Ibrox.

'I was fortunate that living in London gave me a head start, but it was still a long trip. The trains from Glasgow had arrived at Euston station and everyone had to head across to

Victoria, where I started my own journey. It took me from Victoria to Dover by train, connecting to the ferry to Calais and then back onto the French trains to go through to Paris. From the Gare Du Nord we picked up an overnight sleeper that took us straight to Barcelona. We were making really good time until we hit the Spanish border, where they changed engine and we slowed right down. We stopped at every little station there was once we got into Spain, so it took us four hours to cover the distance to the centre of Barcelona.

'There were hundreds of Rangers supporters on the same train. In those days you used to get platform tickets for a penny – those were supposed to give you access to the platform, but not the trains. I met a couple of guys who had got all the way from Glasgow to London on a platform ticket and were hoping to get to Barcelona on the same one. Every time a guard appeared they would duck out of the way. I lost track of them, but they were determined to make it all the way.

'There were plenty of crates of beer taken on board but there was no trouble on the journey down. It was a great atmosphere on the trains, with plenty of holidaymakers on their way to the Costa Brava alongside the football fans. The Costa Brava was a big favourite with the Brits, probably the most popular of the Spanish destinations, but not everyone could afford to fly. My return train ticket cost me £20. I set off at 10 a.m. on Monday and arrived at 1 p.m. the following day, but it was worth the long journey.'

The Rangers players, no matter how well shielded from the intense interest by manager Waddell, were greeted by well-wishers at every turn and buoyed by the carefree spirit of their followers. That was in stark contrast to their Russian opponents, who travelled from beyond the Iron Curtain without a travelling support to talk of. While the Gers stars were sent forth to compete with the raucous chants still ringing in their ears, the Moscow men's minds were dominated by the ideological speeches, or *nakachkas*, that had been delivered by the Communist officials before the Dynamo squad departed for what proved to be mission impossible.

The Scottish contingent had no shackles and were welcomed with open arms as the first plane, bus and train loads disembarked on Spanish soil. It was as the week progressed that the atmosphere began to darken in the country's second city, something the players tucked away in their hotel hideaway were not aware of.

Gault says: 'Everything was fine on the Tuesday when we arrived. On the Wednesday there were thousands pouring into the city for the game and the mood changed as the week went on, with the police and the Spanish people becoming more hostile. There was a girl who was a Rangers supporter working in one of the shops in the city, married to a Spaniard. She pointed out that a newspaper article had basically said all Rangers supporters were Protestants who hated Catholics. It was during General Franco's era and the special police, with their distinctive triangular hats, were a fearsome bunch. They had obviously taken exception to the headlines – they were looking for trouble, waiting for it.'

Even before a ball had been kicked the Bears in Barcelona city centre had been put on edge by increasingly strong-armed tactics from the host police forces. Inside the Nou Camp on the night of the final, they discovered that the approach to crowd control was no softer than it had been on the streets. The sour taste lingers on for those who became embroiled in the trouble.

Gault continues: 'The first time what we thought was the full-time whistle sounded, people ran onto the pitch. I can still picture one guy with long hair, a white t-shirt and jeans. The police grabbed him by his hair and pulled him across the park – it was brutal. That was when the first bottles started flying from the upper tiers and a few of the Rangers supporters ran on to rescue him from the police. There were no

Russian supporters and very few Spaniards in for the game, so it's ridiculous for the police to have been so heavy handed. They had a ground full of Rangers supporters waiting to celebrate a huge occasion, and nobody was looking for trouble.

'After the game we hitched a ride on a supporters' bus out to the airport and stayed there overnight – we figured it would be the safest place to be. We went back into Barcelona the next day ready to catch our train but made sure we weren't wearing any colours. One big guy wearing a kilt wasn't so lucky. It was unusual in those days to see supporters wearing the kilt and obviously he stood out from the crowd as a Scotsman – the police spotted him and dragged him into the back of their car, gave him a good beating and then threw him back on the street. That was the way it was unfortunately – it didn't matter if you were minding your own business.

'The Rangers support's reputation had been damaged by what happened. I was at the game when Rangers returned to European football, playing Borussia Monchengladbach in 1973. The club was fined after a bottle was thrown onto the pitch during that game – what was never reported was that it wasn't actually one of our fans who threw it. It was a soldier from Liverpool, who was standing just along from where I was. He was stationed with the army, who had a big presence at the British headquarters on the Rhine, and had come along for the game.'

Gault made it back to London from Barcelona unscathed, able to celebrate the victory over Dynamo during the long journey back through France and on to his home in the capital city. It had been a trip full of amazing contrasts, from the highs of the triumph to the lows of the crowd trouble that marred the occasion and prevented the post-match party from hitting top gear.

The mixed experience has not soured his affection for the area and he has been back to Barcelona several times since

1972, both as a holidaymaker and football fan. When the Champions League draw paired Rangers with Barcelona in the group stages of the competition in 2007/08 there was the ideal opportunity for the Invernessian and hundreds of fellow veterans of the '72 expedition to revisit their old haunt. It was in November 2007 that Walter Smith took his Euro-hopefuls back to the hallowed turf, lifted by the dogged 0–0 draw in the home encounter against the revered Catalonian entertainers at Ibrox a fortnight earlier. Just as Rennes had criticised Rangers in 1972 for their stubborn streak, the giants of Barca had also hit out at the modern-day Rangers for having the temerity to shut out their millionaire superstars at Ibrox.

The war of words, which had seen Lionel Messi describe Smith's team's style as 'anti-football', stoked the passions as the big match loomed.

Not that it needed an extra injection of interest. The game's setting and the history surrounding Rangers at the Nou Camp added extra significance to the tie, and the build-up to the match, falling during the 35th anniversary year of the European Cup Winners' Cup victory, brought the ideal opportunity for plentiful flashbacks in the media.

The presence of the '72 squad for the match added extra spice to the occasion, with John Greig and his squad of veteran stars invited by the club to make the nostalgic return visit to their old stomping ground and soak up the big match atmosphere once again. They walked the pitch and rolled back the years, replaying the action in their minds as they once again took centre stage.

Only Tommy McLean, who was on duty as a coach in Scotland's youth set-up at the time, was absent from the roll-call, while Colin Jackson and Gerry Neef, reserve goalkeeper in 1972, joined the cast.

Goal heroes Willie Johnston and Colin Stein were the men in greatest demand, but in keeping with the spirit of '72 the team made the sojourn as a unit and the years were rolled back as the banter flew and memories were jogged. In pre-match interviews, Stein was quick to stress that the focus should remain on the present rather than the past and that Barcelona v Rangers was top of the agenda. But it was a losing battle. With the Barca Bears in town, the attention was always going to be divided and the golden oldies received their fair share of adulation.

While the players were on a trip down memory lane, so too were the fans. Gault says: 'For the last game to Barcelona the Inverness supporters' club had a plane full, with 238 making the trip. We had the members from our club as well as supporters from all across the north. We left at 8.30 a.m., flew into Girona to the north of the city and arrived in our hotels by 12.30 p.m. Quite a few of the boys on that trip had been in Barcelona in 1972 and it was a very different journey, not least for the ones who had driven all the way from the Highlands back then.

'There was no need to buy a ticket in '72 – I remember just paying on the gate. We were up in the second tier, opposite the covered section of the ground where the players emerged from. The Nou Camp's a big, big ground and we had it all to ourselves that night. For Rangers to have taken 25 or 30,000 across to Spain was a phenomenal achievement in those days because it was so expensive for the average supporter.

'The Nou Camp hasn't changed much from 1972, although it has expanded with an extra tier. I've been back to Barcelona quite a few times and to the Nou Camp while we've been out there, including for a stadium tour and then again for the Champions League game in 2007. It really hasn't changed much at all, it still feels like the same stadium. Barcelona itself is a lovely city and the experience of the policing at the final never put me off going back for a holiday or from following Rangers abroad again.'

The match in 2007 ended in a 2–0 defeat for the Light Blues, but the thousands who made the trip had at least returned with their own set of memories of the Nou Camp.

For those who did not make that trip but fancy a pilgrimage back to the land of sun, sea and celebrations there are plentiful opportunities for blasts from the past.

For example, if you fancy recreating the famous pictures of the players lounging beside the pool at the Hotel Rey Don Jaime in Castelldefels, you can go right ahead and do it. The hotel chosen by Willie Waddell for his players still stands proud on a hillside overlooking the Balearic sea to the south of neighbouring Barcelona. It is owned and operated by the Soteras group, and a one-night stay during May in the traditional four-star establishment will set you back as little as £75.

Once you have slept and dined like the kings of Ibrox, you can then make the short trip into the centre of Barcelona and soak up the unique atmosphere of the Nou Camp. A snip at just £16 for an adult ticket, the stadium tour offers the chance to go behind the scenes at the famous old ground.

The Nou Camp, or Camp Nou as it should be known, was, in stadium terms at least, still very much a new-build when the Scots arrived in 1972. Completed in 1957 to replace Barca's previous home at Les Cort, the Camp Nou was a monster of a ground even in its original guise. It cost 288 million pesetas to build, in the region of £1.4 million – a colossal figure in the 1950s and an outlay that left Barcelona nursing a heavy debt for years to come. Nobody, however, could argue with the end result. More than 90,000 crammed in for the opening fixture and 15 years later, when Rangers rolled into town, the sprawling bowl had lost none of its grandeur. Now, 40 years on, it remains standing as a shining icon of the glory days when Rangers took on some of the best in Europe – and won.

CHAPTER FIFTEEN

# MAKING THE HEADLINES

The Nou Camp provided a dramatic and fitting setting for the 1972 final, but the venue was also the reason behind one of the frustrations of that famous night. For Rangers fans there is no opportunity to replay the drama in glorious Technicolor – instead, the grainy black and white footage is all that remains to bring back the memories.

The lack of colour footage is one of the great quirks of the campaign and the Spanish hosts are the reason. While black-and-white broadcasts were rapidly becoming a thing of the past in Britain, the Spanish were not as fast to embrace the concept of colour. Although the 1972 Olympics in Munich later in the year saw the trialling of colour footage for Spanish viewers, it was too late for the fans stranded back in Scotland as the British broadcasters relied on feeds provided by the home crews in Barcelona.

That same season, just weeks earlier, football fans in England were able to watch colour highlights of Tottenham Hotspur's victory over Wolves in the first ever UEFA Cup final. Colour broadcasts in Britain had taken off in 1969, but it took the continental networks years to catch up.

The shades of grey were not the only disappointment for the Bears who were not able to make the pilgrimage to the Nou Camp – fans also had to contend with the lack of live coverage of the game in the country of the eventual cup winners. Because Scotland were in action in a home international fixture against Wales at a sparsely populated Hampden, there was a black-out on coverage of the proceedings in Spain. The SFA had clearly decided the show must go on, another sign of the times. Would Scotland contemplate playing a fixture on the same night as one of the country's club sides contested a European final in the 21st century? On every level the answer today would be no – for one thing, no broadcaster would entertain a clash of dates for two prime live television events with a captive audience. But live coverage, of either the international or cup final, was not a factor to be considered in 1972.

As a secondary issue, it is difficult to imagine the SFA entertaining the prospect of giving in to a match without players from either one of the Old Firm. Yet in 1972 the game's chiefs were not only willing to play Wales with the Rangers contingent absent but also to go through the entire home nations series without the Ibrox stars. Tommy Docherty led his troops to a 2–0 win against Northern Ireland four days prior to the Barcelona final, naturally without a Gers player to be seen, and three days after the win against Dynamo the Scots fell to a 1–0 defeat against England. Again, the celebrating Rangers quota was spared duty.

Rewinding back to 24 May and the clash between the national team's low-key exploits and the Bears in Barcelona, there was a simple choice for the nation's football fans. The majority chose light blue over dark blue. While 22,000 hardy souls watched a national side huff and puff their way to a 1–0 win against the Welsh, with Peter Lorimer scoring the only goal of the game 12 minutes from time, the blue half of the city had to be content with radio coverage of the action unfolding on the continent.

Oddly, the Irish population were treated to live match action from the Moscow Dynamo match on RTE, which was the republic's sole channel in those days. Back in Scotland, there was a specially extended highlights programme scheduled for ITV, allowing the best moments of Scotland's game and the Rangers final to be shown in one hit.

Just as Wolves and Spurs supporters had to be content with highlights, so too did the Gers loyal. It is unthinkable now to contemplate major European finals being contested by three British clubs without a live broadcast, but in 1972 that was the media landscape. The exception to the rule was the European Cup final a week after the Rangers triumph. The Johan Cruyff-inspired Ajax defeated Inter Milan 2–0 in Rotterdam in a match beamed live by both the BBC and ITV.

But then, the European Cup didn't have the tartan twist that Scottish viewers were treated to. The big gun was wheeled out by Scottish Television, with legendary commentator and presenter Arthur Montford sent forth to bring life to the proceedings in his own inimitable style as the party returned to Scottish soil. Montford was the man chosen to accompany the team on the bus journey back from Prestwick airport on the day after the night before and his interviews with the bleary-eyed players have become the stuff of legend, not least his encounter with Colin Stein – asking the Barca hero which of his two goals he felt was best, only to be reminded by the No.9 that he had only scored one.

That faux pas mattered not a bit to the Bears lapping up the coverage of their team's greatest night, with Willie Johnston and John Greig among the other players getting the Montford treatment during that special STV film.

Montford, the grand old man of Scottish football broadcasting, later reflected on the advances in match coverage. You may expect a character who rose to prominence in the primal days of the 1970s to hark back to the good old days, peering through sepia-tinted glasses at the film reels from the distant past. Not a bit of it. Instead he has been heard to extol the virtues of multi-camera coverage, with bird's eye views and goalmouth action captured pin-sharp from close range. Instead of those many and varied options, it was left to the humble commentator or reporter to paint a picture with words – and Scotland had world-class operators.

Of course the BBC had their own big name to provide dulcet tones to the corporation's coverage of the events. It is the commentary of Archie Macpherson that is well worn, having accompanied various video and DVD releases of the highlights. The packaging may have changed, but the same original black-and-white footage remains at the centre as a permanent reminder of the challenges facing the media covering the cup final.

Those challenges extended to the written press. It is impossible to overstate the impact technology has had on journalism in the past two decades, let alone in the 40 years which have elapsed since the Scottish media crew earned their corn in the Nou Camp.

When I covered my first football match in 1996 there were three tools of the trade. A notepad, a pen and a telephone. Not a mobile phone, but a fixed landline with shiny red BT handset that could be plugged in at the sockets lining the press area. Just as the reporters who covered the final in Barcelona would have done, the match report would be phoned through section by section as the game unfolded from the notes scribbled on the pad. At the other end of the line, at head office, was a team of copy-takers whose sole job was to type the report being read down the line to them. From there it would be put into the system, placed on the page and eventually put into print. Reading copy is fast becoming a lost art form, with the best exponents able to dictate their prose with the ease and confidence of a concert musician. It is one thing performing when you are dealing with a team full of Smiths, Johnstones, Jardines or Steins. Quite another when you are dealing in names like Pilguj, Zhikov, Makovikov and Vryouzhikhine. Spelling each one meticulously to a typist hundreds of miles away over a crackling phone line and ensuring that a system was in place so that the process did not have to be repeated time and time again during the course of the match was the complication for the 1972 media corps.

Now the middle man, the copy-taker, has been cut out of the loop completely. The humble notepad has been usurped by the all-singing, all-dancing laptop computer. Reports are typed there and then by the reporter and filed, in an instant, using mobile phone connections or the wi-fi internet access provided at most major football grounds.

During my days as a rookie reporter there was a routine to be followed. Reference books had to be studied, statistics prepared and notes meticulously made to ensure that all the information on both teams was available at the turn of a page. It was the same for the 1970s reporter, who would have arrived at the Nou Camp armed with their own research. Mind you, finding out the vital statistics of mysterious figures like the Russian defender Vladimir Basalev or midfielder Oleg Dolmatov was no mean feat in the days when Google was no more than a misspelt cricketing term.

Now, again thanks to the wonders of wi-fi and remote web access, the internet is just a click away. Every statistic, every goal, every game, every age, every transfer is available in an instant. Of course there's no substitute for preparation, and research is not a lost art in sporting journalism, but the internet offers a rather substantial safety net.

The ease and speed of delivering copy is the biggest benefit technology has brought to the football writer's party. That is not to suggest that the modern journalist's life is an easy one. The advent of the super-fast laptop means that fewer bodies can produce and file more copy in less time. Coverage has become more comprehensive, with opinion pieces side by side with match reports and quotes from key protagonists all done and dusted within minutes of the final whistle to ensure that it is on the page and rolling off the printing press in double quick time.

Mind you, unlike in 1972, the football fan of the 2000s doesn't have to wait until the following day to read all about it. The advance of the internet and mobile technology in the past decade, with instant updates online and to phones, has challenged the newspaper industry in a way that the industry moguls of the 1970s could never even have dreamt of.

Before supporters have even left the ground there are clips, pictures, reports, blogs, statistical round-ups and message-board debates flying through the ether ready to be digested by fans in every corner of the globe.

Then it was more defined, a simpler existence for the football supporter. If you wanted to get information, insight and a feel for the atmosphere in the ground the only place to turn to was the newspapers.

There was a captive audience to play to and the competition was fierce. The Scottish press travelled mob-handed to Spain to provide the best, quickest and most comprehensive coverage from the game. As the game ebbed and flowed, so too did the copy. Phone lines between Barcelona and Glasgow were red hot as the copy-takers furiously tapped out the reports being dictated with staccato rhythm from the media section of the Nou Camp.

Words were one thing, bringing the powerful images of the pulsating match to a Scottish readership was quite another. The still pictures of Willie Johnston scoring, Colin Stein celebrating and the supporters rejoicing have become some of the most iconic in the history of the football club. There was no digital technology, electronic auto-focus or any other gadgetry – but those incredible visions have stood the test of time.

The finest photographers in the nation's press were flown to the continent for the biggest assignment of the sporting calendar. They found they had to be street-smart to get the pictures they craved, having to go elbow to elbow with the European lensmen who were also crowding the prime vantage points around the pitch. Having jostled for position throughout the evening to get the shots in the bag, the race was then on to get the film back home to processing. Reels were rushed through Barcelona's airport and flown back to Scotland to be processed and hurriedly prepared for print. It was an operation planned with military precision.

The newspapers on 25 May had two stories to cover and

very little time in which to put together the coverage. It was not a time for measured analysis, more of a rush to get copy on the pages. The pitch invasion and clashes with police became inextricably linked with the match that had preceded those incidents – scenes which, incidentally, were not caught in their entirety by the television cameras as the Spanish director chose to order the lenses to be turned away while the drama unfolded. It was a form of frontline censorship, presumably designed to protect the sensibilities of the armchair fan, but it was also argued that it was a method of protecting the local police force.

The *Evening Times* left readers in no doubt that the activity on the terraces, spilling onto the pitch, had detracted from the main event. Jim Blair's match report pointed out: 'It was a night to remember – but, sadly, for all the wrong reasons. Rangers' 3–2 win, which gave them their first trophy in Europe at the third attempt, was virtually overshadowed by a running riot at the end of the game.'

Blair went on to point out: 'To put the matter in its proper perspective, however, the Spanish police were far from blameless. Their actions to "charge" the fans and wield batons came, quite significantly, when television coverage stopped.'

The *Evening Times* writer described the events of the night as the worst football riots he had ever seen, adding: 'I deplored the way the Rangers fans took up a fighting challenge with the police after they had been chased on the final whistle – but really, this was the one time they seemed "justified" in coming over the wall. After all, their team had just won a European trophy for the first time.'

As far as the football was concerned, Blair heaped praised on the performance from the Ibrox men in the Nou Camp. He said: 'Their performance in this tournament has been particularly outstanding in view of their lack of domestic success. Their game seems suited to Europe – and the fact they now have a trophy to prove it rather bears out the theory. Star men in the Rangers side last night were Peter McCloy, Derek Johnstone and Dave Smith, and those two tireless front runners, Colin Stein and Willie Johnston.'

By the time the journalistic core had returned to Scottish soil along with the team on the day after the Barcelona final, the coverage swung back to concentrate largely on the scale of the accomplishment by the boys in light blue.

The *Daily Record* on 26 May devoted its front page to the triumphant homecoming of Willie Waddell's troops. The headline screamed 'Revels in the Rain', sitting above a full-width picture of the team carrying the trophy on their lap of honour around the Ibrox pitch upon the return to Glasgow.

The report, by Ken Stein, kicked off: 'This was it! The moment Rangers brought the European Cup Winners' Cup home to Ibrox – with 20,000 fans revelling in the rain. On a red, white and blue decked lorry, captain John Greig, his team-mates clustered around him, held the cup aloft. And slowly, proudly, the triumphant progress began – two circuits of the stadium with cheering, cheering, all the way. Many of the fans, just back from Barcelona, were still wearing souvenir sombreros. They waved them and their banners and their scarves – and yelled themselves hoarse.'

There was a party atmosphere at the ground as the tens of thousands filtered in to catch sight of the prize that had been hidden from view in Spain. Only two arrests were reported, both outside the ground, as police praised the good nature of the supporters gathered for the celebration in Govan.

While the front page of the *Record* was devoted to the team's success, the back page also majored on the win over the Russians. A picture of Willie Johnston, complete with obligatory sombrero and sipping champagne from the cup, led readers to the inside coverage which featured more images of the celebrations in the Nou Camp dressing room in the aftermath of the match. A report by Alex Cameron extolled the virtues of Derek Johnstone, quoting Willie Waddell and John Greig to support his assertion that the teenager had been one of the players to have shone brightest during the run to victory.

Still, there was no hiding from the impact the confrontation between police and supporters had on the proceedings. Cameron noted: 'What a shame that Rangers' fine play against the Moscow side had to be so miserably K.O.d by the unruly fans. There was the opportunism of Colin Stein and his splendid first goal. There was the cool and calm of Davie Smith in his sweeping role and the speed and dash of Willie Johnston on the wing.'

While Cameron's piece touched on the crowd trouble, the lead on the inside back page was devoted solely to the situation. Penned by Ken Gallacher, the headline read: 'Europe ban: Ibrox men will know next week.' Gallacher reported that a special meeting of the UEFA disciplinary committee would be held in Rotterdam the following week to determine the club's future in continental competition.

In Rangers' favour was the fact that the match referee, Spaniard Jose Maria Ortez de Mendibil, had come out in support of the Scottish followers. He was quoted in the *Record* as saying: 'I did not think at any time that I would have to stop the game. The Russians may protest. But they protest only against happy fans. I did not think they were going to be violent. They were excited. They were exuberant. Probably too exuberant, but I was never concerned.'

The last word went to Willie Waddell, who spoke frankly when he said: 'There were fans on the field at Wembley last year when Ajax won the European Cup. There were fans on the field at Nuremberg in 1967 when Bayern Munich beat Rangers in the European Cup Winners' Cup final. There were Celtic fans on the field at Lisbon when they won the European Cup. I don't see how Rangers FC can be discriminated against when this has happened before.'

Of course the history books show that the club was indeed punished heavily. Although the two-year ban initially handed down by UEFA was cut to a single season on appeal, the damage was serious as the Barca Bears were prevented from defending their crown. Instead, the team quickly began to break up, and by the time the club returned to European competition it was a very different side to the one that had played in the last tie in Barcelona.

There was a real sense of injustice within the dressing room and the corridors of power. While that faded for the Rangers contingent, it appears the similar simmering resentment held by their Russian counterparts has not cooled in the slightest.

In the build-up to the UEFA Cup final against Zenit St Petersburg in 2008, attention naturally turned to the last Scotland v Russia contest in a major European final. Vladimir Pilguj, the Dynamo goalkeeper who picked the ball out of his net three times in 1972, gave a revealing interview to the *Guardian*.

He said: 'I don't think we were weaker than the famous Scottish club. But not having experience of such matches, we were overly worried and as a result froze before our appearance on the pitch. We didn't manage to show over the 90 minutes the sort of football we were capable of playing.'

He went on to address the pitch invasion, claiming: 'They (the Rangers supporters) had mad faces, with bulging eyes. They had to be cleared from the field and although they didn't really do us any harm, it meant the game was held up. That was a big advantage for our opponents. They were exhausted by that stage and could hardly drag their legs, and I'm sure in that final four minutes we'd have scored a third.'

The Russians, it would appear, did not make for gracious losers and the disappointment of their defeat still rankles. In truth it was not the final few minutes that cost the Moscow side the tie – more the imperious manner in which Rangers galloped ahead in the first half, blowing Dynamo away with pace and style.

It was no surprise that that pace was not carried through to the final furlong, but Waddell's team, renowned for their fitness, dug in to keep their noses in front and accomplish the mission they had set out to complete. Rangers were European winners, and for everyone involved in the marathon effort it was a night for celebration, not for sour grapes.

CHAPTER 16

# The Business of Barcelona

How would you like a replica of the famous blue jersey from the 1972 final to wear to the big match? Not a problem – yours for £24.99 from JJB Sports. How about the same shirt signed by skipper John Greig as well as goal-scorers Colin Stein and Willie Johnston? A snip at £124.99 from one of the many online businesses that have popped up trading in cherished memorabilia. While you are in the spending mood, why not go the whole hog and plump for a replica shirt signed by all 11 of the Barca Bears? Part with £199.99 and it will be on your wall before you know it.

Welcome to the wonderful world of the commercial maze that has sprung up around the adventures of 1972. As every anniversary passes the gravity of the success intensifies and the unquenchable thirst for mementoes of the occasion grows. In response a flood of items have made their way onto the open market for Gers fans to peruse and purchase.

From pin badges and mugs to photographs and caricatures, separating the good from the bad and the ugly is fast developing into a new art form for the discerning fan attempting to negotiate a path through the thousands of opportunities to buy a small slice of '72 for posterity. Whether genuine slices of history from the 1970s or mass-produced modern takes on the offerings from that period, the opportunities are near to boundless and there is something to suit every budget.

While for most people the search for memorabilia is little more than a pleasurable pastime, for some the sporting memory lane has become a profitable avenue to go down.

An industry devoted to the past has sprung up and profitable, not to mention long-lasting and well-established, businesses have been built upon the demand from supporters.

The boom in retro relics can be traced back to the humble replica shirt and to London, not Glasgow. It was Vic Groves, Arsenal star of the 1950s, who inspired the bright idea when a Gunners fan, Alan Finch, decided to ditch his itchy polyester football kit and seek out a local seamstress to make him a replica of the red shirt made famous by his hero, Groves.

Soon enough Finch quit his career in the music industry and founded The Old Fashioned Football Shirt company, or TOFFS as it is better known to football fans across the globe. The empire began in his dining room, with just Finch and his wife as the team behind it, but now is based in a Newcastle factory with a staff of 30 and a multi-million-pound turnover.

Its cotton kits have travelled around the globe and been sported on the high street and in the bars of every major city in the land, as much as on the playing fields. They cornered the market for fashionable replica shirts with the all-important retro twist.

Of course no company lasts long without competition and TOFFS is no different. Over the past decade a plethora of firms have entered the market, producing and selling vintage-style shirts. Naturally, Rangers and the JJB club shops have claimed 1972 as their own, not only marketing the now familiar replica shirts but also creating a whole range of '72 branded leisurewear targeted at a generation not even born when those digits took on special significance.

The creation of Bar '72 at Ibrox provides the current generation of supporters with a link to the glorious past, a venue that has given the drama of four decades ago a modern twist and a permanent place at the stadium.

Downstairs at the club shop, retro footballs and mouse mats emblazoned with flashbacks to 1972 and other landmark occasions are among the other souvenirs – but for those wishing to find something original, the search must go far deeper than a quick glance through the pages of the Rangers website or browse through the shelves in the store.

The key words are 'retro' and 'replica'. While those items are in plentiful supply, manufactured to keep pace with demand, the trickle of original pieces from 1972 is far slower. The occasional photograph or magazine from the time can be picked up for relatively little – anything from 50p to £50, depending on the rarity of the publication.

Of course the players are the ones who were best placed to build a stock of collectable items, from the sublime, headed by the distinctive rectangular gold winners' medal to sit side by side with the silver version my dad collected in the 1967 European Cup Winners' Cup defeat against Bayern Munich, to the curious – which includes the menu from the victory banquet hosted by Glasgow's Lord Provost, William Gray, at the City Chambers. In many ways it is slices of history like that glossy menu that stand out from the jerseys, newspaper cuttings and other trinkets associated with the run. It's a little slice of history that could so easily have been lost. For the record, the team sat down to dinner for that celebration on 18 September and were treated to a grapefruit and melon cocktail, celery soup, baked rainbow trout, a mixed grill and the intriguingly titled Rangers' Delight for pudding. Washed down with a 1967 Chateau de la Tour Clos-Vougeot and a 1970 Piesporter Goldtrophen, it was a banquet fit for the men who had been crowned European Cup Winners' Cup kings just months earlier. Soprano Helen MacArthur and accompanist Jill Stewart were entrusted with providing the entertainment while the Drambuie and Courvoisier cognac was being sipped.

Those incidental pieces of memorabilia from the time capture the essence of the era and the sense of occasion surrounding the perfect European season. For every glance at the medal, the dusty old clippings from papers and magazines hold the attention for twice as long. Those are the pieces of nostalgia that are worth pennies, certainly in comparison with the more precious items collected by the stars of the side, but the old chestnut about sentimental value rings true. A menu here or a photograph from one of the foreign excursions there, those are the snippets that bring the memories flooding back and help to bring a sense of realism to an event which has taken on almost mythical qualities as the years roll past.

Programme hunters will be left disappointed, though. There was no match-day publication produced for the final, leaving a huge void in that distinct collectors' market. Instead, posters used to publicise the final around Barcelona have emerged as the next best thing, having been brought back in limited numbers by jubilant Bears. An even rarer batch of signed posters can still be found, dotted around the country.

Those signatures add value, even when added to reproduction items. How those autographs are obtained varies, although for the companies who specialise in memorabilia the most transparent way is by organising sessions with the players in question and ensuring they are paid for their services.

Terry Baker, founder of www.a1sportingmemorabilia.co.uk, is one of the businessmen to have enlisted the Barca Bears to provide a limited edition set of signed reproduction shirts commemorating the win over Moscow Dynamo. Baker says: 'The squad-signed shirt from the 1972 final has sold well. We have the shirt signed by the captain and goal-scorers too, but I think the one signed by the whole group is quite attractive because it does not cost too much more. If you are a fan of a certain age, maybe somebody who was in Barcelona for the final, then to have a jersey signed by the whole squad is a fantastic memento. A lot of our sales are as gifts – they make a very impressive present when they are framed up and signed. The demand comes mainly from Scotland, but there are also fans all over the UK and other parts of the world. There are also some very serious collectors out there, including some who buy one of every shirt and item we sell.'

The market for signed memorabilia from all clubs is strong. At every auction at every sporting dinner up and down the land there are bidding wars breaking out and the trade online is just as brisk. While a relatively new phenomenon on British shores, it is not entirely new.

Baker says: 'I'm Jimmy Greaves' agent and when he was speaking at dinners he would sign a shirt and gift it to the club organising the event. It would always cover his fee when it was auctioned and it was Jimmy who suggested that really the proceeds should be split between the company and the club. It wasn't for his benefit, but he hit upon the idea and it grew from there. Signed sporting items have been hyped up in America for a while. We tend to hang on their coat-tails a bit in the UK and the market here has quickly built up.'

Through his work with Greaves, Baker was able to branch out and tap into a lucrative stream of customers when he moved to secure one of British football's most revered groups of players. 'I've looked after all of the English 1966 World Cup-winning squad and memorabilia from that team is by far the biggest seller we have ever had. I remember doing a signing event at Birmingham one weekend and Ray Wilson said he had earned more from those few days than he had in his whole career at Everton – even as a World Cup winner. I think it is important that the former players are well rewarded for the part they play, particularly those in their sixties and seventies who perhaps did not make a fortune from the game in their playing days. Of course it isn't altruistic on our part – it is a commercial operation.

'There are people who call themselves dealers who hang around outside training grounds or stadiums asking for autographs. To me that is just about as bad as those who are selling forgeries. Our items are sourced from organised signings where the players are paid and know exactly what they are signing and that it is for a commercial use.

'I have a contract with Sir Henry Cooper and pay him well to sign for us. Yet he receives hundreds of items every week from people claiming to be fans who are looking for free signings. I would imagine many of those items would quickly end up for sale online or elsewhere if he went ahead and signed them.

'Even though it can be rewarding to take part in organised signing sessions, some players are still reluctant to do it. Spurs has always been a big market for me, but Alan Gilzean, one of the most popular players from the past, is a virtual recluse. Frank Saul, from the 1967 FA Cup-winning team, is another one who simply isn't interested, while Jimmy Armfield is happy to sign but never on a commercial basis – he just doesn't like the idea of anyone having to pay for his autograph. Steven Gerrard will conduct signing sessions for a significant fee – but in his case, the cheque is written straight to his charitable foundation.'

The memorabilia industry has its dark sides. As someone heavily involved in the sector, Baker has experience of many of the less savoury aspects and knows it is impossible to prevent his industry from being tarnished.

He recalls: 'When Alan Ball died, Geoff Hurst called me at 4.30 a.m. to break the news. By 6.45 a.m. it was public knowledge and almost immediately I had a couple of dealers on the phone trying to buy Alan Ball memorabilia. I told them to clear off, or words to that effect. For people to be so quick to try and profiteer was disappointing. What we decided to do was to keep the items we had on sale available, making sure the price did not increase, and donated the proceeds to Alan's charity.

'We are there as a commercial entity and it is very competitive, not least because of some of the unscrupulous operators out there. There have been people who have been convicted of forging wholesale signed squad shirts. I have a very good relationship with both Manchester United and Liverpool, through the likes of Wayne Rooney and Steven Gerrard. Even with those contacts we are lucky if we see four squad-signed shirts from each of the clubs in a season – yet there are hundreds of them out there purporting to be genuine.

'The question of proving authenticity is the biggest challenge we face. We got a long way down the line with John Lewis, who were going to stock our memorabilia in their stores. Unfortunately, they could not see a way of guaranteeing authenticity and the proposal stalled. Everything we sell is something we have seen signed and wherever possible we try to provide photographs of the signing sessions.

'My advice to anyone preparing to buy signed memorabilia would be that if something looks too good to be true then it generally is. I've had people contacting me by phone to say "I've bought a Jimmy Greaves autograph for £2 in an online auction – can you tell me if it is genuine?" My response would always be that if it only cost £2 then it is not genuine. Then they ask if I can get Jimmy to sign them a real autograph for free. Generally my advice is not to buy anything unless you feel confident about it.

'There are probably four or five major companies operating in the UK at the moment who operate a similar model to ourselves. The biggest threat to all of those firms is from the forgers, who undermine the confidence of the public. They also stop the ex-players earning a bit of money, which I feel they all deserve to do. It's not like the modern wealthy players who are millionaires – the older guys deserve opportunities and the forgeries take that away from them.'

Most of the key artefacts from 1972, including the precious medals and original shirts, remain firmly under lock and key. Some have been displayed as museum pieces, with Peter McCloy among those to have loaned his mementoes to the Scottish Football Museum at Hampden Park in the past to give fans at least an opportunity to have a glimpse at the glorious past.

If that calibre of memorabilia were to reach the open market there would be a ready market. Late in 2009, the Glasgow auction house McTear's handled the sale of a selection of football trinkets from the incredible career of the late, great Alan Morton.

The Wee Blue Devil's collection, put up for sale by a descendant of the legendary Ibrox star of the 1920s and 30s, brought a wave of interest and sale prices exceeded the expert opinion of the auctioneers charged with producing estimates for the list, which included league championship medals and Scotland jerseys. One of the medals, from the 1926/27 title success, raised £2,585 alone while the 14 lots submitted to the sale by the family member totalled £16,238 by the time the hammer fell to signal the end of the sale. It was a pleasant surprise for the auctioneers and the selling party alike, although perhaps not totally unexpected given Morton's status as an all-time hero to the Ibrox loyal. If original Barcelona lots were to go under the hammer it is easy to predict that they too would sell at a premium.

You make think the memorabilia merry-go-round is not for you. Too expensive perhaps, or even too risky? Think again. By picking up this book you have already plunged into the pool of Barcelona-related products swimming around on the open market, with the publishing industry happy to embrace the feel-good factor that all-things-1972 bring.

*To Barcelona and Beyond* began life as a labour of love back in 2005. As a journalist by trade, I had long harboured the idea of creating a lasting tribute to the greatest achievement in my father's professional life, the sporting success that has defined his career since he stepped forward to collect his winners' medal in the Nou Camp on 24 May 1972.

But would any publisher be willing to commit to the project? Yes. In fact there was a reassuring response from both sides of the border, demonstrating a real confidence in the demand for fresh material on the historic events in Barcelona. Of course it was far from the first proposal for a book attempting to capture the essence of the triumph and far from the last, but it is one from the heart.

From histories devoting large sections to the Barca Bears to more specific titles, the challenge is to find a new and attention-grabbing way to cover the big event. One book to achieve that was *The Waddell Years*, which naturally leans heavily on the legendary manager's finest hour. Complete with replica souvenirs from 1972, including a match ticket and other Barcelona paraphernalia, that 1999 offering from author Stephen Halliday through publisher Andre Deutsch included contributions from several of Waddell's former charges.

The memories and observations of the 1972 squad have been heavily leant upon in many books, including this one. Many of the squad have had the opportunity to put their recollections into print in far greater depth than a mere soundbite by penning their autobiographies.

The ball was set rolling just seven years after the trophy was collected, when Derek Johnstone released his autobiography, *My Team: Rangers*. He was still a young man with years ahead of him in the game but, at the peak of his powers, it was an opportune time to hit the stands of the bookshops and take advantage of his popularity. In 2007 a more in-depth look at his exploits was released when *DJ: The Derek Johnstone Story* was commissioned.

Next to appear was Willie Johnston's life story in 1983, when he reflected on the highs and lows of his time in the game in *On the Wing*. Johnston returned to the literary fold in 2009 with *Sent Off at Gunpoint*, recapping on the period covered in his first book and catching up with the events of the 26 years that elapsed between the two publications.

John Greig's tome *My Story* was published in 2006. Three years later it was the turn of Colin Stein to look back on his greatest achievements, including his goal in Barcelona, in the pages of *Shooting Star*. As co-author with Stein on his project, I know at firsthand the warmth with which 1972 is recalled by those who were closest to it.

The tales of Barcelona featured prominently in all of those books and ensured demand from publishers and readers alike, a demand that has also been borne out at various reunion events which have been opened up to an appreciative public to join their cup-winning heroes.

In 2007, to mark the 35th anniversary, the programme of testimonial events arranged by supporters to honour the squad was widely welcomed. The reception the team received at the main testimonial dinner at the Hilton in Glasgow brought the house down, serving as a reminder if any was needed that the passing decades have done nothing to dampen the enthusiasm from the supporters. With the 40th anniversary celebrations looming, there is no sign of that enthusiasm abating any time soon.

# INDEX